TRUSTS AND ESTATES

THIRD EDITION

MELANIE B. LESLIE

Dean and Professor of Law

Benjamin Cardozo School of Law, Yeshiva University

STEWART E. STERK

H. Bert and Ruth Mack Professor of Law

Benjamin Cardozo School of Law, Yeshiva University

CONCEPTS AND INSIGHTS SERIES®

FOUNDATION
PRESS

Concepts and Insights Series is a trademark registered in the U.S. Patent and Trademark Office.

Printed in the United States of America

ISBN: 978-1-63460-300-3

TABLE OF CONTENTS

TRUSTS AND ESTATES

THIRD EDITION

Chapter One

INTRODUCTION

How best can I arrange the transfer of my wealth to my chosen beneficiaries? That's the practical question that clients want their estates and trusts lawyer to answer. Much of the Estates and Trusts course, much of this book—and some of this introductory chapter—is devoted to that question. But this very practical question assumes that the client will be able to, and should be able to, transfer her wealth as she sees fit. Many distinguished people—including some noted capitalists—have questioned the wisdom of unlimited inheritance rights. Andrew Carnegie wrote that

> "[t]he parent who leaves his son enormous wealth generally deadens the talents and energies of the son, and tempts him to lead a less useful and less worthy life than he otherwise would."

Despite Carnegie's warnings, most people—rich and not-so-rich—want to leave property to close family members. For the most part, Americans are free to dispose of their property as they see fit, both during their lifetimes and at death. But let's first explore why a client should be able to dictate what happens to "her" money after her death.

I. The Uneasy Case for Inheritance

Consider the case against inheritance. First, inherited wealth is inconsistent with the American ideal of equal opportunity. If wealthy parents can leave their money to their children or other descendants, those descendants will enjoy advantages not shared by those with less well-endowed parents. Abolishing inherited wealth would level the playing field (at least to some degree). Second, inherited wealth may reduce the incentive for children of the rich to use their talents productively, because they can choose instead to live off the efforts of their parents.

In light of these powerful objections, the case for inheritance is far from ironclad. A first defense of inheritance focuses on the incentive to productive activity that would be lost if people were not entitled to pass their assets on to descendants. Because people derive satisfaction from passing property to the recipients they have chosen, abolishing inheritance rights would make accumulation of wealth less attractive, and would therefore reduce the level of productive activity necessary to accumulate that wealth. At the margin, this analysis is undoubtedly correct. The more significant question concerns the magnitude of the impact inheritance rights might have on patterns of work and savings. People do not know how much money they will need to provide for themselves. Life is unpredictable. We do not control our health or the duration of our own lives, and we cannot control for external economic factors—inflation, for instance—that might have a significant impact on our future financial needs. As a result, even without the prospect of passing on inherited wealth, most people would have incentives to produce and save more than they expect to consume during their own lives.

A second defense of inheritance rights recognizes that a person who accumulates wealth relies on the contribution and support of other people, typically close family members. Those contributions often increase as a person ages and needs additional care and support from family members. The prospect of inheritance leads family members to be more attentive to the needs of their elderly parents and grandparents. On the other hand, elderly people who are poor also need and receive assistance from close family members, even without the prospect of inheritance. Moreover, although a person's spouse often contributes to the person's capacity to accumulate wealth, significant contributions by children and other family members are less common, reducing the persuasiveness of desert-based claims to inheritance rights.

One of the most powerful arguments for inheritance is a practical one: we wouldn't be able to stop inheritance even if we tried. A prohibition on inheritance at death would lead people to give away property during their lifetimes. A prohibition on lifetime gifts would be virtually impossible to police. Moreover, a prohibition on inheritance would lead wealthy people to spend large sums of money on devices designed to evade the prohibition (as wealthy people already spend large sums to reduce estate tax liability). Ultimately, the argument runs, a prohibition on inheritance would result in significant waste of resources.

Finally, inheritance rights are politically popular. That the wealthy—who make up a large percentage of public officials—should support inheritance rights is easy to understand. But support for inheritance is more widespread. Scholars have noted with puzzlement the fact that voters oppose inheritance taxes, even when most of them have so few assets that the tax is unlikely ever to affect them or their families. Professor Graetz has suggested that this support for inheritance rights (and opposition to inheritance taxes) reflects the optimism of the American people: most Americans believe they ultimately will be wealthier than they have any reason to expect.[1]

Whatever the ultimate merits of these arguments for inheritance, there is little likelihood that inheritance will be abolished or curtailed in the near future. Indeed, in recent years the pendulum has been swinging the other way, with reduction in estate taxes and a consequent increase in the amount of wealth that a person can pass to potential beneficiaries. Against that background, then, it is time to turn to the mechanics of intergenerational wealth transfers.

II. Probate and Non-Probate Transfers

Two separate systems—the probate system and the non-probate system—have developed to facilitate the transfer of wealth. Although the two systems accomplish similar objectives, they operate in very different ways. An understanding of the differences is basic to the study of estates and trusts.

Historically, the probate system has been the heart of the wealth transmission process. The probate system is fraught with formality. The death of a property owner triggers a judicial proceeding. If the property owner has left a will, the person named as executor in that will starts the process by petitioning for authorization to act on behalf of the deceased property owner's estate. The executor must submit proof that the will was properly executed (in accordance with statutory formalities, which typically require at least two witnesses). The executor must also notify decedent's closest living relatives of the proceeding, and those relatives have the opportunity to challenge, or "contest" the will, contending either that the will was not properly executed, that the decedent lacked mental capacity to execute the will, or that the will was the product of undue influence. If no one objects, the court admits the will to probate, and the executor distributes the estate assets as the decedent has directed in the will (after payment of any outstanding claims).

The process is similar if the property owner dies without a will. A close relative seeks judicial appointment as "administrator" or "personal representative." The appointment authorizes her to act on behalf of the estate, performing the same functions as the executor performs when decedent has left a will. The personal representative then distributes the estate in accordance with the intestate succession statutes enacted by the legislature—statutes which typically award the bulk of the estate to decedent's spouse and

---

[1]   Michael Graetz, *To Praise the Estate Tax, Not to Bury It*, 93 YALE L. J. 259, 285 (1983).

descendants, if the decedent has left a surviving spouse or descendants.

Several factors explain the formality of the probate system. First, ascertaining the property owner's intent is difficult after the owner's death. When a donor gives a diamond ring to his wife or a watch to his daughter, the donor's intent is not difficult to ascertain. There is little ambiguity in the donor's behavior, and if there were any doubt, donor would be available to explain his action. By contrast, written instructions by the donor about how his property should be distributed after his death raise a host of questions: did the donor give the instructions (or were they forged)? If donor did write the instructions, were those instructions designed to represent his final, deliberate decision about how his property should be distributed, or were they merely preliminary reflections? When decedent wrote the instructions, did he have adequate capacity? Was he free from any undue influence? After death, the donor is not around to shed light on these questions.

Second, title issues arise when a property owner attempts to make a transfer effective only after her death. Suppose a property owner leaves real property to her daughter by will. How would a prospective purchaser from the daughter assure that the daughter had good title to convey? The daughter could not satisfy a prospective purchaser by showing the purchaser a signed copy of the property owner's will, because the purchaser would have no way of ascertaining that the will is genuine, or that the property owner did not subsequently change her will. Some final determination that the estate should be distributed in accordance with the will would be necessary to reassure prospective purchasers. And it is that final determination that the probate process provides. Moreover, title issues like these are not limited to real estate; purchasers of securities need similar assurances that the will was effective to pass title.

The probate system, however, applies only to assets owned by the decedent at death. A property owner can bypass the probate system by transferring assets before his or her death. As most of us have experienced first-hand, birthday gifts do not require judicial supervision. Even more significant gifts can be completed by simple delivery of the subject of the gift, or of a written instrument that serves as the substitute for the subject in cases where physical delivery would be impractical—as in the case of land or intangible property.

Lifetime gifts are the most obvious form of non-probate transfer, but they are not nearly as important in the wealth transmission process as another form of non-probate transfer: transfer by the terms of an instrument creating a tenancy by the entireties or a joint tenancy with right of survivorship. If two parties hold property as joint tenants or as tenants by the entireties, when the first of the two dies, the property passes to the other automatically. The transfer that occurs is a non-probate transfer, because the surviving owner takes the property not as decedent's heir or by the terms of decedent's will, but by the terms of the instrument that created the joint tenancy or tenancies by the entireties.

The law has long recognized lifetime gifts and joint tenancies as non-probate transfers. The notorious costs and delays associated with the probate system have, however, led increasing numbers of property owners to invent and use newer forms of non-probate transfers, particularly forms that enable property owners to reap most of the benefits associated with disposing of the property by will: retention by the property owner of substantial control over the property during the owner's lifetime, and freedom to revoke the transfer until death. Although courts and legislatures once exhibited hostility toward these efforts, the legal system has gradually become more hospitable to transfers designed to avoid probate.

The first probate avoidance device to generate widespread acceptance was the "bank account trust," also known as the "Totten Trust", after In re Totten,[2] a leading case enforcing the device. Property owner opens a bank account in her own name, "in trust for" a designated beneficiary. By the terms of the account agreement, the account will pass to the beneficiary at the depositor's death, but the beneficiary enjoys no rights in the account until the depositor's death; depositor remains free to withdraw and spend all of the money, or to give it to another beneficiary. Most courts routinely treat the deposits in bank account trusts as assets that pass outside the depositor's probate estate, even though the beneficiary had no significant rights in the property until the moment of the depositor's death.

In more recent decades, courts and legislatures have generalized the rule that applies to bank account trusts. First, statutes authorize accounts that explicitly make assets "payable on death" to designated beneficiaries. These accounts are not limited to savings banks, but can be used to arrange non-probate transfer of a wide variety of investments. Second, courts have upheld revocable lifetime trusts that reserve for the trust's creator all significant powers of ownership. That is, a property owner can create a lifetime trust, reserving to himself the power to act as "trustee" and life beneficiary of the trust property, and also reserving a power to revoke the trust. The trust "beneficiary" does not acquire a significant interest until the property owner's death, and then only if the property owner has

---

[2]   179 N.Y. 112, 71 N.E. 748 (1904).

not previously revoked or modified the beneficiary's interest in the trust. As a result, revocable lifetime trusts have become popular vehicles for avoiding probate; courts treat the transfer as effective when the trust was created, not when the dispositions became irrevocable. Therefore, the trust property does not pass through the property owner's estate, and does not enter the probate system.

The first portion of this book, dealing with intestate succession and the law of wills, deals largely with probate transfers. The book then returns to examine non-probate transfers in the later chapters.

Chapter Two

INTESTATE SUCCESSION

I. Introduction

Most Americans die without wills. The property of a person who dies without a will—that is, of a person who dies *intestate*—is distributed in accordance with the intestate succession statutes enacted by the state legislature. Those statutes invariably direct decedent's property to close family members.

The preference for family members reflects a number of factors. Perhaps most important is the presumed intent of the decedent. Most decedents who write wills leave the bulk of their estates to family members. People who don't write wills often are too poor or uninformed to seek legal advice. Sometimes, contemplating their own deaths makes them uncomfortable. In either event, there appears little reason to believe that people who don't write wills have preferences significantly different from those held by people who do write wills. Because legislatures have little reason to "punish" decedents who fail to write wills, intestate succession statutes typically reflect legislative guesses about how decedents would want to have their estates distributed, and those guesses generally lead to close family members.

Reasons of policy also support the legislative preference for close family members. Those are the very people most likely to have contributed to the accumulation of decedent's property, and they are also the people most likely to be dependent on that property. Moreover, administrative convenience supports the preference for close family members: how would courts determine how much decedent would want to leave to which charities and which friends? Intestate succession statutes do not focus on the intent of the particular decedent; instead, they provide a "one size fits all" framework. This approach consumes fewer judicial resources in evaluating the intent of particular decedents; a decedent who wants to make an unusual disposition of her property is free to do so, but only by writing a will.

Although intestate succession statutes operate primarily to distribute the property of people who die without a valid will, their importance extends beyond people who die intestate. Sometimes, a poorly drafted will fails to distribute all of decedent's estate. In that case, property that is not devised by testator's will is distributed to testator's intestate heirs. For instance, suppose decedent executes a will making a number of charitable gifts, and leaving the remainder of her property "to my husband." If the husband dies before decedent, the remainder of decedent's estate will be distributed in accordance with the intestate succession statute. Second, a will or other instrument sometimes makes a disposition to the "heirs" of the decedent or some other person. Who are a person's heirs? The people who would succeed to that person's estate by intestate succession. Third, intestate succession statutes often determine who has standing to contest a will. Suppose decedent has written a will leaving his entire estate to a religious organization. Suppose further that decedent's sister believes the decedent lacked mental capacity to execute that will. Unless the sister was the beneficiary of a prior will, the sister would have standing to contest the will benefitting the religious organization only if the sister would share in decedent's estate by intestate succession.

II. Terminology

The language of intestate succession is in many respects the product of history. The common law developed two different intestate succession systems, one for real property and the other for personal property. Real property passed by **descent** to the decedent's **heirs** or **heirs at law**. By contrast, a decedent's personal property passed by **distribution** to decedent's **next of kin** or **distributees**. Most modern intestate succession statutes use the same scheme for all property, real and personal. For practical purposes, "next of kin" and "heirs" have become synonymous. Nevertheless, a number of statutes (and court decisions) continue to use language that reflects the historical distinctions between real and personal property.

Intestate succession schemes invariably give a decedent's **descendants** or **issue** priority over **collateral relatives** in the distribution of an intestate estate. Descendants or issue, sometimes called **lineals** or **lineal descendants**, include a person's children, grandchildren, great-grandchildren and others who can trace their lineage directly to the decedent. Collateral relatives, by contrast, are those who share a common ancestor with decedent, but who cannot trace their lineage directly to the decedent. Decedent's siblings, cousins, nieces and nephews, and uncles and aunts are examples of collateral relatives. Siblings, nieces, and nephews can trace their lineage to decedent's parent or parents; first cousins, uncles, and aunts can trace their lineage to decedent's grandparent or grandparents.

III. The Share of the Surviving Spouse

A. In General

1. *Common Law States*

Every intestate succession statute provides the decedent's surviving spouse with a share of decedent's estate. The size of that share, however, is subject to considerable variation. Historically, the common law did not treat decedent's spouse as decedent's heir, and the spouse did not inherit a decedent's real estate. Instead, the spouse was entitled to dower or curtesy rights in real estate, which permitted the spouse to enjoy the fruits of that real estate during the spouse's life, but which gave the spouse no right to dispose of the real estate after death. By contrast, the common law did treat the spouse as a distributee of personal property. As we have seen, however, modern intestate succession statutes do not distinguish between real and personal property; the surviving spouse is generally entitled to share in all of decedent's property.

Nevertheless, the size of the spouse's share depends on the decedent's family situation. If decedent died survived by the spouse and issue, the statute often (but not always) requires the spouse to share the estate with the issue; how much the spouse takes varies considerably from state to state. If decedent is not survived by issue, some statutes give the entire estate to the spouse, while others require the spouse to share the estate with decedent's parents, or even with decedent's siblings.

A surviving spouse is generally entitled to an intestate share even if the decedent and the spouse were separated at the time of the decedent's death. Equitable distribution rules in most states assure, upon a final judgment of divorce, that the couple's property will be divided between them without regard to formal title. But before a final judgment of divorce, one party might hold all of the couple's assets, even though the other contributed substantially to those assets. Permitting the surviving spouse to take an intestate share— even if the couple has been separated—assures that the surviving spouse will not be left without a fair share of the marital assets.

2. *Community Property States*

A number of American states, including the two largest— California and Texas—have community property laws. These states treat property acquired during the marriage (other than by gift or inheritance) as the product of joint efforts of the husband and wife. Each, therefore, has a half share. Property acquired before marriage or by gift or inheritance is the separate property of the respective spouse.

Each spouse has a power of testamentary disposition only over his or her half of the community property. Thus, the surviving spouse has a guaranteed half interest in all community property, whether or not decedent has left a will. When the decedent spouse has not left a will, the remaining half of the decedent spouse's estate passes through the intestate succession statute.

B. The Uniform Probate Code

The Uniform Probate Code incorporates two distinctive features in its treatment of the surviving spouse's intestate share. First, the spouse's share is larger than is typical of other intestate succession statutes. Second, the UPC takes into account the large number of blended families, and adjusts the share of the surviving spouse to reflect the composition of those blended families. UPC § 2–102 determines the share of the surviving spouse in a variety of family situations, but that section does not indicate how to distribute the balance of the estate; for that, one must examine section 2–103.

In two circumstances, UPC § 2–102(1) provides that a surviving spouse shall take the entire estate of an intestate decedent. The first, more traditional circumstance, is when decedent is survived by neither descendants nor parents. But Section 2–102(1) also provides that the surviving spouse shall take decedent's entire estate in the case of the "traditional" family, in which the decedent is survived by descendants, but the only surviving descendants of either spouse are the descendants of both spouses. The assumption underlying this provision is that the decedent and the surviving spouse have a common interest in providing for their children, and that the spouse can be counted upon to provide for those children after the decedent's death. The UPC provision tracks the general preferences of "traditional family" decedents who write wills, most of whom leave the vast bulk of their estates to their spouses because they do trust those spouses to provide for the couple's common descendants.

By contrast, when the decedent is survived by descendants who are not descendants of the surviving spouse, or when the surviving spouse has both descendants who are descendants of the decedent and descendants who are not descendants of the decedent, the UPC does not assume that the surviving spouse will provide adequately for decedent's descendants. As a result, the UPC provides the surviving spouse with a significant share of the intestate estate, but not the entire estate.

The statute differentiates between two types of blended families. First, when the descendants who are not common to the decedent and the spouse are all descendants of the surviving spouse, UPC § 2–102(3) allocates to the surviving spouse the first $225,000 of the estate, plus one-half of the balance. In this circumstance, the surviving spouse has every reason to provide for decedent's descendants (all of whom are also the spouse's own descendants), but the spouse might be more generous to the spouse's own descendants than the decedent would prefer. As a result, the UPC provides that the spouse must share the estate balance above $225,000 with decedent's issue, limiting the spouse's freedom to treat the spouse's own children more favorably than decedent might want.

Second, when the decedent has descendants who are not also the surviving spouse's descendants, UPC § 2–102(4) recognizes the danger that the surviving spouse might disadvantage those descendants. As a result, after giving the surviving spouse the first $150,000 of the intestate estate, the statute permits decedent's descendants to share equally with the spouse in the balance above $150,000.

Finally, in those cases where decedent is not survived by any descendants, but is survived by a parent or parents, UPC § 2–102(2) gives the spouse the first $300,000 of the intestate estate, plus three-fourths of the balance above $300,000.

IV. Distribution Among Decedent's Descendants

As we have seen, when a decedent dies survived by descendants—often called "issue"—those descendants take to the exclusion of all collateral relatives. In the ordinary course, the descendants who survive the decedent will be the decedent's children. Intestate succession statutes invariably provide for equal treatment of children, principally because equal treatment reflects the preferences of most decedents. Moreover, when the decedent's children survive the decedent, decedent's grandchildren and great-grandchildren do not share in decedent's estate. This exclusion of more remote descendants reflects a more general principle of intestate succession law: whenever decedent is survived by a family member—whether it be a descendant or a collateral relative—the intestate succession statute excludes descendants of that family member from any portion of the intestate estate.

Often, however, one or more of a decedent's children will have predeceased the child, leaving descendants. In these circumstances, equality of treatment becomes more complicated, and states have taken different approaches about how decedent's estate should be distributed. The most traditional approach, the one embodied in the English Statute of Distributions, is a **strict *per stirpes* distribution**. The strict *per stirpes* approach divides the intestate estate at the level of decedent's children, whether or not decedent has any surviving children, and then divides the share of each deceased child among that child's descendants. To illustrate, consider the following family tree:

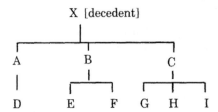

Assume that X's children, A, B, and C, have all died before X. If a jurisdiction provides for strict *per stirpes* distribution, the estate will be divided into three shares—one each for A, B, and C. D will take A's share, E and F will split B's share, and G, H, and I will divide C's share.

The strict *per stirpes* distribution treats X's children equally; X's grandchildren take the shares they would have received if A, B, and C had survived X, and then passed their inheritances on to their respective children. But note the disadvantage of the strict *per stirpes* scheme: testator's closest living relatives, her grandchildren, are treated *un*equally; D takes three times as large a share of X's estate as do G, H, or I.

In reaction to this inequality, many intestate succession statutes adopted an alternative approach, known as a **modern *per stirpes* distribution**. The modern *per stirpes* approach divides the intestate estate at the closest level of descendants in which there is at least one person alive at decedent's death, and then divides the share of each deceased descendant in that generation among the descendants of that deceased descendant. Thus, in the family tree reproduced above, if A, B, and C all died before X, a modern *per stirpes* distribution would divide X's estate at the level of grandchildren; D, E, F, G, H, and I would each take 1/6 of X's estate.

Note, however, that the modern *per stirpes* distribution treats X's grandchildren equally only if all of X's children die before X. If B, for instance, has survived X, a modern *per stirpes* distribution divides X's estate at the level of children—the closest generation to X in which there is at least one surviving descendant. B takes one share, D takes A's share, and G, H, and I divide C's share—the same result that would apply in a strict *per stirpes* distribution.

The Uniform Probate Code takes yet a third approach, which the Code labels **distribution "by representation"** (the Code's approach is sometimes called **distribution "*per capita* at each generation"**). This approach, embodied in section 2–106(b) of the UPC, assures that all members of any generation of descendants who share in a decedent's estate will share equally. UPC § 2–106(b) starts, as does a modern *per stirpes* distribution, by dividing the estate at the closest level of descendants in which there is at least one person alive at decedent's death. For instance, in the family tree above, if X were survived by B and by the children of A and C, the estate would be divided into three shares. Also like a modern *per stirpes* distribution, UPC § 2–106(b) would allocate one of those three shares to B, the only person alive in the generation of children. At that point, however, the approach of UPC § 2–106(b) diverges from the modern *per stirpes* approach. The UPC provides that the shares allocated to deceased members of the closest generation with at least one person alive should then be recombined, and distributed as if the persons already allocated a share, and their descendants, had predeceased the decedent. Thus, in the family tree above, two-thirds of X's estate would be distributed as if X had been survived only by D, G, H, and I. But if X had been survived only by those four people— all of whom are X's grandchildren—X's estate would have been divided at the level of grandchildren, and all of those grandchildren would take equal shares. Thus, D, G, H, and I would each take one-quarter of two-thirds of X's estate, which computes to one-sixth of the estate each. If, however, any of these grandchildren had themselves predeceased X, leaving issue, their shares would be recombined, and distributed in the same manner. For instance, if D and I had died before X, their shares would be recombined, and divided among their issue as if their issue were X's only surviving descendants. Thus, if D left two children and I left one, each of the three great-grandchildren would take one-ninth of X's total estate (one third of two-sixths).

A number of states have adopted the UPC, and with it, section 2–106(b). Some other states have adopted the representation provision even though they have not adopted the remainder of the UPC. Many other states, however have retained a strict *per stirpes* or modern *per stirpes* approach, making it essential for a Trusts and Estates lawyer to understand each alternative. The terms "*per stirpes*" or "representation" are not terms of art. State statutes vary in how they define those words. As a result, careful reading of the applicable statute is always essential.

V. Distribution Among Ancestors and Collateral Relatives

A. In General

When an intestate decedent is not survived by a spouse or descendants, most intestate succession statutes award the entire estate to decedent's surviving parents, if there are any. If decedent is survived by both parents, the parents typically share equally in the decedent's estate. In a few states, decedent's siblings share equally with decedent's parents.

When the decedent is not survived by parents, most intestate statutes distribute the estate to descendants of parents, excluding other collateral relatives. When all of decedent's siblings survive decedent, the siblings share equally. When some or all of decedent's siblings have predeceased decedent, leaving issue, the distribution questions that arise are similar to those that arise when decedent leaves surviving descendants. The basic question is whether the initial division should be made at the level closest to the decedent (here, siblings), or at the level closest to the decedent in which there is a surviving descendant (which, if all decedent's siblings predecease decedent, would be the level of nieces and nephews, or, if nieces and nephews have died, grandnieces and grandnephews). Jurisdictions that take a strict *per stirpes* approach divide at the level of siblings; jurisdictions that take a modern *per stirpes* approach or the UPC's "by representation" approach make the initial division at the closest level with surviving descendants. Once the initial division is made, the differences between a modern *per stirpes* approach and the UPC's "by representation" approach are the same as those that arise with respect to decedent's descendants.

When decedent is not survived by descendants of parents, most intestate succession statutes distribute the estate to grandparents, or descendants of decedent's grandparents—uncles and aunts and their descendants. Distribution among issue of decedent's grandparents, however, raises a host of questions. The first of them is whether there should be a preliminary division of the intestate estate into two halves—one for issue of decedent's maternal grandparents and the other for issue of decedent's paternal grandparents? Consider a hypothetical family situation:

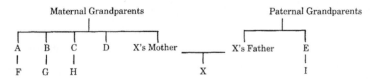

Assume X has died, survived by five uncles and aunts, A, B, C, D, and E. In jurisdictions that do not distinguish between issue of maternal grandparents and issue of paternal grandparents, X's estate would be divided into five equal shares. Some states, however, mandate an equal division of the estate between the maternal side of the family and the paternal side. In these states, E, as the only surviving issue of paternal grandparents, would take one-half of X's estate; the other half would be divided equally among A, B, C, and D. States that mandate an equal division, however, permit the issue of one set of grandparents to take the entire estate when there are no surviving issue of the other set of grandparents.

The second issue involves distribution of assets among descendants of grandparents who are of different generations. Many jurisdictions follow the same pattern that they use for distribution among issue of parents; depending on the statute, distribution could follow a strict *per stirpes* pattern, a modern *per stirpes* pattern, or the UPC's "by representation" pattern.

Other jurisdictions, however, take a different approach, holding that surviving relatives closer in kinship to the decedent take to the exclusion of descendants of deceased relatives with that same degree of kinship to the decedent. The New Hampshire statute (NH RSA 561:3) is illustrative. The statute provides that "no representation shall be allowed among collaterals beyond the fourth degree of relationship to the decedent." The statute's reference to the "fourth degree of relationship" requires an understanding of the Table of Consanguinity:

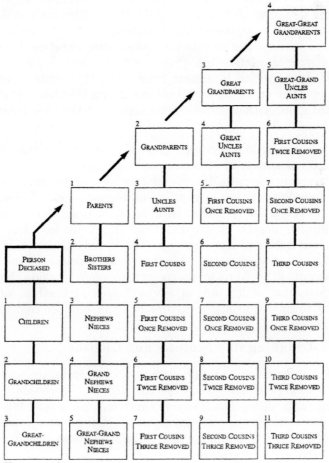

TABLE OF CONSANGUINITY
(Showing Degrees of Relationship)

The Table is not itself law in most jurisdictions; instead, it represents background information that assists in interpretation of statutes. The table operates as follows: to determine how many degrees of kinship separate a decedent from a particular relative, first count up to the common ancestor of the decedent and the relative, and then continue counting down from the common ancestor to the relative. For example to determine the degrees of kinship between decedent and a first cousin, count up two degrees to decedent's grandparent (the common ancestor), and then count down two more degrees from the grandparent to the first cousin, for a total of four degrees.

Against that background, consider the New Hampshire statute, which precludes representation beyond the fourth degree of relationship. Suppose in the hypothetical family situation above, decedent X is survived by three maternal first cousins, F, G, and H, and no one else. F, G, and H would take equally under any statutory scheme. Now suppose, however, that H had predeceased X, leaving a surviving daughter, J. Under the New Hampshire statute, J would not take as H's representative. Instead, J would be excluded altogether because the statute precludes representation beyond the fourth degree of relationship. Only if F and G had also predeceased X would J be entitled to inherit, because in that event J would be taking in her own right, as X's closest living relative, and not "by representation." Other states use variations on the New Hampshire approach.

The Table of Consanguinity plays an even more significant role in some other states; in Massachusetts, for instance, if decedent is not survived by a spouse, descendants, or issue of parents, the estate is distributed to decedent's "next of kin in equal degree." Mass. Gen. L., ch. 190B, § 2–103 (4). That is, if decedent is survived by a great uncle (fourth degree of kinship), the great uncle takes to the exclusion of a child of decedent's first cousin (fifth degree of kinship), even though the great uncle is not a descendant of decedent's grandparent. (The Massachusetts statute does provide, however, that when next of kin are of equal degree of kinship, relatives claiming through the nearest ancestor shall be preferred to those claiming through a more remote ancestor).

B. Laughing Heir Statutes and Escheat

As the preceding section demonstrates, intestate succession statutes diverge more sharply as the distance increases between decedent and decedent's closest surviving relatives. When the distance becomes sufficiently great, many jurisdictions provide that decedent's relatives should not share in the estate at all; instead, the estate "escheats" to the state.

This decision to cut off inheritance when decedent's survivors become too distant rests on two grounds. First, the more distant the survivors, the more difficult (and costly) it becomes to determine who the closest survivors are, and to locate them. Second, as the survivors become more distant, it becomes increasingly less likely that there was a close connection between the decedent and the survivors. Hence, there is little reason to infer that decedent would have cared whether those survivors shared in the estate.

Although the common law assumed that a decedent always had heirs, the statutory limitations on inheritance rights by distant relatives are often referred to as "laughing heir" provisions because they preclude inheritance by relatives whose glee at receiving an inheritance would not be mitigated by any grief over the decedent's death (although the more compelling reason for such statutes is that they reduce the costs and delay associated with tracking down the decedent's long-lost relatives). Jurisdictions differ, however, on precisely how distant a decedent's nearest survivors must be to avoid escheat of decedent's estate.

C.   The Uniform Probate Code

Uniform Probate Code § 2–103, like most other intestate succession statutes, provides that when a decedent is survived by parents, but by no spouse or issue, decedent's estate should be distributed to decedent's parents equally, if both survive, and to the surviving parent if only one survives. (Indeed, even if decedent is survived by a spouse but no issue, parents will share in a large intestate estate; UPC § 2–102(2) combines with UPC § 2–103(a)(2) to give the parents one-quarter of the amount by which the estate exceeds $300,000).

When decedent is not survived by parents, UPC § 2–103(a)(3) provides for distribution to descendants of parents—brothers, sisters, and their issue. As with distribution to lineal descendants, the UPC provides that distribution to descendants of parents should be "by representation" as that term is defined in UPC § 2–106. In other words, distribution should be per capita at each generation. (*See generally* the discussion in section IV, supra).

When decedent is not survived by descendants of parents, UPC § 2–103(a)(4) provides for distribution to descendants of grandparents. If decedent is survived both by descendants of maternal grandparents and by descendants of paternal grandparents, decedent's estate is first cut in half, with one-half allocated to each set of descendants. Then, each half is distributed to descendants "by representation." If, on the other hand, decedent is survived only by descendants of one set of grandparents, then the entire estate passes to that half.

The 2008 revisions to the UPC provide that when decedent is not survived by any descendants of grandparents, decedent's step children and their descendants will take decedent's estate. *See* UPC § 2–103(b). In the absence of step-descendants, UPC § 2–105 provides for escheat to the state. More remote relatives do not inherit.

VI.   Defining the Modern Family: Halfbloods, Adoptees, and Non-Marital Children

The American family is not always a simple entity composed of parents married for life and children born within the marital relationship. For many, the family is a complex web of relationships affected by divorce, remarriage, adoption, and non-marital relationships. Through a combination of legislation, common law adaptation, and constitutional mandate, intestate succession law has adapted to reflect the dynamic nature of the American family.

A.   Halfbloods

When two people share one parent, but not the other, they are "halfblood" siblings. Often, halfblood siblings grow up in the same household, developing relationships indistinguishable from "wholeblood" siblings. In other circumstances, however, halfblood siblings share few common experiences. Consider, for instance, a divorce that leaves the couple's children in the custody of their mother. If the father moves elsewhere, remarries, and starts a new family, the children of the first marriage may have little relationship to the children of the second marriage.

Moreover, the halfblood problem is not restricted to siblings. For example, a person may have a halfblood niece or nephew (the child of a halfblood sibling), or a halfblood first cousin (the child of a halfblood sibling of decedent's mother or father).

The modern trend—reflected in Uniform Probate Code § 2–107—is to treat halfbloods equally with wholebloods. Treating halfbloods and wholebloods equally reflects the realities of many, but not all, halfblood relationships, and also has the advantage of simplicity. In those states that opt against equal treatment, the question becomes what inheritance rights should halfbloods receive?

Some statutes provide that when a decedent is survived by relatives of the half blood and relatives of the whole blood in the same degree, half blood relatives take half as much as whole blood relatives. So, for instance, if decedent were survived by a halfblood brother and two wholeblood sisters, the sisters would each take two-fifths of the estate, and the brother would take one-fifth.

Other statutes provide that wholeblood relatives take to the exclusion of halfblood relatives of the same degree. Courts have sometimes construed these statutes to exclude halfblood relatives even when they are of a closer degree of kinship than the wholebloods. Thus, one court has concluded that wholeblood nieces and nephews take to the exclusion of a halfblood sister, because the nieces and nephews step into the shoes of their deceased parents.

Still other jurisdictions treat halfbloods and wholebloods equally, except in the case of property that has come to the decedent by inheritance from one of his ancestors, in which case those halfbloods who are not of the blood of the ancestor are precluded from inheritance. These "ancestral property" statutes have been heavily criticized, both because they create administrative headaches and because they make no logical sense: whole blood relatives of decedent who were not related at all to the ancestor are nevertheless entitled to inherit!

B. Adoption

Adoption statutes typically attempt to transplant adopted children from their biological families into their adoptive families. To that end, intestate succession statutes almost invariably provide that adoptive children inherit from their adoptive parents, and also from other members of the adoptive family—siblings, grandparents, aunts, uncles, and more distant collateral relatives.

At the same time, intestate succession statutes typically preclude adopted children from inheriting from their biological parents. In the case of the child given up for adoption at birth, this result makes some sense; the biological family often loses touch with the child, and policy suggests that the child should be transplanted as completely as possible into its new family. But many adoptions are not intended to remove the child from its natural family. The most common example involves the stepparent adoption that occurs when a child is adopted by a parent's second spouse after the first spouse has died or after the child's parents were divorced. In that instance, there is little reason to believe that the death or divorce severed the ties of affection that bound the child and his or her natural relatives.

In recognition of the continuing ties between a child and his or her natural parents in cases of stepparent adoptions, UPC § 2–119(b) provides explicitly that adoption by the spouse of either natural parent has no effect on the relationship between the child and that natural parent, and no effect on the right of the child to inherit from or through the other natural parent. To illustrate the statute's application, consider a child adopted by its mother's second husband after the death of the child's father. UPC § 2–119(b)(1) makes the child the heir of his or her mother, and § 2–119(b)(2) makes the child an heir of his or her adoptive father, and of the parents (and potentially, the siblings and other collateral relatives) of his or her natural father. That is, if the natural father's mother were to die intestate, the adoptive child would be entitled to take an intestate share. But the inheritance rights are not reciprocal. UPC § 2–119(b)(2) does not permit the blood relatives of the natural father to take by intestacy from the adopted child.

On occasion, a child who is orphaned will be adopted by a grandmother, aunt, uncle or other relative. This can cause complications in intestacy proceedings. For example, if an orphaned child is adopted by her father's mother, is she still an heir of her own mother's relatives? And if her father's sister dies, is the child a sibling or a niece of that sister? UPC § 2–119(c) addresses this issue, providing that an adoption by a relative of the child's genetic parent does not cut off the child's rights (or the rights of the adopted child's descendants) to inherit from either genetic parent. Section 2–113 directs that an individual who is related to a decedent through two lines of relationship is entitled only to a single share, based on the relationship that would entitle the individual to the larger share.

Not all state statutes track the Uniform Probate Code, but the sensible results the statute reaches are likely to make these provisions of the UPC increasingly influential, both in the legislatures and in the courts.

Most adoptions occur when the adopted child is a minor. A number of statutes, however, permit adoption of adults, often subject to limitations. Should a child adopted as an adult be entitled to inherit through its adoptive parent? When intestate succession statutes deal with adopted children, they do not distinguish between children adopted as minors and children adopted as adults. As a result, the persons adopted as adults would appear entitled to the same treatment as persons adopted as children. In general, this rule is not subject to abuse: a person who seeks to preclude inheritance by adopted adults can achieve that objective by writing a will that cuts out the adopted adult. In circumstances where it is clear, however, that an adult adoption is motivated by a desire to procure an inheritance from a decedent who would not want the adopted adult to inherit, courts might decline to apply the general rule.

As with childhood adoptions, adult adoptions can preclude the adoptee and the adoptee's issue from inheriting from the adoptee's biological relatives. For instance, in Kummer v. Donak, decedent's biological sister had been adopted, at age 53, by her husband's aunt. When decedent died, the Virginia Supreme Court held that the sister's adoption precluded her three children from inheriting from decedent.[1]

C.   Inheritance from Stepparents and Other Caretakers

Suppose a child has grown up in a decedent's home, and the decedent had cared for the child and treated the child as his or her own, but the relationship between caretaker and child had never been legally formalized. Should the child be entitled to inherit from the caretaker? In general, the answer has been no, subject to significant exceptions.

One issue involves the right to inherit from a stepparent: a parent's spouse who has not adopted the child. In most states, a child does not inherit from or through its stepparents. In cases where the child's absent biological parent has died, this result would generally appear to reflect the stepparent's intent: if the stepparent had wanted to be treated as a parent, the stepparent could have adopted the child. Failure to adopt generates an inference that the stepparent did not consider the child as his or her own. But when the absent biological parent is alive, adoption by a stepparent requires the consent of the biological parent or termination of parental rights. In that situation, the failure of the stepparent to adopt sheds no light on the closeness of the relationship between stepparent and stepchild. California has dealt with this situation by permitting inheritance by intestate succession from a stepparent (or a foster parent) when two conditions are met: first, the relationship between the parties must have begun during the child's minority and continued through the joint lifetimes of the parties, and second, clear and convincing evidence establishes that the stepparent or foster parent would have adopted but for a legal barrier. In 2008, the UPC was amended to give step-children inheritance rights in rare circumstances—if the deceased is not survived by a spouse, descendants, parents, siblings, descendants of siblings, grandparents or descendants of grandparents, but decedent's predeceased spouse (or spouses) have surviving children, those children will take to avoid escheat. In most states, however, the stepparent would have to write a will to enable the stepchild to inherit.

In other circumstances, a child may be raised by a caretaker who has no formal legal relationship to either the child or its natural parents. In these circumstances, some states have developed a doctrine of "equitable adoption" to permit the child to inherit from the caretaker by intestate succession. The equitable adoption doctrine rests on the fiction that when a caretaker takes a child into his or her home, the caretaker impliedly agrees with the child's

---

[1]   Kummer v. Donak, 715 S.E.2d 7 (Va. 2011).

natural parents that he or she will adopt the child. If the parties rely on this agreement, the child will be entitled to whatever benefits flow from status as the caretaker's child, even if the caretaker never performs the implied "agreement." Among those benefits is inheritance by intestate succession. Equitable adoption doctrine, however, is not reciprocal. In the absence of a formal adoption, the caretaker is not entitled to inherit from the child.

D. Non-Marital Children and Proof of Paternity

Historically, inheritance law discriminated against children born outside of marriage. At common law, non-marital children (often labeled "bastards" or, later, "illegitimates") were not entitled to inherit from or through either parent. Intestate succession statutes generally ameliorated that harsh treatment, permitting non-marital children to inherit from or through their mothers. Most states, however, placed significant restrictions on the right of non-marital children to inherit from or through their fathers.

The United States Supreme Court, however, transformed the law in this area. In Trimble v. Gordon,[2] the Court held unconstitutional an Illinois statute that permitted a non-marital child to inherit from his or her father only if the parents had legitimated the child by marrying each other and the father had acknowledged the child as his during the child's lifetime. The Court rejected altogether one of the justifications the state offered for the statute—the statute encouraged legitimate family relationships—questioning the premise that "persons will shun illicit relations because the offspring may not one day reap the benefits." By contrast, the Court acknowledged the force of the state's other justification: the statute facilitated orderly transmission of decedent's property. But the Court concluded that the justification could not support the statute as drafted, because the statute excluded some categories of non-marital children whose inheritance rights could have been recognized without jeopardizing the orderly settlement of estates.

In effect, Trimble and a successor case, Lalli v. Lalli,[3] established that the states could justify excluding non-marital children from intestate succession rights only by applying procedural rules designed to assure adequate proof of paternity. In light of these cases, states reformed their intestate succession statutes to permit non-marital children to inherit from their fathers, subject to requirements designed to ensure adequate proof of paternity.

As DNA testing becomes more sophisticated and available, proving paternity should serve as less of an obstacle to intestate

---

[2]   430 U.S. 762 (1977).

[3]   439 U.S. 259 (1978).

succession from biological fathers. Technology, however, raises new problems for courts and legislatures to solve. First, what impact should DNA testing have on the presumption of legitimacy that arises when a child is born to a married woman? Legislatures and courts have long treated the husband of a child's biological mother as the child's father. And, indeed, in most cases, the husband treats the child as his own, and may believe the child is his own. Should such a child be entitled to inherit from the husband if the husband's other intestate heirs prove that the husband is not the child's father? And should the child be entitled to inherit from its biological father—in addition to or instead of any rights the child has to inherit from its mother's husband? These issues raise basic questions about the importance of biology in determining family relationships.

Modern reproductive technology will also have an impact on intestate succession law. The 2008 amendments to the UPC deal explicitly and in great detail with the parentage issues presented by reproductive technology. Parties engaged in procreation through assisted reproduction can eliminate issues by identifying the parents on the birth certificate or setting forth their understandings in writing. In the absence of such measures, UPC sections 2–120 and 2–121 set forth a detailed framework for resolving parentage issues. The statute ties the definition of "parent" to the intentions and actions of the parties involved in the process. Those who intend to function as "donors"—of eggs, sperm or womb—are not presumed to be parents of the subsequently born child, while those who use (or support someone who is using) reproductive technologies with the intent to become a parent are deemed "parents." The UPC sets forth factors to assist a court in determining "intent."

VII. Simultaneous Death

To share in a decedent's intestate estate, a prospective heir must be alive at the time of decedent's death. Suppose, however, decedent and the prospective heir die in a common accident, making it difficult to determine who died first. How should decedent's intestate estate be distributed? Note the alternatives. If the law were to treat the prospective heir as surviving the decedent, then the heir's share of the decedent's estate would be distributed to the heir's heirs, or to the beneficiaries of the heir's will—not to decedent's closest living relatives. For instance, if a wealthy decedent and her less wealthy husband were to die in a common car crash, a rule that treated the husband as surviving the decedent would mean that the decedent's assets would pass to the husband's blood relatives, while the husband's smaller estate would pass to the decedent's relatives—an anomalous result.

To avoid this problem, simultaneous death statutes universally provide that when an intestate decedent dies simultaneously with one of decedent's heirs, the decedent should be treated as having survived the prospective heir. Thus, if husband and wife die in a common accident, and both are intestate and childless at the time of the accident, the husband's estate will be distributed as if the husband survived the wife (so that the husband's blood relatives share his estate), while the wife's estate will be distributed as if the wife survived the husband (assuring that the wife's blood relatives take her estate).

Simultaneous death statutes have generated far too much litigation about whether death of decedent and heir was in fact simultaneous. A number of statutes apply when "there is no sufficient evidence that the persons have died otherwise than simultaneously." This formulation leads to disputes in which thousands of dollars turn on minute differences in time of death, leading to extensive testimony by medical experts. Yet even if the heir survived decedent by three minutes—or three days—the decedent's intent would, in general, be advanced by treating the decedent as if the decedent survived, so that the decedent's estate passes to decedent's relatives and not the relatives (or will beneficiaries) of the heir.

Section 2–104 of the Uniform Probate Code has responded to this problem by requiring a prospective heir to survive decedent by 120 hours in order to qualify for distribution of an intestate estate. It also directs that one who is in gestation at decedent's death is presumed to survive the decedent if she lives for 120 hours after birth. The UPC provision is designed to reduce litigation over the precise order of death, and to give effect to intestate decedent's presumed wishes in a broader range of cases. The statute is inapplicable if its application would cause decedent's estate to escheat.

VIII. Disclaimer

At common law, title vested in an intestate heir automatically at the decedent's death; the heir was free to give away the inherited property, but could not "disclaim" or "renounce" the inheritance. Modern statutes have reversed the common law rule, and uniformly permit disclaimer by an intestate heir.

An heir might want to disclaim for any of three principal reasons. The first—of little practical importance—is that the heir's relationship with the intestate decedent was such that the heir wanted nothing to do with the decedent's property. The second reason is to direct the inherited assets away from creditors. The third is to minimize tax burdens.

Consider first the problem of creditor claims. If an heir is in debt when the decedent dies, the heir's creditors will have a claim against the inherited assets, perhaps leaving the heir with little benefit from the inheritance. If, by contrast, a disclaimer would prevent the heir's creditors from reaching the property, the heir might be better off, especially if the disclaimed property would pass to the heir's own children or grandchildren.

Most courts have held that if an heir executes a disclaimer, creditors cannot reach the disclaimed interest. These courts treat the disclaimed property as if it never reached the heir, and therefore never became available to the creditor. Other courts have permitted an heir's creditors to reach disclaimed assets. Whether a bankrupt heir may cut off the rights of a bankruptcy trustee by disclaiming an inheritance remains an open question. The timing of the disclaimer may matter; several courts of appeals have held that a disclaimer executed before the disclaiming heir petitions for bankruptcy is effective to cut off the rights of the bankruptcy trustee. There is more disagreement over whether a post-petition disclaimer can cut off the trustee's rights. The United States Supreme Court has held that a disclaimer does not defeat a federal tax lien, emphasizing that the power to channel estate assets constitutes property subject to the government's tax lien.[4]

Consider next the heir who disclaims for tax reasons. The heir may have a substantial estate of her own, and may want to assure that the inheritance does not become part of her own estate for federal estate tax purposes. By disclaiming, the heir may channel the disclaimed inheritance to her own children, without having the property pass through her estate.

The value of disclaimer to the disclaiming heir depends in large measure on the effect of a disclaimer. In general, when an heir disclaims, the intestate decedent's property will be distributed as if the disclaiming heir had predeceased the decedent. If the heir has issue, the disclaiming heir's share will pass to the heir's issue.

Section 2–1106(b)(3)(C) of the Uniform Probate Code includes a provision designed to prevent an heir from using disclaimer to pervert the UPC's "by representation" provisions. Imagine an intestate decedent who is survived by a son and the daughter of a deceased daughter. Imagine further that the son has four sons. Under the UPC (and all other intestate succession schemes), the son would divide the estate equally with the daughter's daughter. But suppose the son disclaims. Should the five grandchildren now divide the estate equally? That result would follow if we simply treated the son as having predeceased the decedent. But that result would

---

[4]   Drye v. United States, 528 U.S. 49 (1999).

encourage the son to disclaim to benefit his own children at the expense of his niece. But the statute prevents the son from enlarging his family's share in this way. Section 2–1106(b)(3)(C) provides:

> If by law or under the instrument, the descendants of the disclaimant would share in the disclaimed interest by any method of representation had the disclaimant died before the time of distribution, the disclaimed interest passes only to the descendants of the disclaimant who survive to the time of distribution.

In the comments to the section, the drafters explain that the "time of distribution" in an intestacy proceeding is the time of decedent's death.

IX. Disqualification from Inheritance: The Problem of the Murdering Heir

Should an heir who kills an intestate decedent be entitled to inherit from that decedent? The answer to that question is more complicated than it might seem at first glance. One problem is that many intestate succession statutes—enacted by state legislatures— do not include explicit exceptions for heirs who kill decedents. Nevertheless, courts have overcome that obstacle in a number of cases. And many state legislatures have enacted statutes preventing slayers from inheriting from the person they have killed.

These prohibitions rest on three policies. The first is that the slayer should not profit from his own wrong. The second involves deterrence: permitting the slayer to profit creates an unfortunate incentive to engage in murderous behavior. The third focuses on the intention of the decedent: it is a rare decedent who would want his killer to share in his estate.

These policies, however, suggest that not all killings should be treated alike. First, not all wrongs are equally blameworthy, and the principle that one should not profit from his own wrong carries more moral force with respect to intentional killings. Second, it is not clear that a prohibition on inheritance would effectively deter negligent or reckless killings (even if we assume that a prohibition would deter intentional killings). Finally, if the heir kills an intestate decedent negligently, or even recklessly, it is not clear that decedent would want to cut the killer out of his estate. As a result of these differences, some slayer statutes prohibit inheritance only in cases of murder, or in cases of intentional killing.

Note also that a slayer can be disqualified from inheriting even if the slayer has not been convicted in a criminal proceeding. An acquittal in a criminal trial establishes only the existence of reasonable doubt; heirs other than the slayer remain free, in a civil proceeding, to prove by a preponderance of the evidence that the slayer has killed the intestate decedent. By contrast, a criminal conviction bars the slayer from denying that he killed the decedent.

Uniform Probate Code section 2–803 embodies many of these principles. The statute provides for forfeiture of an intestate share (as well as any benefits under a will), when an heir "feloniously and intentionally kills the decedent." The killer is then treated as if he disclaimed his interest in the estate. Finally, UPC § 2–803(g) provides that a judgment of conviction establishing "criminal accountability for the felonious and intentional killing of the decedent conclusively establishes the convicted individual as the decedent's killer," while in the absence of a conviction, the probate court must determine, by a preponderance of the evidence, whether the heir "would be found criminally accountable" for a felonious and intentional killing.

X. Advancements

At common law, if an intestate decedent had made a substantial gift to an heir during decedent's lifetime, a presumption arose that the gift was an advancement of the heir's inheritance, and that the gift should be charged against the heir's intestate share. The presumption was rebuttable, but the burden of proof was on the heir to prove that the decedent did not intend an advancement.

Uniform Probate Code section 2–109, like many state statutes, reverses the common law presumption that a lifetime gift should be treated as an advancement. Under the UPC formulation, a gift is treated as an advancement only if (1) either the decedent or the heir acknowledges in writing that the gift is an advancement, or (2) the decedent or the heir indicates in writing that the gift is to be taken into account in computing division and distribution of decedent's intestate estate.

If a lifetime gift is to be treated as an advancement, the value of the property distributed to heirs as advancements should be added to the value of decedent's estate. That total is often referred to as the "hotchpot." The hotchpot should then be divided among the heirs in accordance with the provisions of the intestate succession statute. Amounts received during lifetime should then be charged against the shares of the heirs who received those amounts. If however, a particular heir received more than her intestate share as a lifetime gift, the heir would not be required to give back any of the advancement. Instead, that heir's share would be removed from the hotchpot, and the remainder of the hotchpot would be allocated as if that heir had predeceased the decedent, leaving no issue.

Problems

1.   Decedent, I, dies intestate, survived by her husband H, by the couple's children, A and B, by a child, C, born to her prior marriage to J, and by H's child D, born to H's prior marriage to K. I's net probate estate equals $300,000. Assuming the Uniform Probate Code is in force, how should the $300,000 be distributed?

How, if at all, would your answer change if C had never been born?

2.   Decedent, I, dies intestate, survived by a paternal first cousin, Z, and by a maternal uncle, A, three maternal first cousins Y, T, and S (all born to different parents), and three first cousins once removed, Q, R, and P, as illustrated on the chart at the top of the following page. I's net probate estate equals $300,000. Assuming the Uniform Probate Code is in force, how should the $300,000 estate be distributed?

How, if at all, would your answer change if Z also had predeceased I, and the jurisdiction's intestate succession statute provided for strict *per stirpes* distribution?

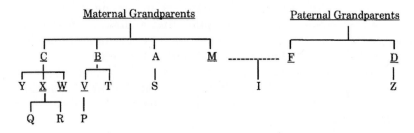

3.   Suppose, using the chart in Problem 2, P were the only relative to survive I. How would I's estate be distributed? Suppose now that P died, leaving I as her only surviving relative. How would P's estate be distributed?

4.   H and W, a married couple, died intestate as a result of an automobile accident. Other than W, H's closest surviving relatives were his sisters, Y and Z. Other than H, W's closest surviving relatives were a daughter, A, born to a prior marriage, and a brother, X, as illustrated on the chart below. Assume that the accident killed W instantly, but H survived for 10 days. If H had an estate of $100,000, and W had an estate of $500,000, how should their estates be distributed if the Uniform Probate Code is in effect?

How, if at all, would your answer change if H has survived W by 2 days instead of 10 days?

H's Parents   W's Parents

Y   Z   H —— W ⊤ J   X
                   A

5.   Decedent, I, dies intestate, survived by her daughter B, and six grandchildren, D, G, H, J, E, and F, as illustrated on the chart below. How should I's estate be distributed under the Uniform Probate Code?

How, if at all, would your answer change if B were to disclaim her inheritance?

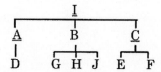

6.   Decedent, I, and her sister, C, are the offspring of a marriage between W and H. Before W married H, she had been married to G. W and G had a son, A. After W died, H married X, and the couple had a son, B. Suppose I died, survived by A, B, C, and X. How should I's estate be distributed if the Uniform Probate Code is in effect?

G —— W ⊤ H —— X
          ⊤   ⊤
    A   C I   B

How, if at all, would your answer change if X had adopted I and C after X's marriage to H?

How, if at all, would your answer change if, X adopted I and C, but died before I, so that I was survived only by A, B, and C?

Chapter Three

PROTECTION OF THE FAMILY

I. Introduction and Rationale

Within the United States, decedents are generally free to dispose of their property as they wish. All states provide one important qualification to testamentary freedom: decedent is not free to disinherit a spouse. This qualification has operated most frequently to protect wives against disinheritance by their husbands, largely because as a matter of history and culture, wives have been at a financial disadvantage with respect to their husbands. Men tended to be the family "breadwinners", and often held title to family assets in their own name. Traditional notions of fairness required that men support their wives, and those support obligations did not end at death.

In recent decades, the emerging "partnership" theory of marriage has provided the foundation for protecting spouses—husbands as well as wives—from disinheritance. That theory recognizes that spouses contribute to the well-being of a family in different ways. One spouse may earn more income while the other takes on a disproportionate share of family and household responsibilities. Each spouse's contribution to the family's well-being entitles that spouse to a share of the family assets, even if legal title to those assets may be in the name of the other spouse. If the parties divorce, equitable distribution laws implement the partnership theory by assuring that each spouse receives a share of marital assets. But partnership theory also mandates that upon death of a spouse with significant assets, the surviving spouse should end up with a share of those assets.

The mechanisms for protecting spouses against disinheritance vary from state to state. In community property states, assets acquired by either spouse during the marriage (subject to some exceptions) are treated as "community property." Each spouse has a one-half interest in community property. Neither spouse may transfer community property without the consent of the other. Each spouse is free to devise his or her half of community property, but the surviving spouse's half remains with the surviving spouse, regardless of the provisions in the decedent spouse's will. Community property law, then, embraces a theory of marriage as a fully-equal partnership, and provides maximum protection to the surviving spouse.

Common law states, by contrast, have treated property as individually owned, unless husband and wife take title as tenants by the entirety or as joint tenants. Historically, the principal protection for the surviving spouse came in the form of dower and curtesy. Dower gave a widow a life interest in one-third of her deceased husband's lands. Curtesy gave the husband a life interest in all of his wife's lands, but only if children were born to the marriage.

Dower and curtesy provided reasonable, albeit imperfect, protection in a culture where most wealth consisted of real property owned by men. But dower and curtesy provided no protection with respect to personal property. And as Americans began to hold more wealth in stocks, bonds, and bank accounts, dower and curtesy became less effective mechanisms for protecting spouses against disinheritance.

To deal with this gap in protection, most states enacted "elective share" statutes which permitted the surviving spouse to elect to take a statutory percentage (generally one-third) of decedent spouse's probate estate, even if the decedent spouse tried to limit the surviving spouse to a smaller share. Elective share statutes apply both to personal property and to land.

II. Elective Share Statutes: Typical Problems and Solutions

Unfortunately, people intent on disinheriting their spouses do not give up easily. If an elective share statute guarantees the surviving spouse one-third of decedent's probate estate, some disenchanted spouses will seek to pass their property outside of the probate process, so that the elective share statute will not apply.

Consider a simple case: a decedent who wants to disinherit his wife gives all of his property, during his lifetime, to his only child (perhaps a child by a prior marriage). At decedent's death, the decedent has no probate estate, because all of his assets have already passed to his child. Although the surviving spouse is entitled to an elective share, the share is a percentage of decedent's estate. If the estate is zero, the elective share is also zero. Decedent has effectively disinherited his wife, despite the existence of an elective share statute.

Most decedents, however, are not willing to divest themselves of all of their assets. A decedent who gives all of his property away during his lifetime leaves himself at the mercy of the people to whom he has given the money; the decedent has no assurance that they will provide for him. As a result, self-interest provides a check against decedents evading the elective share statute by making large outright gifts.

As courts became more willing to enforce revocable living trusts, however, more decedents saw a way to have their cake and eat it too. A decedent could create a trust, reserving to himself a right to income from the trust, together with a power to revoke the trust whenever the decedent found it convenient to revoke. If a decedent were to create such a trust, and a court were to enforce the trust, all of decedent's assets would pass outside of the probate process. Decedent's net probate estate would be zero, even though decedent retained complete control over decedent's assets until decedent's death. If these revocable trusts were effective to cut off the surviving spouse's elective share, any decedent could effectively disinherit his or her spouse. That, of course, would defeat the purpose of the elective share statute.

In some states, courts dealt with this problem by developing an "illusory transfer" doctrine. Although the standards for determining whether a transfer was illusory differed from state to state, the basic principle was the same: if the decedent created a trust over which he exercised too much control during his lifetime, the trust assets would be considered part of the probate estate for elective share purposes.

Although this approach addressed the most flagrant attempts to evade the elective share statute, it did not provide a comprehensive solution to the problem. For instance, if a decedent had enough money that he could comfortably live on the income generated by his property, decedent could create a trust, reserve no control over the property but reserve a right to receive income for his life, and name his child as the remainder beneficiary. Transfer to such a trust would not be illusory: the child received an irrevocable right to the property as soon as the transfer was complete, subject only to decedent's reserved life interest. Yet such a transfer, if effective, would defeat the surviving spouse's elective share rights.

To deal with these problems, states turned to legislative solutions. A number of states enacted statutes giving the surviving spouse a right to invalidate transfers made "in fraud of the marital rights"[1] of the surviving spouse, or transfers made "with an intent to defeat the surviving spouse of his distributive or elective share."[2] These statutes made it more difficult for the decedent spouse to evade the surviving spouse's elective share rights, but the statutes are sufficiently vague that they have engendered considerable litigation. Suppose, for instance, decedent spouse makes significant outright transfers, during his lifetime, to his children. Was the transfer made in fraud of marital rights, or was it made out of love for decedent's children?

---

[1]   *See* Mo. Rev. Stat. § 474.150.

[2]   *See* Tenn. Code Ann. § 31–1–105.

Aside from the potential for evasion inherent in many elective share statutes, many of them were drafted before the ascendancy of the partnership theory of marriage. They rested instead on vague notions that the decedent spouse (typically the husband) had an obligation to support the surviving spouse. As a result, they often entitled the surviving spouse to an arbitrary ⅓ of the decedent's estate—a figure carried over from common law dower and curtesy. Moreover, early elective share statutes ignored the surviving spouse's own assets—a critical component of the couple's wealth.

To deal with possibilities of evasion, modern elective share statutes have become more comprehensive and precise. These statutes typically treat specified non-probate transfers as if they are a part of the probate estate for elective share purposes. New York was a pioneer in enacting such a statute, but today the leading comprehensive statute is the Uniform Probate Code. Moreover, the Uniform Probate Code—unlike other elective share statutes—accounts for the value of the surviving spouse's own assets in determining whether that spouse has a right to upset the decedent spouse's testamentary scheme.

III. The Uniform Probate Code's Elective Share Provisions

A. Overview

The Uniform Probate Code's elective share provisions attempt to implement the partnership theory of marriage. For couples who have been married for at least 15 years, the Code essentially treats all of the property of both spouses (and most of the property either spouse has transferred without consideration) as "marital property"—a pot of resources owned equally by the two spouses. Once we figure out what is in the pot at the death of the first spouse to die, the surviving spouse is entitled to at least half of that pot. If the various *inter vivos* and testamentary transfers made by the decedent spouse have left the spouse with less than half, the surviving spouse has a right to elect to obtain a full 50% of the joint assets.

Thus, if the surviving spouse holds the bulk of the couple's assets in his or her own name, the surviving spouse will not generally have a right to elect, even if the decedent spouse left nothing to the survivor. By contrast, if the surviving spouse held no assets in his or her own name, the surviving spouse will have a right to elect unless the decedent spouse left the survivor with at least 50% of the joint assets.

For marriages shorter than 15 years, the amount of property categorized as "marital property" is smaller. The theory behind these provisions is that the marriage has not yet generated a full and equal financial partnership, so that each spouse should be able to shield more of his or her own assets, often earned before the marriage, from claims by the surviving spouse. The percentage of the spouses' property categorized as "marital property" increases gradually, from 3% of the estate in a marriage that has lasted less than one year, to 100% in a 15-year marriage.

By limiting surviving spouse protection until the marriage has endured for a significant period, the Uniform Probate Code takes account of the situation of a late-in-life marriage between spouses each of whom have had children before entering into the marriage, and each of whom would like those children to be principal beneficiaries of their respective estates. Thus, until the marriage has endured for a significant period, the surviving spouse has only a limited right to upset the testamentary scheme of a testator who has chosen to make his or her children the principal beneficiaries of his or her estate.

B. The Statutory Scheme

The UPC's elective share provisions are complex. Determining whether a surviving spouse has a right to elect requires several steps: (1) compute the value of the decedent spouse's "augmented estate"— the pot of money the spouses have a right to share; (2) determine how much of the augmented estate is "marital property"; (3) compute the surviving spouse's elective share (1/2 of the marital property portion of the augmented estate); (4) determine whether the dispositions already made for the surviving spouse, taken in combination with the marital property portion of the spouse's own assets, are sufficient to eliminate any right to elect; and (5) if the dispositions made for the surviving spouse are inadequate, determine how other dispositions abate to satisfy that spouse's elective share.

Section 2–203 includes four broad categories of property in the augmented estate, each of which is described in greater detail in another section. Thus, the augmented estate includes decedent's net probate estate (Section 2–204); decedent's lifetime transfers to people other than the surviving spouse, as described in section 2–205; decedent's lifetime transfers to the surviving spouse, as described in section 2–206; and the surviving spouse's own property, as described and limited by section 2–207.

Once we ascertain the value of the augmented estate, section 2–203(b) instructs us to determine the marital property portion of the augmented estate. We do this by multiplying the augmented estate by the applicable percentage, which depends on the duration of the marriage. Section 2–202(a) then instructs that the elective share amount is 50% of the marital property portion of the augmented estate.

Section 2–209 then determines which amounts should be applied in satisfaction of the surviving spouse's elective share. Dispositions made to the surviving spouse through intestate succession, the will, or by nonprobate transfer, are applied first to satisfy the elective share. If those dispositions are adequate, the spouse has no right to an additional elective share amount. If those dispositions are inadequate, section 2–209 provides instructions about how to adjust dispositions to others to satisfy the elective share.

C. Composition of the Augmented Estate

Determining what property is included within the augmented estate is the heart of the UPC elective share statute. The Code reaches beyond the assets in which the decedent spouse held formal legal title at the time of his death, and also includes assets owned by decedent spouse in form but not in substance, and assets transferred by the decedent spouse in ways that suggest that the assets should be treated as assets of the marital partnership. The augmented estate also includes assets held or transferred by the surviving spouse in order to obtain a more accurate picture of the assets of the marital partnership.

The augmented estate includes four broad categories of assets, several of which are divided into subcategories. For ease of administration, the UPC does not focus on the decedent's intent in making transfers, but rather on the powers and rights held by the decedent in particular forms of property.

1. The Net Probate Estate

Section 2–204 includes the value of decedent's net probate estate in the augmented estate. Section 2–204 is the simplest and most intuitive of the augmented estate provisions: any assets formally owned by decedent at his death—assets that pass through the decedent's probate estate—are included as part of the augmented estate. The net probate estate serves as the starting point for assembling the augmented estate. Thus, any assets that would pass by decedent's will, or by intestate succession, are part of the net probate estate, and are therefore included in the augmented estate. What is included, however, is the *net* probate estate; creditor claims, funeral and administrative expenses, and any homestead allowance, family allowance, and exempt property must be subtracted from the probate estate before reaching the value of the net probate estate.

2. Decedent's Non-Probate Transfers to Others

With the explosion in recent decades of non-probate transfers— trusts, POD and TOD accounts, life insurance, and even outright gifts—the net probate estate reflects only a small percentage of the resources available to many decedents. Section 2–205 includes in the augmented estate the value of a variety of specified non-probate transfers—but only when those transfers are made to persons *other than the surviving spouse*. Many, but not all, of the same types of non-probate transfers are included when made to the surviving spouse, but those transfers are included by the terms of section 2–206, not 2–205. Non-probate transfers within the meaning of section 2–205 fall into three separate categories, each of which is treated in a separate subsection.

 a. Property Owned in Substance by the Decedent at the Time of Death

 Suppose decedent holds property with a sister, as a joint tenant with right of survivorship. If decedent dies before the sister, decedent's share of the property does not pass through decedent's net probate estate, but instead passes to the sister by the terms of the instrument that created the joint tenancy. Yet the decedent could, at any time before death, transfer decedent's joint tenancy interest to a third party. That interest is a resource available to decedent, even though the interest does not pass through the net probate estate. The same is true for property held in a POD or TOD account. Similarly, if decedent creates a trust, and reserves a power to revoke the trust, decedent is free to use the property as he or she sees fit. The UPC treats revocable trusts as property over which decedent holds a general, presently exercisable power of appointment, and includes that property within the augmented estate.

 Thus, section 2–205(1) includes within the augmented estate "[p]roperty owned or owned in substance by the decedent immediately before death that passed outside probate . . . " Within that category are four types of property:

  A. Property over which decedent held a general power of appointment (which includes property held by decedent in a revocable living trust);

  B. Decedent's interest in property held in joint tenancy with right of survivorship;

  C. Decedent's interest in accounts held in POD, TOD or co-ownership registration with right of survivorship; and

  D. Proceeds of life insurance on the death of the decedent, to the extent that decedent owned the life insurance policy before his death.

Section 2–205(1) includes this property in the augmented estate to the extent that decedent's interest in this property passes at death to someone other than the surviving spouse. If the property passes to the surviving spouse, the property would be included within the augmented estate, but under the terms of section 2–206, not 2–205.

b.   *Transfers over Which Decedent Reserves Powers or Interests*

The property included in section 2–205(1) is property over which the decedent has complete control until the moment of his death. By contrast, section 2–205(2) deals with property over which decedent has relinquished some control, while retaining significant rights of enjoyment. Suppose, for instance, decedent owns a home, and conveys the home to a daughter, reserving to the decedent a life interest. Even though the decedent has relinquished control—the decedent cannot later decide to convey the house to someone else— the decedent is entitled to live in the house just as if decedent had retained ownership, and left the house to the daughter by will. Similarly, if decedent places property into an irrevocable trust, and reserves a right to income for decedent's life, the decedent retains considerable enjoyment of the trust property, even if decedent has relinquished control. In these circumstances, section 2–205(2) directs that if the decedent has reserved the "right to the possession or enjoyment of, or to the income from" property until the moment of his death, then the property—and not just the value of the right to income—will be included within the augmented estate. Thus, section 2–205(2) includes real property in which decedent has retained a life interest, and also includes trusts in which decedent has retained an income interest for life.

Suppose a decedent were to attempt to avoid inclusion of trust property by not reserving to himself a right to income, but by instead reserving a power to demand income in the future. That is, suppose decedent creates an irrevocable trust, with income to be paid to decedent's daughter for life, remainder to the daughter's children. Suppose further that the trust instrument reserves for the decedent a power to name decedent as the income beneficiary at any point during decedent's lifetime. Such a trust would leave decedent with a safety net: if decedent's other resources proved insufficient to meet decedent's needs, the trust income would be available. Under the terms of section 2–205(2)(B), the trust property would be included within the augmented estate, because decedent has created a power over income, exercisable by decedent for decedent's benefit. That is, the drafters made sure that so long as decedent could choose to use income from the property to provide for decedent's own needs, the property would be included within the augmented estate.

c. Outright Transfers During Two Years Before Death

In general, if a decedent makes outright transfers of property to persons other than the surviving spouse, the value of those transfers is not included within the augmented estate. That is, UPC § 2–205 does not generally limit the power of a decedent to make gifts during his or her lifetime.

Section 2–205(3) accords different treatment to outright gifts made within two years of decedent's death. At that time, the outright gifts begin to look more like testamentary substitutes, perhaps designed to reduce the surviving spouse's share, than like gifts made out of ordinary love and affection.

Section 2–205(3), therefore, includes within the augmented estate three categories of property in which decedent has disposed of all interest and control. First, section 2–205(3)(A) includes property that passed, within two years of decedent's death, as a result of the termination of decedent's right, interest or power in property that would have been included within the augmented estate had decedent retained an interest until death. For instance, if decedent transferred his life interest in an irrevocable trust, the trust property would be included within the augmented estate if the release occurred within two years of decedent's death. Or if decedent held a general, presently exercisable power of appointment over a trust created by decedent's mother, decedent's release of the power within two years of decedent's death would cause the trust property to be included within decedent's augmented estate.

Second, section 2–205(3)(B) includes within the augmented estate any transfer relating to a life insurance policy if the proceeds of the policy would have been included had the transfer not occurred. That is, if decedent owned a $100,000 life insurance policy on his own life, and transferred that property to his son within two years of the time of his death, the entire $100,000 proceeds would be included in the augmented estate.

Third, section 2–205(3)(C) includes all other transfers made to persons other than the surviving spouse if those transfers are made within two years of decedent's death. The decedent may, however, make gifts of up the amount excludable from taxable gifts under the Internal Revenue Code ($14,000 as of the date of this writing) without having those gifts included in the augmented estate. For gifts larger than the excludable amount, the amount by which the gift exceeds that amount will be included within the augmented estate.

These outright transfers are included in the augmented estate only if they meet one additional qualification: the transfers were made during marriage. That is, if decedent makes a number of outright transfers, then marries, and dies within two years of the transfers, the transfers would not be included in the augmented estate because they were made before the marriage.

3.   Nonprobate Transfers to the Surviving Spouse

Recall that the design of the UPC's elective share provisions is to include all partnership assets within the augmented estate, and then to assure that the surviving spouse receives a half share in those assets. To realize the UPC's objectives, the augmented estate must include non-probate transfers made to the surviving spouse as well as non-probate transfers made to others. (Probate transfers to the surviving spouse are already included, as are all other probate transfers, by virtue of Section 2–204). UPC Section 2–206 includes non-probate transfers made to the surviving spouse.

Thus, the statute includes all property that would have been included in the augmented estate under sections 2–205(1) or 2–205(2) if the property had passed to the benefit of some person other than the surviving spouse. In other words, if decedent held property in a POD account with decedent's spouse as a beneficiary, the property would be included within the augmented estate. Similarly, if decedent held property as a joint tenant or tenant by the entirety with decedent's spouse, the decedent's share of the property would be included in the augmented estate under section 2–206. (Note that the spouse's own share would not be included under section 2–206, but would be included, in whole or in part, under section 2–207).

Absolute transfers made by the decedent to the surviving spouse within two years of death are not included under section 2–206. That property would, however, be included under section 2–207.

4.   Surviving Spouse's Property (and Transfers to Others)

Because the partnership theory is designed to treat all assets of each spouse as marital assets, the surviving spouse's own assets are included within the augmented estate. Section 2–207 includes all property owned by the surviving spouse at the decedent's death, except to the extent that property is already included under sections 2–204 or 2–206.

The statute also includes within the augmented estate transfers made by the surviving spouse that would be included within the spouse's augmented estate had the spouse been the decedent. The purpose of this provision is to avoid enabling the surviving spouse to increase the elective share by divesting herself or himself of formal legal title to property. For example, if the surviving spouse held a general, presently exercisable power of appointment, the appointive property would be included as the surviving spouse's property. If the surviving spouse had created an irrevocable trust, reserving a right to income for life, the trust property would be treated as the surviving spouse's property, and would be included in the decedent spouse's augmented estate.

D. Determining Whether the Surviving Spouse Has a Right to Elect

Computing the augmented estate is the first step in determining whether a surviving spouse has a right to elect. The next step is determining how much of that augmented estate is marital property. Section 2–203(b) addresses that issue. The statute operates on the premise that marriage gradually builds a full economic partnership; in the early years, much of the property owned by each of the parties is the equivalent of "separate property." The UPC, however, does not require us to trace the origins of particular property to determine whether it constitutes separate or marital property. Instead, the UPC includes all of the property owned by either spouse in the augmented estate, but ties the percentage of the property that is marital property to the length of the marriage. For a marriage that has lasted 15 years or longer, all of the property is marital property, and the surviving spouse is entitled to half of it. For marriages of shorter duration, the percentage is smaller. In effect, the statute gives each spouse a 50% share in marital property, but presumes that a decreasing percentage of the couple's assets is separate property with each passing year of marriage.

Determining the surviving spouse's elective share is easy: multiply the marital property portion of the augmented estate by 50%. More complicated, however, is determining whether the decedent spouse has left the surviving spouse with enough assets to satisfy the elective share. The goal of the Uniform Probate Code's elective share provisions is to upset the decedent spouse's testamentary scheme as little as possible, so long as the decedent spouse has provided adequately for the surviving spouse. So, to determine whether the surviving spouse can elect anything beyond what the decedent has provided, one must determine whether the decedent spouse has provided the survivor with the elective share amount.

Section 2–209 addresses this problem. In general outline, the statute provides that amounts included in the augmented estate that pass to the surviving spouse are applied first to make up the surviving spouse's elective share. Consider first how the statute applies to a marriage that has lasted at least 15 years. The statute requires that we add three quantities:

    i.   the value of property passing to the spouse through the net probate estate;

    ii.   the value of non-probate transfers to the spouse included under 2–206; and

    iii. the value of the marital property portion of the surviving spouse's own property.

Those three values are applied first to satisfy the surviving spouse's elective share. If the sum of those three values exceeds the surviving spouse's elective share, the surviving spouse may not upset any of the decedent spouse's testamentary scheme; the surviving spouse has been provided for adequately. Only if the sum of those three values is smaller than the elective share may the surviving spouse obtain more than the spouse would receive if the decedent spouse's dispositions remained intact.

When the sum of the three quantities is too small—cases where the decedent spouse has not adequately provided for the survivor—UPC 2–209(c) provides that the surviving spouse can obtain the unsatisfied balance of the elective share from two sources: amounts included in the decedent's probate estate, and amounts included in those of decedent's non-probate transfers to others that come within sections 2–205(1), (2) and (3)(B). Those transfers then abate proportionately to satisfy the elective share. For instance, if the net probate estate (other than provisions for the surviving spouse) and the non-probate transfers to others total $500,000, and the unsatisfied balance of the elective share totals $200,000, then the surviving spouse is entitled to 40% of the value of each disposition. If, during the last two years before death, the decedent spouse made significant outright gifts to persons other than the surviving spouse, it is possible that even if the spouse receives 100% of the net probate estate and the non-probate transfers to others included in section 2–209(b), the elective share will still not be satisfied. In that event, and only in that event, UPC § 2–209(c) directs that outright gifts be used to satisfy the remaining balance of the spouse's elective share.

So far, discussion has focused on the marriage that has lasted at least 15 years. The statute adjusts the analysis in one significant way for marriages of shorter duration. When computing the amounts applied against the surviving spouse's elective share, the statute includes only a percentage of the value of the surviving spouse's own property. This reflects the premise that in the early years of the marriage, the financial partnership of the parties is incomplete; some of the resources of each spouse should be treated as separate property.

To capture the idea that some of the surviving spouse's own assets are not marital assets, and therefore should not be counted as assuring that the survivor obtains an equal share of marital assets, section 2–209 applies only the marital property portion of the surviving spouse's assets toward satisfaction of the elective share. Thus, in a ten-year marriage, 60% of the value of the surviving spouse's assets would be considered marital property and would be applied toward satisfying her elective share amount; the remainder would be treated as the equivalent of separate assets. Subject to this single exception, section 2–209 treats short-term marriages in the same way the statute treats long-term marriages.

E. Life Interests in Trust

Suppose a decedent provides for a spouse by giving the spouse a life interest in trust, rather than by giving the spouse property outright. Many decedents, for instance, create QTIP trusts, especially when the decedent has children by a prior marriage. The UPC's elective share provisions are a muddle when it comes to life interests in trust. Nevertheless, although the drafting is unclear, the Code's legislative history clarifies its intent. The drafters intended that if a decedent provided for the surviving spouse by creating life interests in trust, the surviving spouse could disclaim those interests. As a result, neither the trust principal nor the present value of the surviving spouse's income interest would be applied against the elective share. The surviving spouse would be entitled to take the elective share outright.

Note, however, that the surviving spouse may have a difficult decision to make: if the decedent spouse has left a significant portion of the estate in trust, and made the surviving spouse a life beneficiary, disclaiming the interest in trust and electing to take an outright share may leave the surviving spouse less well off than forgoing the elective share right and leaving the trust intact. Much will depend on the spouse's life expectancy and the duration of the marriage.

Conversely, the decedent spouse also faces difficult decisions. If the decedent spouse chooses to provide for the surviving spouse only by creating a life interest in trust, the decedent spouse takes the risk that the surviving spouse will elect and upset decedent's testamentary scheme (which may also have adverse tax consequences). In that situation, decedent spouse would be well advised to consider seeking a waiver of elective share rights.

Invoking the support theory of marriage, section 2–202(b) provides that the surviving spouse is entitled to own at least $75,000 after the deceased spouse's death. If the total of the elective share amount and all of the spouse's own assets is less than $75,000, the surviving spouse has a right to elect an additional sum to bring her total take to $75,000.

IV. Waiver of Elective Share Rights

All states enforce waivers of elective share rights, whether executed before or after the marriage. At the same time, however, courts recognize that such waivers are hardly arms-length bargains. The party seeking a waiver may have more information, and more leverage, than his or her spouse or future spouse.

States have dealt with these problems in a variety of ways. All states require that the waiver be "voluntary", but it is often difficult to conclude that a waiver is voluntary when the waiving party does not know the value of the rights he or she is waiving. As a result, some provide that waivers of elective share rights will be enforced only after fair disclosure of assets by the beneficiary of the waiver. That approach, however, generates litigation over whether disclosure has been fair. Even a spouse seeking to provide full and fair disclosure is likely to err in some of the particulars. When the surviving spouse demonstrates that the assets held by the decedent spouse differed in some respect from the assets disclosed, how material must the differences be to set aside the waiver?

Other states focus on whether the waiving spouse had counsel at the time the waiver was executed. That approach, too, leads to litigation when the spouse has expressly declined counsel, even when the beneficiary of the waiver has suggested use of independent counsel.

The Uniform Probate Code approach, embodied in section 2–213, provides that elective share rights, and other rights accruing to a surviving spouse, may be waived by written agreement signed by that spouse. The surviving spouse can prevent enforcement of the waiver if the spouse can prove that the waiver was not voluntary. Alternatively, even if the waiver was voluntary, the surviving spouse can prevent enforcement if the spouse can prove that the waiver was unconscionable when executed *and* three additional elements: (1) the surviving spouse did not receive fair and reasonable disclosure or assets; (2) the surviving spouse did not waive, in writing, a right to disclosure of assets; and (3) the surviving spouse did not have, or reasonably could not have had, adequate knowledge of the property of the decedent spouse.

In other words, in cases where waiver was voluntary, the UPC places a number of significant hurdles in front of a spouse who seeks to set aside a waiver of elective share rights. If the spouse knew of the decedent's property, or waived in writing any right to know, the spouse cannot set aside the waiver even if the waiver was unconscionable when executed.

V. Other Protections for the Surviving Spouse

A. Protection Against Creditors

Generally, a decedent's creditors enjoy priority over the beneficiaries of decedent's estate. That is, a decedent who has fallen into debt must pay off creditors before disposing of property to family members, charities, or other beneficiaries. State law, however, typically places some of a decedent's property beyond the reach of creditors. In many states, the surviving spouse, and often minor children, are entitled to a homestead exemption, which limits the right of creditors to reach the family home (often up to some specified value). The surviving spouse may also be entitled to keep some personal property away from creditors.

Section 2–402 of the Uniform Probate Code gives the surviving spouse a homestead allowance of $22,500. The allowance is a cash allowance; it does not give the surviving spouse a right to any particular piece of property. The allowance, however, takes priority over all claims against the estate, and is in addition to any share the surviving spouse would take under decedent's will, unless the will provides otherwise. If decedent is not survived by a spouse, minor children are entitled to share the homestead allowance.

The UPC also includes a provision for exempt property, which entitles the surviving spouse to an additional $15,000, and which also takes priority over creditor claims. (UPC § 2–403). If there is no surviving spouse, all children, whether minors are not, are entitled to share in the exempt property.

Finally, UPC § 2–404 entitles the surviving spouse and any minor children to a reasonable allowance in money out of the estate for maintenance during the period of administration of the estate— but not for longer than one year if the estate is inadequate to satisfy creditor claims. This provision accounts for the fact that the spouse will need funds to live on during that period, and if all of the family's funds were in the decedent's name, the spouse would not otherwise be entitled to money until estate administration was completed. The UPC limits the family allowance to a maximum of $27,000 for the one year period provided in the statute.

B. Inadvertent Disinheritance: Pre-Marital Wills

Elective share statutes primarily protect a surviving spouse against the decedent spouse who actively tries to disinherit the survivor. Sometimes, however, decedent has written a will before decedent's marriage, leaving his or her estate to someone other than the future spouse. Decedent did not change the will after the marriage, perhaps out of inertia, or out of procrastination. In most circumstances, however, the failure to change the will does not signal an intent by the decedent to leave a new spouse with nothing.

States have developed a number of mechanisms for dealing with this problem. Some states assume that a decedent who failed to change his or her will did so inadvertently. Statutes in those states provide that marriage automatically revokes a pre-marital will—at least as far as the spouse is concerned. As a result, the new spouse takes an intestate share—which will often be the entire estate (in most states adopting this approach, the will is effective to distribute the balance of the estate remaining after the spouse takes her intestate share).

Other states leave the elective share provisions as the principal protection of the surviving spouse, and hold that the premarital will remains in force, subject to the surviving spouse's right to elect. In these states, the surviving spouse might receive far less than what the decedent spouse actually intended.

The Uniform Probate Code takes a more complicated approach. When the decedent married the surviving spouse after execution of the decedent's will, the will remains effective with respect to the portion of the estate devised to children born to decedent before the marriage and to descendants of such children. As to the remainder of the estate, section 2–301 entitles the surviving spouse to receive the value the spouse would have received if the decedent had died intestate with respect to that portion of the estate. The surviving spouse is not entitled to this portion if it appears from the will that the will was made in contemplation of the marriage, or if the will expresses an intention that it be effective notwithstanding the marriage, or if the testator provided for the spouse by transfer outside the will, and evidence establishes the intent that the transfer be in lieu of a testamentary provision. Of course, if the amount provided for the surviving spouse under section 2–301 is smaller than the spouse's elective share, the spouse may take the elective share.

VI. Protection of Children

Every state but Louisiana permits a decedent to disinherit children; even Louisiana permits a decedent to disinherit children over the age of 24, unless those children are permanently incapable of administering their property.

Many states, however, protect children against unintentional disinheritance. Of these, some states protect all children, whether born before or after execution of decedent's will, against unintentional disinheritance. Others limit protection to children born after execution of the will.

In those states that protect all children against unintentional disinheritance, questions arise about how to determine decedent's intention. Some statutes avoid focus on intention by providing that the child is entitled to an intestate share whenever the child is omitted from a parent's will. In those states, if the parent wants to disinherit a child, the parent must make explicit provision for the child. Language such as "I make no provision for any other child of mine" or "I make no provision for my son Sam" would operate to disinherit Sam; by contrast, if the will made no mention of Sam, Sam would be entitled to an intestate share.

Other states permit an omitted child to take unless the omission is intentional. In these states, extrinsic evidence is typically admissible to prove intention. It is not always clear what sort of evidence is relevant in proving that the omission was intentional.

The Uniform Probate Code, together with statutes in a number of other states, protects only children born after execution of the will. Children born before execution of the will do not take unless the will makes express provision for those children. In cases where a child is born after execution of the will, and testator had no children born before execution of the will, section 2–302(1) of the Uniform Probate Code entitles the afterborn child to his or her intestate share, unless the will devises all or substantially all of the estate to the other parent of the omitted afterborn child. Thus, if testator's will effectively assures that the afterborn will be provided for—because the estate passes to the afterborn's other parent—then the afterborn is not entitled to share in the estate.

UPC § 2–302(2) treats afterborn children differently when testator had living children at the time testator executed the will. In that event, the statute effectively divides decedent's estate into two portions: that portion devised to children and that portion devised to others. The afterborn child is not entitled to share in the portion of the estate devised to others. Instead, the statute directs that after isolating the property devised to children in the will, the afterborn child (or afterborn children) should receive a proportionate share of that property. For instance, if the will devises $10,000 to child A and $20,000 to child B, and testator then has another child, C, born after execution of the will, C is entitled to a proportionate share (⅓) of the $30,000 devised to children. C, therefore, receives $10,000. The shares devised to A and B abate ratably. Because C takes ⅓ of the amount devised to children, C effectively takes ⅓ of A's $10,000 and ⅓ of B's $20,000.

Section 2–302(2) rests on the premise that if testator thought A deserved or needed less than B before the birth of C, then C's birth would not affect that belief, so that the relative proportions allocated to A and B should remain constant. Because testator could not and did not provide any indication about his beliefs with respect to C, C is entitled to an average of the total amount allocated to children.

Problems

1.   In 2006, W created a revocable trust, naming herself as trustee and providing that trust income should be paid to her daughter, D, for life, with a remainder at D's death to D's children. W funded the trust with $500,000. In 2008, W created an irrevocable trust with the Faithful Trust Company as trustee, reserving income to W for life, and directing that at W's death, the trust principal should be paid to D. W funded this trust with $800,000. W also owned a family beach house with her sister S, as joint tenants with right of survivorship. Finally, in 2010, W released her right to revoke the 2006 trust. W dies in 2011 with a will leaving all of her property to her husband, H.

Assume that the value of the two trusts at W's death was identical to their value when W created them, that the house was valued at $400,000, and that W's net probate estate was valued at $500,000. If H and W had been married for 30 years, and if H had assets in his own name valued at $600,000, does the Uniform Probate Code give H a right to elect more than W has provided for him? If so, how much is he entitled to take beyond what W has provided, and what assets would be used to satisfy H's elective share?

How, if at all, would your answer be different if H and W had been married for 10 years rather than 30?

How, if at all, would your answer be different if W's 2006 trust had been made irrevocable when it was created?

2.   Husband, H, dies in 2011 with a 2010 will leaving his wife, W, $100,000, and leaving the residue of his estate in trust, with income from the trust to be paid to W for life, remainder at W's death to H's son, S. H also owned two life insurance policies, one, in the amount of $300,000, payable to W, and the other, in the amount of $500,000, payable to S. In addition, H had established a POD account with a broker, and the account directed the broker to pay the account proceeds to S upon H's death. The account was valued at $200,000.

Assume that the value of H's net probate estate was $2,000,000, that W had no assets of her own, and that H had been married to W for five years. W is now fifty years old. Does the Uniform Probate Code give W a right to elect more than H has provided for her? If so, would you advise W to take advantage of that right? Why or why not?

3.   Husband H executed a will two years before his marriage to W. The will leaves $100,000 to H's son, S, and the balance to the American Red Cross. H did not execute a new will after the marriage. He died five years after the marriage, with an estate valued at $1,000,000. At H's death, W had assets of her own valued at $200,000. Does the Uniform Probate Code give W a right to elect against H's estate? Does the Uniform Probate Code give W any more attractive options? Explain.

4.   T's last will leaves "all of my property in equal shares to my husband, H, and the Roman Catholic Church." T's net probate estate is valued at $400,000. If, after execution of the will, T and H had a child, A, would the Uniform Probate Code entitle A to share in T's estate? If the answer is yes, to how much would A be entitled?

How, if at all, would your answer be different if T had another child, B, born before execution of T's last will?

How, if at all, would your answer be different if T had another child, B, born before execution of T's last will, and the will made a general bequest of $10,000 to B, and then directed that the remainder of T's estate be divided equally between H and the Roman Catholic Church?

Chapter Four

WILLS

I. Will Execution

A. The Purpose of Formalities

When a testator dies and a loved one offers a will for probate, how does a court determine whether the document is valid? After all, testator is not present to testify that she executed the document, and that it really does memorialize her final intentions. The document could be a forgery. Or, testator might have lacked the capacity to formulate a thoughtful distribution plan. Perhaps testator was coerced into signing the document.

To address this problem, statutes have long required that wills be in writing and executed in accordance with several formal requirements,[1] such as signing in the presence of witnesses. These statutes, often referred to as "formalities statutes", have several objectives. First, they serve a *protective* function. By requiring witnesses and other safeguards, the statutes attempt to protect the testator from fraud and overreaching by greedy relatives and acquaintances. Second, the statutes serve a *ritual* function; requiring a testator to participate in a ceremonial occasion impresses upon the testator the finality and importance of the act she is performing. The will should control distribution of testator's assets only if it is a carefully considered, formal document, not a hastily scribbled product of a momentary whim. Third, formalities statutes serve an *evidentiary* function: the formal document serves as conclusive evidence of the testator's wishes, and the witness requirement ensures that others will be available to testify if the will's authenticity is in doubt. Fourth, the *channeling* function simplifies the probate process: all wills have a similar form and structure, which helps the court recognize a document as a "will" and facilitates the probate process.

Although state statutes share similar objectives, they vary in the number and content of the formal requirements they impose. Some statutes create virtual obstacle courses. For example, the New York statute requires that the testator sign a written document, at the end of the document, in the presence of at least two witnesses; that testator declare to those witnesses that the document they are about to sign is testator's will; and that the witnesses affix their names in the testator's presence. If the testator is physically unable

---

[1]   English Wills Act, 1837.

to sign the document, she may direct someone else to sign the will as her proxy, but the proxy must sign in the testator's presence.[2]

Not all statutes are quite so complicated, but most create ample opportunities for testator error. For example, many statutes require the testator to sign in the presence of two witnesses, and for the two witnesses to sign their names in testator's presence. Legions of cases involve testators who failed strictly to comply with these requirements. For instance, a common fact pattern involves witnesses who were present when testator signed his or her name, but then carried the will out of testator's line of vision before affixing their own signatures. As a result of these types of inadvertent errors, documents that testators intended to function as wills have been denied probate. This has led some scholars to argue that will formalities statutes should be simplified to reduce the risk that careless mistakes will doom a will. If the purpose of the formalities statutes is to effectuate testator's intent, they argue, then rejecting wills that manifest intent because they fail to comply strictly with formalities statutes frustrates the statutes' principal objective.

This argument has produced significant changes in statutory law. First, current Uniform Probate Code section 2–502, the formalities provision, is notable for its simplicity. It requires only that the testator sign a written document, and that at least two other individuals sign the document within a reasonable time after witnessing the testator's execution or acknowledgment of the will. Witnesses need not be present during testator's execution of the will, nor must witnesses sign in the testator's presence. Section 2–502 even permits a testator to dispense with traditional witnesses altogether if the testator acknowledges her signature on the will before a notary. The drafters of the UPC added this provision in 2008 in recognition that notarization is a sufficient means of executing many other estate planning documents (including durable powers of attorney and living wills). The drafters concluded that permitting the same formalities to suffice for all estate planning documents would reduce the likelihood that testators would inadvertently use the wrong formalities in executing particular documents.

The Uniform Probate Code contains a second provision intended to give effect to informal documents that express a decedent's testamentary intent. Section 2–503 authorizes a court to probate a will that fails to comply with section 2–502 as long as the person offering the document for probate (the "proponent") can prove, by clear and convincing evidence, that the testator intended that the document function as a will. This provision, often referred to as the

---

[2]   N.Y. E.P.T.L. section 3–2.1.

"dispensing power" (because it enables courts to "dispense" with formalities requirements) has been adopted by many states.

Even in states that have not adopted UPC § 2–503, courts have been increasingly willing to excuse "harmless" error in will execution, provided that 1) the document offered for probate substantially complies with will formalities, and 2) the proponent of the nonconforming will can establish, by clear and convincing evidence, that the testator intended the document to function as her will. For example, in *Estate of Ranney*,[3] the court admitted a will to probate despite the fact that the drafting attorney instructed the witnesses to sign only the self-proving affidavit and not the will itself. Other courts have invoked substantial compliance to validate wills when the witnesses were out of testator's sight, but in the same building.

But whether sections 2–502, 2–503 and the substantial compliance doctrine will cause greater numbers of wills to be admitted to probate remains to be seen. There is evidence that courts have been more inclined to insist on strict compliance, and to deny probate on this ground, when wills deviate from established social norms by devising testators' property to individuals other than family members who appear "deserving." When wills *do* conform to social norms by devising property to deserving relatives, courts often validate them even when they fail to comply strictly with formalities statutes. To the extent that courts and juries are inclined to enforce social norms, reforms that seek to facilitate probate of wills will be ineffective.

Neither section 2–503 nor the substantial compliance doctrine are of importance to the estate planner. The estate planner's objective should be to guarantee that probate of the will without fuss or controversy. Creating the grounds for a legal battle by failing to comply scrupulously with the formalities statute does not serve the client. Even if the court ultimately admits the will, the litigation expenses will have reduced the value of testator's estate. It is therefore important to pay careful attention to the execution ceremony.

B.   The Execution Ceremony: Procedure

1.   *The Testator's Signature*

The testator must sign her will to indicate that the will is a final expression of her testamentary wishes. Almost any mark on the paper can function as a signature, provided that the testator made the mark with the intent that it serve as a signature. If a testator needs assistance, someone may help the testator sign her name. In

---

[3]   124 N.J. 1, 589 A.2d 1339 (1991).

addition, most execution statutes allow the testator to sign by proxy if the proxy signs at the request and direction of the testator in the testator's presence. Needless to say, a signature that is assisted or by proxy might make the will vulnerable to later allegations that the testator did not freely sign the will. Consequently, the lawyer should take extra precautions to avoid a will contest.

Although not all statutes require that the testator's signature appear at the end of the document, it is wise to follow that custom. A signature at the end establishes a presumption that the testator intended to give life to the entire will. If the signature is not at the end, the will's proponent must prove that testator so intended.

2. Witnesses

Until the Uniform Probate Code introduced notarization as an alternative, statutes universally required that a will be witnessed by at least two people. (An exception in about of a third of the states permits probate of a holographic will). The witness requirement seeks to ensure that testator signs the will freely and without coercion, and that the document reflects testator's intent, not the intent of some other person. There is some question about how effectively the witness requirement accomplishes this task. Because statutes do not require that the testator reveal the will's contents to the witnesses, witnesses may be unaware that the will's contents are a result of pressure by a scheming beneficiary. Moreover, the scheming beneficiary can often arrange to have witnesses who are sympathetic to the beneficiary. Yet because witnesses provide some measure of protection and also further the ritual function of formalities, the requirement is probably here to stay.

A significant minority of states recognize an exception to the witness requirement for **holographic wills**. A holographic will is one that is unwitnessed but written entirely in the testator's hand. Although the recognition of holographic wills enables unsophisticated or uncounseled testators to control the distribution of their estates, it undermines many of the objectives of the formalities statutes. For instance, it is said that the extended handwriting sample that the will provides substitutes for the *protection* traditionally provided by witnesses. Although the handwriting sample may provide strong evidence that the document was written by the testator, it provides no evidence that the document was a result of testator's exercise of free will. Additionally, the holographic will doctrine undermines the *channeling* and *ritual* functions. Case law is replete with litigants offering everything from envelopes to grocery lists to cocktail napkins as wills. Courts often find themselves considering whether scribblings were intended to have testamentary effect, or whether unattached scraps and pieces of paper should be considered one integrated will. It goes without saying that no competent attorney would recommend that a client use a holographic will.

Witnesses should be competent adults who will be easy to locate once the will is offered for probate. If the will embodies a conventional estate plan, in which the bulk of testator's assets are devised to those who would otherwise take as intestate heirs, a will contest is unlikely, and any two competent people who will later be easy to locate will suffice. For this reason, lawyers often use office personnel as witnesses in routine cases. But if the will makes dispositions that could provoke a will contest, good lawyers take extra care to find witnesses who can later provide credible evidence of testator's sound mind and freedom from coercion. Although it is unwise to use will beneficiaries as witnesses in any case, it is extremely bad practice when the will makes an unorthodox disposition. Doing so will fuel the argument that the witness/beneficiary improperly influenced the testator. In fact, many states have "interested witness" statutes to deal with these problems. The statutes vary in detail. Some direct courts to render such a will void, others to strike the disposition in favor of the interested witness. Still other statutes prohibit an interested witness from receiving any probate assets that exceed in value the amount to which the witness would be entitled under the intestacy statute.

The **attestation clause** is a boilerplate provision that immediately precedes the witness signature lines. It recites the circumstances of the execution, stipulates that the testator signed the document freely without coercion and in the absence of undue influence, and provides a place for the witnesses to sign their names. Although states do not require an attestation clause, lawyers include it because in most states it creates a rebuttable presumption that the will was properly executed.

At first glance, it might be hard to distinguish the **self-proving affidavit** from an attestation clause. Following is a typical affidavit:

> [Testator], [first witness] and [second witness], the testator and witnesses, respectively, whose names are signed to the attached instrument, being first duly sworn, do hereby declare to the undersigned authority that the Testator signed and executed the instrument as his Last Will and Testament, and that he signed willingly and that he executed it as a free and voluntary act for the purposes therein expressed; and that each witness states that she or he signed the Will as witnesses in the presence and hearing of the testator, and that to the best of her knowledge, the

Testator was at the time 18 years of age or older, of sound mind, and under no constraint or undue influence.

The Affidavit then provides signature lines for the Testator, Witnesses, and the Notary's signature and seal.

A careful comparison of the self-proving affidavit to the attestation clause reveals that the attestation clause speaks of the action of witnesses in the present tense, while the affidavit uses the past tense. By signing her name after the attestation clause, the witness affirms her present intent to act as a witness to the will. When she signs the self-proving affidavit, she swears that she has already performed the act of witnessing and signing the will. In other words, the self-proving affidavit has the same function as any other type of affidavit—it is a substitute for witness testimony at a hearing or other legal proceeding. In many cases, the self-proving affidavit will eliminate the need to find the witness to establish a foundation for the will. The affidavit itself is sufficient to get the will admitted to probate. Of course, if someone contests the will, then the witnesses will have to be located.

Section 2–504 of the Uniform Probate Code provides that witnesses may simultaneously sign as attesting witnesses and execute a self-proving affidavit—all on a single form. The statute itself includes the language necessary to accomplish that result. Section 2–504 was drafted in response to cases in which a lawyer had inadvertently instructed the testator and witnesses to sign the self-proving affidavit, but not the will itself.

3. A Foolproof Procedure

Although statutory requirements vary, a lawyer who adopts the following procedure as a routine will greatly reduce the chance that a court will reject a will for non-compliance with formalities.

1. The will should be in final form, pages securely fastened and numbered 1 of ___.

2. The will should contain an attestation clause, and, if the state authorizes it, a self-proving affidavit (or, in a jurisdiction that has adopted UPC § 2–504, the statutory language that serves both purposes).

3. There should be at least two disinterested and competent witnesses present. Use three witnesses if there is a risk of a will contest.

4. Prior to the execution ceremony, allow the witnesses time to form an opinion about the capacity and mental state of the testator.

5. Bar will beneficiaries from the room during the execution ceremony.

6. Once the ceremony begins, allow no interruptions and let no one leave the room.

7. Ensure that testator, witnesses and the attorney can see and hear one another.

8. Ask the testator if the document is her will, and if she wants to sign it; once the witnesses have heard the answer, the testator should sign the will under the witnesses' careful gaze.

9. Ask the testator to declare to the witnesses that the instrument is her will, and to ask them to sign the will. Read the attestation clause aloud to the witnesses before they sign it.

10. Have the witnesses sign their names and addresses. As they sign, witnesses should be able to see the testator's signature.

C. Will Software and Electronic Wills

In a world where consumers are used to transacting business online, a number of entrepreneurs have developed software to simplify the process of preparing and executing wills. The software typically prompts the customer to answer a series of questions, and then generates a complete will based on the answers. Once the will is completed, the testator must still print it out and execute it in accordance with testamentary formalities. Of course, if the jurisdiction has a dispensing power similar to UPC § 2–503, the will might be admitted to probate even without compliance with all statutory formalities.

In 2001, Nevada enacted a statute authorizing electronic wills that include at least one "authentication characteristic" of the testator. Nev. Rev. Stat. § 133.085. Fingerprints, retinal scans, voice recognition, and facial recognition all qualify as authentication characteristics. To date, other states have not followed Nevada's lead.

II. What Constitutes a Will? Integration, Incorporation by Reference, and Facts of Independent Significance

A. Integration, Incorporation by Reference, UPC § 2–513

People often write wills without the supervision of an attorney. Ignorance of the law not only causes some testators to fail to comply with formalities, but can cause other problems as well. Some testators, for example, neglect to fasten all of the pages of the will together prior to executing the signature page. Because there is often a significant time lag between the drafting of the will and testator's death, it may not be clear which pieces of paper offered for probate comprise the testator's will, and which were written by the testator or someone else at other times. The doctrine of **integration** attempts to solve this problem.

Even when it is clear which pages were present at the will's execution, a related problem occurs if the will directs that part of testator's estate be distributed in accordance with a second, un-executed document. Should the probate court give that second, un-executed document testamentary effect? A few doctrines grapple with this problem: the common-law doctrine of **incorporation by reference** (codified at UPC § 2–510), the UPC's **§ 2–513**, and **the Uniform Testamentary Additions to Trusts Act**.

First, consider the doctrine of **integration**. Suppose that a testator executes a will, keeps the unfastened pages in an envelope, and later adds or subtracts pages to the envelope, but fails to re-execute the will. Or, perhaps testator creates substitute pages that he keeps in a separate place, such as a desk drawer. If all pages are offered for probate, how should the court determine which pages should be given effect? The doctrine of integration answers this question by providing that *only those pages that were present at the will's execution comprise the final will.* The doctrine is designed to effectuate decedent's intent; by denying probate to those pages that were not in testator's presence at the execution, the doctrine guards against fraud, forgery, mistake, or lack of seriousness of intention.

Sometimes, the will offered for probate is complete, but a provision directs that particular estate assets be distributed in accordance with some other document that was not executed simultaneously with the will. Consider some examples: testator's will might direct that certain items be distributed in accordance with a list that she keeps in her bedside table drawer, or as her husband's last will and testament directs, or that her residuary estate is to become an asset of her inter vivos trust, to be managed and distributed together with trust assets. If the separate document was not executed with testamentary formalities, can the court determine whether it was a product of testator's final, deliberate intent, or whether it was the product of coercion or a forgery produced by a meddling beneficiary? If the separate document was not present at the execution and physically made a part of testator's will, can the court determine with certainty which document testator intended to describe? If the document was written after the testator executed her will, can the court be sure that testator seriously intended it to govern the disposition of her assets?

The common law doctrine that first evolved to solve this problem is the doctrine of **incorporation by reference**. That doctrine allows the court to give effect to the separate document if three conditions are met: first, the document to which the will refers must have been *in existence, and complete, prior to, or contemporaneously with, the will's execution.* Second, the testator's will must evince a *clear intent to incorporate* the document into her will. Third, the testator's will must *clearly and specifically describe* the document so that there is no doubt about the identity of the document to which testator's will refers. UPC § 2–510 codifies the common law doctrine.

To give an example, suppose testator's will, executed on April 2, 2016, directs that the family home be "distributed in accordance with a letter written by me and dated March 15, 2013, which is located in my safe deposit box." If, at the testator's death, a letter fitting that description is found in testator's safe deposit box, then it can be incorporated by reference into testator's will.

Now suppose instead that testator's will directs that "certain items of my personal property should be distributed in accordance with a list that can be found in my bedside table drawer." Suppose further that on testator's death, a list is found in that drawer. The list contains bequests of items such as paintings and jewelry to different friends and relatives. The entries were made at different times, and the list contains strike outs and amendments. It is not dated or signed. This list cannot be incorporated by reference into testator's will because it is not clear that the final version of the list was made prior to or contemporaneously with the will.

Testators often attempt to bequeath items of personal property on separate lists so that they may remove or add bequests without having to re-execute their wills. Such lists are problematic. On one hand, there is no way to ensure that all of the entries were made by the testator, reflect deliberation instead of whim, and were not the result of fraud or undue influence. On the other hand, when extrinsic evidence renders testator's intent clear, it seems a shame to frustrate that intent. Historically, courts faced with such a dilemma could not validate such lists unless they complied with incorporation by reference doctrine,[4] or the jurisdiction recognized holographic wills and the list was entirely in testator's handwriting and included testator's signature (in which case the list could be construed as a holographic codicil).

---

[4]   Clark v. Greenhalge, 411 Mass. 410, 582 N.E.2d 949 (1991).

The drafters of the UPC thought that all testators should have the ability to distribute items of personal property by using modifiable lists. Accordingly, **UPC § 2–513** provides that,

> a will may refer to a written statement or list to dispose of items of tangible personal property not otherwise specifically disposed of by will, other than money. To be admissible under this section as evidence of the intended disposition, the writing must be signed by the testator and must describe the items and devisees with reasonable certainty. The writing may be referred to as one to be in existence at the testator's death; it may be prepared before or after the execution of the will; it may be altered by the testator after its preparation; and it may be a writing that has no significance apart from its effect on the dispositions made by the will.

Explore how section 2–513 differs from the incorporation by reference doctrine. The most notable difference is that section 2–513 does not require the un-executed document to be in existence and complete when the will is executed. This allows testator to make changes to the document up to the time of death without having to pay for additional execution ceremonies. On the other hand, section 2–513 is more limited in scope; where incorporation by reference doctrine allows the testator to dispose of any asset through reference to a separate document, section 2–513 is applicable only to devises of tangible personal property.

Note that section 2–513, which allows the list to be modified but requires only testator's signature as a formality, provides slim protection against fraud, undue influence or meddling by those who have access to the list. This might explain why the statute limits items that can be bequeathed to tangible personal property. Stocks, cash, real estate, and all other forms of property must be disposed of by will. Yet even tangible personal property can have great value. In the UPC drafters' view, the lack of protection afforded by section 2–513 is justified by the need to provide people with a simple and inexpensive way to dispose of personal property.

B. Facts of Independent Significance and the Uniform Testamentary Additions to Trusts Act

As we've seen, testators sometimes attempt to dispose of property by referring to documents outside of the will, and courts often use the doctrine of incorporation by reference or section 2–513 to validate those attempts. A related problem arises when testator's will makes a disposition that is affected by acts or events that occur after the will execution but before the testator's death. For instance, suppose testator devises "the stocks in my stock portfolio" to his sister. In the five years between the execution of his will and his death, he buys and sells various investments, and the portfolio appreciates in value. At testator's death, the character of his devise to his sister has changed dramatically; the identity and value of those stocks are different than they were when testator executed his will. To the common law mind, this presented a problem (one not obvious to modern law students): the will had been "changed," but the change had not been accompanied by testamentary formalities. The common law solved this dilemma by developing the doctrine of **facts of independent significance** (sometimes referred to as **acts of independent significance**, or **events of independent significance**). That doctrine provides that a will provision that is affected by outside acts or events is valid if, and only if, *those acts or events have a motive, purpose or significance separate and apart from their effect on the will*. So, for example, our testator's bequest of his stock portfolio would be valid, notwithstanding the changing character of the bequest, because testator's primary motive for selling and purchasing stocks was a desire to increase his wealth, not to change the bequest in the will. This requirement that the changes have an independent lifetime significance provides some protection against coercion and fraud.

The doctrine of facts of independent significance is relevant in two types of circumstances: 1) when life events change a testator's *beneficiary* designation, and 2) when events change the *character of a bequest*. The example concerning testator's stock portfolio is an example of lifetime events that change the character of the bequest. Now consider some examples that affect the identity of the will's beneficiary. Suppose testator's will devises a sum of money to "my employees in equal shares," or to "the members of the Maplewood Garden Club in appreciation for their beautification efforts." Each of these bequests would have been problematic to the common law mind, because membership in those groups might continually change up to the time of testator's death. The devise to testator's employees would be valid because testator's hiring and firing of employees after the will's execution would be primarily motivated by a desire to run a productive business, not to change the bequests in his will. The devise to the Maplewood Garden Club would be valid because people will join and quit the Garden Club for their own personal reasons, not to gain a share of testator's estate.

It is not always clear whether a court should use facts of independent significance to validate a will provision. For example, suppose testator's will devises "all the jewelry in my green jewelry box" to her sister. If testator had only one jewelry box, which happened to be green, a court might validate the bequest because testator had an independent reason (aside from directing the distribution of her jewelry) for placing her jewelry there. But if testator had several jewelry boxes, her acts of adding and removing items to the green one might have been motivated solely by the desire to change what her sister receives. In that case, the bequest would fail. If the testator bequeaths "all of the jewelry in my safe deposit box at First National Bank to my sister", the answer is murkier. On one hand, testator's chief motivation in removing and adding jewelry to the safe deposit box might be to affect what her sister gets under the will. On the other hand, testator may keep all of her expensive jewelry in the box for safekeeping, and may add and remove items as she sells or acquires jewelry.

UPC § 2–512 codifies the doctrine. That section states:

> A will may dispose of property by reference to acts or events that have significance apart from their effect upon the disposition made by the will, whether they occur before or after the execution of the will or before or after the testator's death. The execution or revocation of another individual's will is such an event.

C.   The Problem of the Pour Over Will

Historically, the doctrines of incorporation by reference and facts of independent significance played an important role in a common fact pattern. As the *inter vivos* trust increased in popularity (more about those in Chapter Six), increasing numbers of testators sought to combine their probate assets with those assets that they had placed in trust during their lives. The objective was to consolidate probate and non-probate assets into one trust after testator's death for easy management and distribution. Testators would try to combine their assets by devising the residuary of their estate to the trustee of their *inter vivos* trust.

The provision might look something like this: "all the rest of my estate I hereby devise to First National Bank as trustee of the Teresa Testator Inter Vivos Trust, dated May 3, 1990, to be held and managed according to the terms of the trust." This type of will is often referred to as a "pour over will." By now you can probably spot the problem. The will attempts to dispose of probate assets by reference to a document that is not a part of the will, and which was not executed in compliance with testamentary formalities (because trust law imposed few formal requirements for the creation of a valid trust).

Historically, courts looked to two doctrines to validate pour over wills, but both proved unsatisfactory. Some pour over wills could be validated by application of incorporation by reference doctrine. If the will clearly identified the trust, and the trust was in existence at the time of execution, the trust could be incorporated. However, if the testator modified the trust after the will execution, the trust would not satisfy the doctrine's requirement that the completed document be in existence prior to will execution. So, incorporation by reference doctrine worked only if the trust was never modified or changed.

The doctrine of facts of independent significance sometimes validated trusts that had been modified after will execution. If the testator had *funded the trust during his life,* testator's principal motive or purpose in amending the trust instrument was to change the way the trust funds were being managed, not to change the distribution of probate assets. But many testators failed to fund *inter vivos* trusts during life. Instead, they created lifetime trusts that functioned as **standby trusts**. The function of the standby trust is to receive assets, both probate and non-probate, at testator's death. The standby trust consolidates management of all of testator's assets, such as life insurance and retirement account proceeds and probate assets, after her death. The doctrine of facts of independent significance could not validate an unfunded trust that testator amended after will execution, because testator's sole objective in making the amendments would have been to direct the distribution of his property after death.

There was a strong sense among courts and scholars that pour over wills ought to be valid. The problem was finally solved with the **Uniform Testamentary Additions to Trusts Act** (UTATA), which validates pour over will provisions regardless of whether the receptacle trust is funded or amended after the will execution. **UPC § 2–511** is substantially identical to the UTATA.

III. Construction Problems Created by the Time Gap Between Will Execution and Death

When testators execute their wills they have a solid understanding of their assets and intended beneficiaries. But testators have poor foresight. They cannot predict changes in their assets or family relationships. Of course, testators can amend their wills whenever circumstances render it necessary. But lives are busy, and execution ceremonies cost money. It is not uncommon for people to fail to get around to changing their will even when changing circumstances make it necessary.

This section explores several problems created by the time gap between will execution and death. First, the value of testator's estate might change dramatically, for better or worse. When the estate declines in value, there might not be sufficient assets to fully effectuate testator's estate plan. The rules of **abatement** determine which devises get satisfied. Second, decline in value of the estate may distort the testator's tax objectives. The rules governing **apportionment of taxes** deals with that problem. Third, assets may change in form. The testator may sell or lose property that she specifically devised in her will. The **ademption** doctrine addresses this problem. Fourth, estate beneficiaries might predecease the testator. When this happens, the devise to the predeceased beneficiary **lapses**, unless the relevant jurisdiction has enacted an **anti-lapse statute**.

A. Introduction: Classifying Devises

To understand time-gap doctrines, it is necessary to master terminology that describes the parts of a will. The terms with which you must be familiar are: specific devise, general devise demonstrative devise and residuary devise.

First, a clarification. There is today no meaningful difference between the terms "devise," "bequest," or "legacy." At early common law, "devise" referred to a testamentary gift of real property, and "bequest" or "legacy" were used to distribute personal property. The reasons for the distinction have evaporated, and the terms are used interchangeably.

Specific devise: A specific devise is a testamentary gift of a particularly described item of property. The devise can be satisfied only by distributing that property. Gifts of "my home located at 55 Owen Drive", "my Rolex watch," "my mother's wedding ring," or "the money in my checking account at First National Bank" are specific devises.

If the specifically devised property is subject to a mortgage or other security interest, the rule of **non-exoneration** provides that the specific devisee takes the property subject to the security interest; the estate's personal representative does not pay off the debt from other estate property.

General devise: A general devise, on the other hand, is not a gift of a particular thing, and can be satisfied from the general assets of the estate instead of a particular fund or asset. Devises of sums of money are the most common form of general devise ("$300 to my sister Kate").

Demonstrative devise: A demonstrative devise is a devise of a particular amount of money to be drawn from a specific probate asset or fund. For instance, a devise of "$5,000 to my brother Jim, which shall be satisfied from the sale of my Honda Civic" is a demonstrative devise. What happens if the Honda Civic sells for $4,000? **UPC § 3–902** provides that Jim takes the $4,000 from the sale, and that the remaining $1,000 shall be treated as a general devise to Jim, payable from the probate estate. If the Civic sells for $6,000, however, Jim takes only $5,000.

Residuary devise: A residuary devise is the "sweep up" clause in the will that distributes all of the property that has not been described as either a specific, general or demonstrative devise. It is usually the last dispositive clause in the will.

B. Abatement

The rules of abatement apply when the testator's estate is of insufficient value to satisfy the specific, demonstrative, general and residuary devises in her will. This problem can occur either because testator's assets decline in value after the will's execution, because the testator amasses significant debt prior to her death, or both. When an estate is probated, creditor claims have first priority. In other words, the court will direct that the executor pay creditors prior to satisfying the directives of the will. In reality, the creditor claims reduce the devises to the residuary legatees, because they take what is left over once specific, general and demonstrative devises are satisfied.

If creditor claims are substantial, or if testator's assets have declined in value, there may be insufficient assets to satisfy all of the will provisions. The common law developed an order of abatement: the first to abate are distributions made pursuant to the intestacy statute (these distributions occur when the will fails to make a complete disposition of the estate). Second to abate is the residuary devise, followed by general devises (pro rata) and lastly, specific devises. Another way to state the rule is that the court will satisfy specific devises first, then general devises, then residuary devises, and last, distributions, if any, that occur by application of the intestacy statute. Demonstrative devises are treated as specific devises to the extent that the source of the funding is sufficient to satisfy the devise. To the extent it is not, the devise is treated as a general legacy.

Consider an example. Suppose testator's will devises her wedding ring to her daughter Anna, $2,000 to her son Bart (who has amassed considerable wealth of his own), and the residue of her estate to her son Cain (a poor artist). When testator executes her will, she owns the ring, and has other assets totaling $20,000. Testator intends, therefore, to give Anna and Bart gifts of roughly equivalent value, and to give Cain the bulk of her estate. At her death, however, the ring is worth $4,000, and testator's other probate assets have a total value of $1,000 after creditor claims have been paid. Under the rules of abatement, Anna will receive the $4,000 ring, Bart will take $1,000 cash, and Cain will receive nothing.

The rule provides that gifts of the same classification abate ratably. So, suppose the testator in the above example made, in addition to the general devise of $2,000 to Bart, two more general devises of $1,000 to each of two friends. Under the rules of abatement, Bart takes $500, and each friend receives $250.00.

As our example indicates, the common law rule can frustrate testators' intentions, because most modern testators probably view the residuary legatee as the most important beneficiary under the will. The common law rule probably evolved because historically most family wealth took the form of real estate and tangible personal property, such as family farms and businesses and the accoutrements needed to run them. Bequests of these types of property tended to take the form of specific devises. But as the form of family wealth has changed from real and personal property to intangible assets, the residuary legatee often is the main beneficiary of the estate. The common-law rule, then, often frustrates testator's intent. Although UPC § 3–902 codifies the common-law rule, subsection (b) allows the court to depart from the rules of abatement if departure is necessary to effectuate testator's express or implied intent.

From a drafting perspective, a lawyer should take care to anticipate problems arising from changes in estate size. For instance, the will could avoid specific and general devises in favor of percentage shares of the estate, thus assuring that the residuary devisee does not bear the entire cost of a loss in estate value. Alternatively, the will could provide explicitly that specific and general devises (or particular specific and general devises) should abate whenever the value of the net probate estate falls below a specified amount. Such provisions would avoid application of statutory or common-law abatement rules.

C. Apportionment of Taxes

When a testator dies with debts, the executor typically pays debts "off the top" of the estate so that, as we have seen, the residuary devisee bears much of the cost of satisfying the testator's debts. Most states, however, treat tax obligations differently from debts. Largely as a result of the Great Depression, when many estates decreased dramatically in size, many state legislatures enacted states requiring apportionment of taxes. These statutes provide that when the estate is subject to estate taxes, the tax obligation must be shared proportionately by all estate beneficiaries. Suppose, for instance, an estate of $8,000,000 owes $1,000,000 in estate taxes. Suppose, further, that testator's will left an $80,000 car to her brother, a general devise of $400,000 to her sister, and the remainder of her estate to her children. Because the taxing authorities are entitled to

1/8 of testator's estate, each beneficiary will have to relinquish 1/8 of his or her devise. The brother would have to pay $10,000 in order to take the car; the sister would pay $50,000 in taxes, leaving her with a net of $350,000, and the children would pay the remaining $940,000 out of their residuary devise.

Apportionment, however, is often inconsistent with the testator's intentions. Testators do not expect that the devisee of an $80,000 car will have to pay $10,000 in taxes. To avoid this result, testators may include a **direction against apportionment** in the will. For instance, the will might include a provision directing the executor to treat all estate taxes as expenses of the estate, and to pay those taxes out of the residue of the estate.

D.   Ademption

A second problem that can be created by the time gap between will execution and testator's death occurs when a *specifically devised item of property* is not in testator's estate at testator's death. Courts call this problem **ademption,** or **ademption by extinction**.

Consider some examples: Testator's will devises "my vacation home located in Bayhead, New Jersey, to my daughter Zelda." After will execution but before testator's death, testator sells the vacation home, but neglects to change her will to reflect the fact. At testator's death, should Zelda receive nothing? If testator had purchased a new vacation home with the proceeds from the sale of the first, should Zelda be entitled to the new home? Or, suppose instead that testator had not sold the vacation home, but that it had burned down in a fire. Should Zelda be entitled to the insurance proceeds?

At early common law,[5] the answer to these questions was simple. The rule, termed the **identity theory** of ademption, provided that *if the specifically devised property was no longer part of testator's estate at testator's death, the devise was adeemed,* and the beneficiary received nothing. A qualification to the rule provided that if the change in the property was *a change merely of form, but not of substance,* then the gift would not adeem, and the beneficiary would receive the gift in its new form. As one might imagine, the form v. substance rule gave rise to frequent litigation and established no clear standard.[6]

---

[5]   *See* Ashburner v. MacGuire, 29 Eng. Rep. 62 (Ch. 1786).

[6]   Contrast Willis v. Barrow, 218 Ala. 549, 119 So. 678 (1929) (finding that the gift of money in a specifically described bank account did not adeem when testator transferred the assets to a new bank) with McGee v. McGee, 122 R.I. 837, 413 A.2d 72 (1980) (finding that gift of "all monies, standing in my name at any bank" adeemed when testator's agent withdrew funds from bank account and purchased "flower bonds" with the proceeds).

At first blush, the **identity theory** might be justified as best approximating the intentions of most testators. If a testator takes pains to style a gift as a specific bequest, it must be important to the testator that the beneficiary receive the exact property bequeathed and no other. Gifts of personal property, such as jewelry and paintings, or gifts of real property, such as the family farm, tend to have sentimental or other value. However, courts applying the identity theory generally refused to consider extrinsic evidence of testator's intent in particular cases. As a result, ademption often frustrated, rather than furthered, testator's intent.

In a variety of circumstances, the absence of devised property from testator's estate provides very little evidence that testator intended to leave the devisee with nothing. For example, when specifically devised property is sold by a conservator, the sale provides no evidence that testator wanted to cut out the specific devisee. Courts have refused to apply the identity theory in that circumstance, and UPC § 2–606(b) reaches the same result by statute.

UPC § 2–606(a) modifies common law ademption rules in a number of circumstances. When transfer of the specifically devised property is so recent that decedent has not yet collected the proceeds at the time of his death, the decedent has not had much opportunity to change his will to make alternative provision for the specific devisee. In these circumstances, the UPC entitles the specific devisee at least to any proceeds from the specifically devised property that remain unpaid at testator's death. Thus, UPC § 2–606(a)(2) and (3) entitle the specific devisee to any unpaid condemnation or insurance proceeds resulting from taking of or injury to specifically devised property. Similarly, UPC § 2–606(a)(4) entitles the specific devisee to property acquired by the testator as a result of foreclosure on specifically devised property. These provisions are particularly appealing because testator took no affirmative action to transfer the specifically devised property. UPC § 2–601(a)(1) extends similar rights to the specific devisee even when the transfer is the result of an affirmative act by the testator: the specific devisee is entitled to sale proceeds that remain unpaid at testator's death.

UPC §§ 2–606(a)(5) and (6) intrude further on common law ademption principles. UPC § 2–606(a)(5) deals with the situation in which testator replaces specifically devised property, and it gives the specific devisee a right to the replacement property. Thus, if testator's will leaves "my 2012 Honda Accord to my daughter Barbara," Barbara will be entitled the 2016 Toyota Camry testator purchased to replace the Accord. Finally, UPC § 2–606(a)(6) offers a specific devisee the opportunity to establish that testator did not intend ademption or that ademption would be inconsistent with testator's testamentary plan. A specific devisee who establishes either of those circumstances is entitled to the *value* of specifically devised property.

When testators devise securities, complicated ademption issues can arise. Testator may sell the stock and purchase other stock. Or, the corporation might declare a stock split or dividend, multiplying or reducing the stock held by the testator. Finally, the corporation might be acquired by another company, leaving the testator with stock in that new company. Consequently, drafters would be well advised to steer clear of devises of specifically described stock.

UPC § 2–605 addresses these problems by providing that the beneficiary of specifically named stock is also entitled to additional securities acquired by the testator as a result of testator's ownership of the original stock. Distributions in cash before the testator's death are not considered part of the specific devise.

One final wrinkle created by the ademption doctrine concerns lifetime gifts made by testators to will beneficiaries. If the testator executes a will that devises "my mother's engagement ring" to her daughter Annie, but then gives the ring to Annie before testator's death, the testamentary gift is **adeemed by extinction**. Annie is not entitled, at testator's death, to the value of the ring. The question is trickier if the testator's lifetime gift is to a *general legatee*. Should the lifetime gift of money be deemed to "satisfy" all or part of the testamentary general devise? UPC § 2–609 answers "no;" a general bequest will not be **adeemed by satisfaction** unless the testator or devisee acknowledges in writing that the gift is in satisfaction of a testamentary bequest, or unless the will expressly provides for a deduction of the gift.

E.   Lapse

A third major issue that arises as a result of changes that occur between the will execution and the testator's death is the **lapse** issue. This issue arises when a will beneficiary predeceases the testator. Because the common law resolves lapse issues differently than the statutory law of most states, the following paragraphs set out the common law rules first. Even though 49 states have enacted statutes, the common law rules apply when those statutes fail to save the gifts, so it is important to understand them. We then turn to a discussion of the different approaches taken by state statutes.

1.   *The Common Law Rules*

a.   *Gifts to Individuals*

When a will beneficiary predeceased the testator, the common law generally assumed that a testator would want the gift to lapse.

When the lapsed gift was a specific, general or demonstrative devise to a predeceased individual, the property that is the subject of the gift was distributed according to the will's residuary clause (or, if there was no residuary clause, in accordance with the intestacy statutes). If the predeceased beneficiary was a residuary beneficiary, the property subject to the lapsed residuary gift passed to testator's heirs as determined by the intestacy statute.

Consider the following example: suppose T's will included the following provisions:

1.   I give my Van Gogh painting, Starry Night, to my cook, Mary Smith.

2.   I give $50,000 each to my three sons, John, Jake and James.

3.   All the rest, residue and remainder of my estate I hereby devise and bequeath to my brother, Lucas Tyler, and my sister, Mamie Schwartz, in equal shares.

If Mary Smith predeceased the testator, the specific devise of the Van Gogh would fail. The court would distribute the painting as part of the residuary estate to Lucas and Mamie. If, instead, son John predeceased the testator, Jake and James would each receive $50,000, and the $50,000 gift that was supposed to go to John would be distributed to Lucas and Mamie.

At early common law, if Lucas predeceased the testator, his half of the residuary estate would be distributed to T's intestate heirs (most likely John, Jake and James). Here, however, the law has changed significantly. Most courts and legislatures have abandoned the traditional approach, reasoning that most testators would prefer that the lapsed gift be distributed to the remaining residuary legatees. Thus, in most jurisdictions, if the gift to Lucas lapsed, Mamie would receive the entire residuary estate.

b.   Class Gifts

A class gift is a devise that is given to two or more people to share. Instead of naming the beneficiaries individually, the testator characterizes the devisees as a class, such as "my children" or "my nieces and nephews." The use of class terminology creates a different result when one member of the class predeceases the testator. If the gift lapses (as it would at common law), then that class member's share is distributed to the remaining class members. Only if the entire class predeceases the testator is the gift distributed through the residuary clause or intestacy.

So, in our example above, consider clause two. As currently drafted, clause 2 makes three $50,000 devises, one to each son.

Suppose instead that testator had drafted the devise as a class gift: "I devise $150,000 to be distributed to my children in equal shares." If son John predeceased the testator, and the common law rules applied, John's gift would lapse, and Jake and James would receive $75,000 each.

2.   *State Statutory Approaches*

a.   *Gifts to Individuals*

Most state legislatures have made the determination that testators would not necessarily want all gifts to predeceased devisees to lapse, but would prefer that the lapsed gift be distributed to the devisee's surviving descendants. All states but Louisiana have **anti-lapse statutes**, which "save" certain devisees by designating "substitute takers" who will receive the lapsed gift.

Anti-lapse statutes vary from state to state, but a few generalizations are apt. First, most statutes "save" only devises to specified blood relatives of the testator. Generally, anti-lapse statutes do not protect devises to testator's spouse, the spouses of testator's relatives, or to those unrelated to the testator. The exception to this is New Hampshire, which "saves" all lapsed gifts, regardless of the relationship of the devisee to the testator.

Second, almost all anti-lapse statutes designate the *issue* of predeceased beneficiaries, not the *estates* of those beneficiaries, as substitute takers. The exception to this rule is the Maryland statute, which provides that the deceased devisee's bequest shall be distributed to his estate.

Although statutes vary in terms of which gifts they "save", all statutes save *devises to the testator's predeceased descendants who leave surviving descendants*. To illustrate, return to our original working example. Suppose son John predeceases the testator, and that John is survived by a wife and two daughters. Recall that at common law, John's gift would lapse, and the $50,000 that would have been his is distributed to the residuary legatees, Lucas and Mamie. In all states except Louisiana and Maryland, an anti-lapse statute would "save" John's gift by creating substitute takers in John's daughters.

But what if John had been survived only by his wife? In almost all states, his gift would lapse. In Maryland, however, John's gift would have been distributed as his will directed. If John's residuary devise was to his wife, then she would receive testator's devise. But if John's residuary estate was devised to someone else, that party would take testator's gift.

Although all anti-lapse statutes save gifts to testator's issue, they vary in terms of which other gifts they save. For example, the New York statute applies only to devises to testator's issue or siblings.[7] Others save gifts to testator's "relatives."[8] The Virginia statute applies to devises made to testator's grandparents or to issue of testator's grandparents. This is the approach the UPC takes. Because the UPC creates serious complications for the anti-lapse rules, however, it is discussed separately below.

b.　Class Gifts

Most anti-lapse statutes expressly apply to class gifts in the same way that they apply to gifts to individuals. In states where the statute does not expressly apply to class gifts, courts are willing to read them that way.

Return to our working example. Again, suppose that the gift to testator's sons was fashioned as a class gift, thus: "I devise $150,000 to my children in equal shares." If son John predeceases the testator, leaving two surviving daughters, most statutes would direct that $25,000 would be distributed to each of John's daughters, $50,000 each to Jake and James. If a class gift is not saved by an anti-lapse statute, however, the common law rules apply, and the property is distributed to the surviving class members.

3.　Consequences of Lapse

When a gift is saved by an anti-lapse statute, it is distributed to the substitute takers as directed by the statute. When the anti-lapse statute does not save the gift, the common law rules apply. Thus, lapsed specific, general and demonstrative bequests are distributed pursuant to the residuary clause. Lapsed residuary gifts are, depending on the jurisdiction, distributed either to testator's intestate heirs or to the remaining residuary legatees. A few states have codified this latter approach.[9]

4.　Void vs. Lapsed Devises

At common law, a "void" devise was a devise that was made to someone who was dead at the time of the will's execution; a "lapsed" devise was a devise made to one alive at the will execution, but who died prior to the testator. With respect to individual gifts, most lapse statutes have eliminated the distinction between void and lapsed devises, treating them exactly the same way. In some states, however, the distinction remains with respect to class gifts. In New

---

[7]　*See* N.Y. E.P.T.L. § 3–3.3 (saving gifts to issue and siblings of testator).

[8]　*See* Ohio R.C. § 2107.52; *see also*, Kan. Stat. Ann. § 59–615 (saving devises to a spouse or relative to the sixth degree).

[9]　*See* N.Y. E.P.T.L. § 3–3.4, and UPC § 2–604.

York, for example, void gifts to class members are not saved by the anti-lapse statute.[10] In Virginia, they are.[11]

5. *Construction Question: When Does the Will Override the Anti-Lapse Statute?*

Anti-lapse statutes are "default rules" or "rules of construction." That is, they apply to resolve a dispute when the will contains no directions. It follows that a properly drafted will should contain express directions on how to treat lapsed devises. If the testator wishes to preclude application of the anti-lapse statute, it is important to draft a clear instruction to that effect, and to include an alternate devise that shall take effect if the gift lapses. An example of this might be: "I devise my flat screen television to my daughter, Marla, but if Marla predeceases me, the [anti-lapse statute] shall not apply, the devise shall lapse, and the flat screen television shall become part of my residuary estate to be distributed in accordance with the residuary clause herein."

However, wills are not often this clear. The most common issue concerns will provisions conditioned on survivorship. An example would be, "I devise my flat screen television to my daughter, Marla, if she survives me" with no direction about what the court should do if Marla does not survive the testator. Although most courts have held that words requiring survivorship evince an intent to preclude application of the anti-lapse statute, the issue is frequently litigated, and there is some precedent for the other outcome.

Another typical problem occurs when specific or general bequests have no survivorship requirement, but testator's residuary clause contains language such as, "all the rest, residue and remainder of my estate, including any gifts that may lapse or fail for any reason, I devise to ... " Courts are divided over whether this "boilerplate" language in a residuary clause evinces an intent to preclude application of the anti-lapse statute.[12]

6. *UPC § 2–603*

The 1969 version of the Uniform Probate Code included a relatively simple anti-lapse statute that is still in effect in a number of states. It saved gifts to testator's grandparents, or descendants of testator's grandparents, and provided that a saved gift would be distributed to the issue of the deceased devisee, by representation.

---

[10] *See* N.Y. E.P.T.L. § 3–3.3(a)(3).

[11] *See* Va. Code Ann. § 64.1–64.1.

[12] Compare Blevins v. Moran, 12 S.W.3d 698 (Ky. App. 2000) with Colombo v. Stevenson, 150 N.C.App. 163, 563 S.E.2d 591 (2002).

In 1990, the UPC drafters replaced the anti-lapse statute with an expanded, rather complicated statute. The controversial statute attempts to provide a framework for resolving "a variety of interpretive questions that have arisen under standard anti-lapse statutes."[13] Whether a detailed statutory approach to these construction questions is preferable to allowing judges to decide issues in light of specific factual contexts remains to be seen.

The statute's substantive provisions are contained in section 2–603(b). Subsection (b) saves gifts to testator's grandparents, descendants of testator's grandparents, and testator's stepchildren. Subsection (b)(1) applies to individual gifts, and provides that the predeceased devisee's descendants take, by representation, as substitute takers. Subsection (b)(2) provides that the statute applies to class gifts, and that the descendants of predeceased class members take each class member's share, by representation.

Subsection (b)(3) is the controversial section. It directs that "words of survivorship, such as in a devise to an individual 'if he survives me,' or in a devise to 'my surviving children' are not, in the absence of additional evidence, a sufficient indication of an intent contrary to the application of this statute." In short, the UPC directs the court to ignore testator's clear language, and to apply the anti-lapse statute even if the testator has conditioned a bequest on survival. This is contrary to the view of the majority of courts that have grappled with this issue. From a drafting perspective, the statute requires a drafter who wants to ensure that the testator's survivorship condition is respected to take one of two alternatives: first, to include an alternative gift, or second, to explicitly refer to, and to exclude, descendants of deceased beneficiaries. Thus, the drafter might provide "to my surviving children, and not to descendants of deceased children."

The UPC's approach is probably preferable if one views any lawyer who fails to include an alternative gift as an incompetent who has no idea what he is doing. If we believe that the language used by a lawyer who does not include sufficiently explicit directives is not at all probative of testator's intent (because the lawyer is incompetent), then the UPC's position makes sense. On the other hand, there may be many fair-to-middling lawyers who do not include alternative gifts, and who do not explicitly exclude descendants of deceased beneficiaries, but who use language of survivorship only when testator wants to impose a survivorship condition. For the clients of these lawyers, UPC § 2–603(b)(3) is a disaster.

Even though the statute directs that an alternative devise overrides the anti-lapse statute, the statute qualifies this, in section

---

[13] *See* UPC § 2–603, Official Comment.

2–603(b)(4), when it states that the substitute gift (created by the anti-lapse statute) is superseded by the alternative devise only if someone is entitled to take pursuant to the alternative devise. Thus, if the alternative devisee also has predeceased the testator, the substitute takers, not the alternative devisee's descendants, take the property.

IV. Construction Problems More Generally

A. Incomplete Wills and the Problem of Negative Disinheritance

Typically, a testator's will disposes of testator's entire estate. Most commonly, this is accomplished through the will's residuary clause, which directs the disposition of "the remainder of my estate" to designated residuary beneficiaries. If, however, a will omits a residuary clause, or if the residuary clause is, for some reason, ineffective, the will may make an incomplete disposition of testator's property: some portion of testator's estate has not been left to any beneficiary. In that circumstance, the property not devised passes by intestate succession.

In rare circumstances, testator makes an incomplete disposition of his estate, but clearly articulates an intent to disinherit one of his intestate heirs. For instance, testator's will might leave the family home to his daughter, and provide "I hereby disinherit my son." If testator dies with the house and a $20,000 bank account, who is entitled to the bank account if the will makes no express provision for the account? The orthodox common law rule was that the daughter and the son would split the account, assuming they were testator's only heirs. Courts following that rule gave no effect to words of "negative disinheritance." Testator could disinherit an heir only by making an affirmative provision for some other beneficiary. That result, however, is plainly inconsistent with testator's expressed intent, and has been rejected by UPC § 2–101(b) and a number of modern courts. The UPC provides that in the case of negative disinheritance, any property not devised by will should pass by intestacy as if the disinherited heir predeceased the testator.

B. Ambiguity

1. *The Difference Between Latent and Patent Ambiguity*

If a testator is lucky, her will is perfectly drafted to anticipate all contingencies and provide clear directions to the probate court. Sometimes, however, the will is less than crystal clear, and courts are called upon to determine what the testator meant to express. When the words of the will do not adequately convey testator's intentions, what process should the court use to ascertain them?

Should it stick to the will's "plain meaning," or should it consider extrinsic evidence of testator's intent? This interpretative question has generated controversy in wills law, just as it has in contract law and constitutional law.

At common law, and up until the first half of the twentieth century, the approach a court chose to take depended (at least allegedly) on whether the ambiguity was described as **patent** or **latent**. A **patent ambiguity** is one that appears on the will's face. In other words, the will provision, as written, is not coherent. A **latent ambiguity** occurs when the will is coherent when read, but the meaning becomes uncertain when the court attempts to distribute the property. The black letter rule of construction provided that when the ambiguity was patent, it could be resolved only by examining the "four corners" of the will. The court could not consider extrinsic evidence, such as testimony about statements that testator had made during her life or details about her relationships, to help ascertain testator's meaning. If meaning could not be clarified, the bequest would fail. When the ambiguity was latent, however, the court could consider extrinsic evidence to clarify testator's meaning.

Some examples drawn from cases might be useful. Suppose testator's will created a trust, and provided that on the death of the income beneficiary, the principal amount of $12,000 should "be divided equally, in equal shares, share and share alike between my son Hugh Pfost, and my twelve (12) grandchildren, said grandchildren being the eight (8) children of my daughter Iva L. Foss, and the four (4) children of my son Hugh Pfost." The provision is not clear on its face: did testator mean that his son Hugh should take $6,000, and his grandchildren the other $6,000, or did he mean that Hugh and all of the grandchildren should divide the $12,000 equally? To resolve this question, the court determined first that the ambiguity was **patent**; the will was incoherent on its face. In determining the meaning of the provision, the court announced, it was limited to considering only the "four corners" of the document. The court noted that Hugh was the residuary legatee, and that the testator had disinherited his daughter, Iva Foss, and determined that testator must have meant to distribute $6,000 to his son.[14]

Now consider an example of a **latent ambiguity**. Suppose testator devised his residuary estate to "the Michigan Cancer Society." The provision seems clear on its face. However, it turns out that there are two charities with similar names: The American Cancer Society, Michigan Division, and the Michigan Cancer Society, an affiliate of the Michigan Cancer Foundation. Extrinsic evidence revealed a **latent ambiguity**: testator might have intended to devise

---

[14] In re Estate of Pfost, 139 Neb. 784, 298 N.W. 739 (1941).

the money to the American Cancer Society, not the Michigan Cancer Society. Testator had told people that he intended to benefit the American Cancer Society, the American Cancer Society had helped the testator's wife when she was dying of cancer, testator had made substantial contributions to the American Cancer Society during his wife's life, and testator requested memorials to the American Cancer Society at his death. The court therefore found that the American Cancer Society should receive testator's residuary estate.[15]

2.   Is the Will Ambiguous?

The aura of certainty that these rules purport to give is misleading. First, reasonable minds can disagree about whether a patent or latent ambiguity exists. For example, in *Matter of Marine Midland Bank, N.A.*,[16] four Judges on the New York Court of Appeals found that a will provision was not ambiguous, while three others dissented on the ground that the will was **patently ambiguous**. The provision at issue devised a remainder interest in a residuary trust to "the surviving child or children" of testator's brother Leonard. One of Leonard's two children predeceased the life tenant, leaving surviving children, who argued that they should take their father's share. The majority found that the word "children" should be given its "ordinary and natural meaning," the will clearly limited the devise to "children", and plaintiffs were not entitled to take a share of the trust property. The three dissenting judges argued that the will was patently ambiguous because the will used the terms "issue" and "children" interchangeably throughout, other will provisions manifested a clear intent to benefit the deceased brother's lineal descendants, and the will's entire structure revealed an intent to benefit testator's brothers' family lines equally.

Similarly, courts have disagreed about whether a **latent ambiguity** is present. Suppose that a married couple executes mirror image wills. Each will leaves all property to the surviving spouse, or, if the spouse predeceases the testator, to "my nephews and nieces." Both husband and wife have nephews and nieces with whom the couple have close relationships. When the second spouse dies, should her estate be distributed only to her nieces and nephews by blood, or did she mean to direct that her husband's nieces and nephews should share in her estate? Courts have taken different approaches on substantially similar facts. In *Estate of Carroll*,[17] the court found that no latent ambiguity existed because "nieces and nephews" had a commonly understood legal meaning, and that there was no reason to think that the testator had not intended to use the

---

[15]   Estate of Kremlick, 417 Mich. 237, 331 N.W.2d 228 (1983).

[16]   74 N.Y.2d 448, 547 N.E.2d 1152, 548 N.Y.S.2d 625 (1989).

[17]   764 S.W.2d 736 (Mo.App. 1989).

words in their legal sense. Thus, only testator's nieces and nephews by blood took the property. On the other hand, the court in *Martin v. Palmer*[18] held that whether testator meant to include his wife's nieces and nephews in the bequest was a triable issue of fact because the argument that the term nieces and nephews referred only to blood relatives "lacked merit in current English usage."

3.   *Using Extrinsic Evidence*

The above discussion gives rise to questions: why did courts traditionally bar extrinsic evidence to clear up patent ambiguities? And why did they make an exception for extrinsic evidence in the case of latent ambiguities?

If a primary objective of courts should be to give effect to testator's intent, why is extrinsic evidence not always admissible to clarify testator's meaning? There are some good reasons for courts' reluctance to consider extrinsic evidence. Routine admission of extrinsic evidence would open the floodgates to claims that testator's meaning needs to be clarified. For example, envision a will provision leaving testator's estate "to my children." Should we allow testator's neighbor to argue that testator told her that he had always considered her "his child," and that he would provide for her in his will? Such evidence can be easily fabricated. The result would be an inefficient system where the costs of probate would probably far outweigh the increase in instances where testator's intent was better effectuated. These concerns have motivated courts to make pronouncements such as "parol testimony cannot be [used to] add to, vary, or contradict the language of a will unambiguous on its face."[19]

If admitting extrinsic evidence is potentially problematic, why do courts allow it to reveal and resolve questions of latent ambiguity? Probably because this evidence is more difficult to fabricate, and is likely to be probative. For example, suppose testator's will leaves her estate to "my daughter." But when the court attempts to distribute testator's property, it is revealed that testator in fact has two daughters. Extrinsic evidence establishes that testator lived her entire life with her eldest daughter, but that she cut off all contact with her second daughter after that daughter married out of the faith twenty years before testator's death. Allowing extrinsic evidence in cases of latent ambiguity, then, is unlikely to open the floodgates, overburden the courts, and will often lead to better results.

Why, then did courts traditionally not admit extrinsic evidence to clarify patent ambiguities? After all, patent ambiguities are hard

---

[18]   1 S.W.3d 875 (Tex.App. 1999).

[19]   Detroit Wabeek Bank & Trust Co. v. City of Adrian, 349 Mich. 136, 143, 84 N.W.2d 441 (1957).

to fabricate, so there is hardly a "floodgates" problem. The answer can probably be found in the formal approach of the common law mind. When an ambiguity is patent, and the meaning cannot be determined from reading the "four corners" of the will, a court can only give meaning to the provisions by adding words to the will. To the common law mind, this would be problematic, because the court would be amending the will without testamentary formalities. Thus, the rule that a patent ambiguity can be resolved only by interpreting the will as a whole, but not by resort to extrinsic evidence. Admitting extrinsic evidence to clarify latent ambiguities, however, enables the court to interpret what the testator has written, or to clarify the meaning that the testator attached to particular words.

In recent years, courts have been increasingly willing to admit extrinsic evidence to clarify even patent ambiguities.[20] This trend is consistent with the larger trend in wills law away from rigid rules and towards admitting extrinsic evidence to clarify testator's intent (as exemplified by provisions such as UPC § 2–503, which allows courts to admit improperly executed documents to probate if there is clear and convincing evidence of testator's intent). For obvious reasons, courts still bar the door on admission of extrinsic evidence if it is introduced to contradict the testator's clear directives.

4.   *What Types of Extrinsic Evidence Are Admissible?*

Once a court determines that extrinsic evidence is admissible to clarify testator's intent, another problem arises: what type of extrinsic evidence is admissible? Courts allow evidence tending to show the meaning the testator attached to words used in his will, but often bar evidence of direct statements that testator made about his testamentary intentions. Suppose that testator's will devised "my home place" to his wife, Melba, and the rest of his estate to his son Bruce. Evidence shows that testator owned two adjacent lots, and that his home was built on lot 1, and that lot 2 was overgrown and undeveloped. Both Melba and Bruce claim lot 2. If Melba introduced evidence that testator had refused to sell lot 2 because "it was his home", and that testator had purchased materials to build a fence around lots 1 and 2, most courts would admit this evidence to show that testator meant to refer to both lots 1 and 2 when he used the words "my home place." However, if Bruce offered evidence that

---

[20] *See, e.g.*, First Union Nat'l Bank, N.A. v. Frumkin, 659 So.2d 463 (Fla. App. 1995) (where there is a patent ambiguity as to the testator's intent, the court is free to consider extrinsic evidence on the subject); Parkersburg Nat'l Bank v. United States, 228 F.Supp. 375 (N.D.W.Va. 1964) (Consideration of extrinsic evidence was proper to determine what organization fit the description of "person or persons in charge of the adult choir of the First Methodist Church" regardless of whether ambiguity was latent or patent).

testator had stated to his attorney "I want to give lot 2 to Melba," many courts would bar this evidence. What explains the difference?

Courts often justify their refusal to admit evidence of testator's declarations of intent with statements such as "[t]o permit this would allow one to orally 'rewrite' his will."[21] Note again the common law hesitance to "add" words to the will without testamentary formalities. On the other hand, evidence about the meaning attached to particular words merely "clarifies", but does not re-write, testator's will.

Another justification for barring evidence of testator's declarations of intent is that these statements are easily fabricated and hard to impeach, given that the testator is dead. By contrast, when an allegation is made about testator's usage in other contexts, other acquaintances are more likely to be available to testify about testator's usage.

Increasingly, courts are moving away from the common law prohibition on admission of testator's statements of intent. The trend is to admit such statements, relying on cross examination to uncover misrepresentations.

C.   Mistake

Mistake is a problem closely related to the problem of patent and latent ambiguity. Most ambiguities in a will are a result of a mistake. The following discussion will focus on two distinct types of mistake: **mistake of fact**, which *occurs when a testator is mistaken about a particular fact*, and **scrivener's error**, which *occurs when the will's drafter makes a drafting error.*

1.   *Mistake of Fact*

A testator may write and execute her will while laboring under a mistaken belief about a particular fact. For example, a testator may erroneously believe that her only son is dead, or that her husband is carrying on an extra-marital affair. When testator's mistaken belief influences her decision about how to distribute her property at death, should a court correct the error and rewrite the will to reflect what testator would have done but for her mistaken assumption?

Obviously, courts should be hesitant to entertain many claims of mistake of fact. People often hold mistaken beliefs about the world around them, and allowing disappointed family members to claim that the testator held a mistaken belief that caused their disinheritance would certainly open the door to much litigation. Moreover, evidence of mistake could be easily manufactured; courts

---

[21]   Virginia Nat'l Bank v. United States, 307 F.Supp. 1146 (E.D. Va. 1969), aff'd, 443 F.2d 1030 (4th Cir. 1971).

might be hard pressed to get to the truth. Even if it could be shown that testator harbored a mistaken belief, it might not follow that testator would have made a different will had she known the truth. Generally, then, a rule that allowed people to argue that the testator would have written the will differently but for a mistaken belief would be inefficient and misguided.

Historically, courts have clung to the rule that provides that, where a will is clear on its face, extrinsic evidence shall not be admitted to show that testator held a mistaken belief. Courts have been willing, however, to entertain claims of mistake in rare instances where two conditions are met: 1) the mistaken belief must appear on the face of the will, and 2) the disposition that the testator would have made but for the mistaken belief must be clear on the face of the will. Thus, if testator devised "my entire estate to my maid Ursula" because testator erroneously believed that her husband had recently died overseas, the husband would not succeed on a claim of mistake. On the other hand, if the testator's will declared that "it is my preference to leave my entire estate to my husband; I do not because he recently died overseas", a court would be more willing to distribute testator's estate to her husband.

These traditional standards have made it difficult to obtain reformation on grounds of mistaken belief. The Uniform Probate Code has attempted to liberalize these rules. Section 2–805 authorizes courts to reform unambiguous wills and other dispositive instruments "if it is proved by clear and convincing evidence what the transferor's intention was and that the terms of the instrument were affected by a mistake of fact or law."

2.   Scrivener's Error

Sometimes a mistake occurs through no fault of the testator. The scrivener, usually testator's attorney, simply misdescribes or omits critical information. Traditionally, courts treated these mistakes as ambiguities, and refused to consider extrinsic evidence of testator's intent to create substantive will provisions. For instance, in one (infamous) case, the attorney/drafter failed to include a residuary clause in the final draft of testator's will.[22] The will revoked a previous will that did contain a residuary clause leaving the bulk of testator's estate to his close friend. The attorney admitted to his mistake, and was willing to testify that testator intended to keep the same residuary legatee. The court refused to admit this extrinsic evidence, and distributed testator's estate to the District of Columbia by escheat!

---

[22]   *See* Knupp v. District of Columbia, 578 A.2d 702 (D.C.App. 1990).

There appear to be few sound reasons to prohibit courts from correcting scriveners' errors. Allowing correction for scriveners' errors will not open the floodgates for mistake arguments more generally, since scriveners' errors are limited in number. Moreover, when the evidence of testator's intent is clear, consideration of extrinsic evidence would be consistent with the general trend toward effectuating intent even when formalities are not complied with. Perhaps for these reasons, section 2–805 of the Uniform Probate Code authorizes reformation to correct mistakes in expression so long as clear and convincing evidence exists to establish testator's intent. Moreover, the Restatement (Third) of Property: Donative Transfers (2003) would permit the use of extrinsic evidence to correct a mistaken omission.

V.   Revocation and Revival

A.   Revocation

There are three ways to revoke a will. They are: 1) revocation by subsequent written instrument, 2) revocation by physical act, or 3) revocation by operation of law due to a change in testator's circumstances. A competent lawyer will insist that a client who wishes to revoke his will expressly do so in a writing that is executed in compliance with the applicable will formalities statute. But because testators often attempt to revoke wills without adequate legal advice, doctrines have evolved to address the problems that testators create.

1.   *Revocation by Subsequent Written Instrument*

When will revocation is supervised by a competent attorney, revocation is accomplished by executing a new will that is dated, and announces in the opening paragraph that "I hereby revoke all other wills that I have previously made" or some comparable boilerplate. When a testator executes a subsequent document that fails to expressly revoke a previously executed will, however, complications may arise. If the second will completely disposes of testator's estate, then most courts will find that the second will revokes the first by **inconsistency**. This probably effectuates the intentions of most testators who draft a second, complete will that is inconsistent with the first.

UPC § 2–507 modifies this approach slightly, by providing that the execution of a second will that makes a complete disposition of testator's estate creates a *presumption* that the testator intended to revoke, rather than supplement, the first will. *See* UPC § 2–507(b) & (c). The presumption can only be overcome by clear and convincing evidence that the testator intended the second will to supplement, rather than revoke, the first will. UPC § 2–507(c).

But what happens if the testator executes a second document that does not make a complete disposition of her estate? The second document revokes the first only to the extent that it is inconsistent with the first. Each will is fully operative to the extent it is consistent with the other. Under the UPC, the testator is presumed to have intended the second will to supplement, rather than replace, the first will unless there is clear and convincing evidence to the contrary. UPC § 2–507(b) & (d).

A **codicil** is the most common example of a written instrument that revokes only part of a prior will. When a testator executes a codicil, the testator typically revokes some provision of an existing will, while expressly reaffirming the rest of the will. In the case of the codicil, the express reaffirmation of the remainder of the will constitutes clear and convincing evidence that the codicil is designed only to supplement the existing will. A codicil, like a will, must be executed in accordance with testamentary formalities.

Even when a subsequent written instrument does not expressly ratify an existing will, the UPC presumes that the subsequent instrument revokes the first only to the extent the two documents are inconsistent. Consider some examples: suppose Theresa Testator executes a will on November 1, 2015, that devises her car to her neighbor, Marge, and the rest of her estate to her son Albert. On January 1, 2016, Marge executes a document that devises her car to her granddaughter, Lola. The January 1st document partially **revokes** the November 1st document **by inconsistency**. The car shall be distributed to Lola, and the residuary to Albert.

Consider another example. Suppose testator's first will simply devises "my home to my sister-in-law, Mildred." A second will, properly executed several years later, devises "all of my personal property to my niece Jessie." Which document is testator's will? Both are, because the second is not inconsistent with the first. The court will distribute the home to Mildred, testator's personal property to Jessie, and the residue of her estate, if any, to testator's intestate heirs.

2. *Revocation by Physical Act*

A testator can revoke a will by performing an act of revocation, such as tearing, burning, marking or obliterating, on the will with the intent to revoke, or by directing another to perform one of those acts in testator's presence. Under UPC § 2–507, if the revocatory act destroys or obliterates only part of the will, then only that part of the will is deemed revoked. Some states, however, do not recognize partial revocation by physical act. In those states, a revocatory act on only part of the will gives rise to an issue: should the court find that the entire will is revoked, or that the revocation was ineffective?

The biggest difficulty created by revocation by physical act is that testators often revoke the will when they are alone. At testator's death, the will may be found ripped or burned or with major provisions crossed out. How can the court establish that those acts were performed by the testator, with an intent to revoke, if there were no witnesses to the act and the testator cannot testify? Or, testator's will may be missing. How can a court determine whether it is missing because testator revoked it, or whether it is missing because someone else had a motive to dispose of it?

Courts have developed a burden-shifting construct to deal with these dilemmas. If the testator was known to have executed a will, and the will was known to last be in the testator's possession, there is a presumption that the testator performed the revocatory acts with the intent to revoke. If the will cannot be found, there is a presumption that the testator revoked the will. The strength of the presumption depends on the degree of control the testator had over the will, and whether others who would benefit from the will's revocation had access to the will, either before or after testator's death. The presumption can be overcome if other evidence establishes that testator intended his will to be valid.

If the presumption is rebutted, how can the will be admitted to probate if it is destroyed, damaged or missing? States have "lost wills" statutes that allow witnesses to prove the contents of the will. The statutes vary in their requirements: some require the production of a copy of the will, others allow oral testimony about the will's contents, and some require an additional showing that the testator properly executed the lost will.

Sometimes testators cause problems by performing revocatory acts on photocopies of the original will. Generally speaking, these acts will not be sufficient to revoke the will. The Restatement (Third) of Property, however, provides that if the testator mistakes a copy for the original, and testator's intent to revoke the will can be proven by clear and convincing evidence, the failure to revoke the original will can be excused as harmless error, and the revocation is valid.

3.   Revocation by Operation of Law

Another common revocation problem arises when testators divorce, but fail to change their wills. If a divorced testator's will was executed during marriage and devised property to his ex-spouse, should the court enforce the will? Courts faced with this problem developed a doctrine that allowed them to strike bequests to ex-spouses as long as the divorce had been accompanied by a final property settlement. Most states have now codified the rule, although the statutes differ in significant ways. The pre-1990 UPC § 2–508 is still in effect in many jurisdictions. That statute provides that divorce or annulment revokes any disposition of property made to the ex-spouse, and that the court should distribute the property so devised as though the ex-spouse had predeceased the testator. Also revoked by law are provisions granting an ex-spouse a power of appointment, or naming the ex-spouse as a guardian, trustee, executor or conservator. Again, these provisions are construed as though the ex-spouse had predeceased the testator. Testator's re-marriage to the same spouse revives the will.

If the objective of revoking wills after divorce is to effectuate the intentions of testators who had neglected to change their wills after divorce, the statute arguably has some shortcomings. First, the statute does not revoke bequests to or appointments of the ex-spouse's relatives. Second, it applies only to testamentary bequests, and not to transfers at death that occur outside of probate. The drafters of the 1990 UPC remedied these perceived shortcomings by expanding the statute's reach to all revocable dispositions to the ex-spouse, and to the ex-spouse's relatives, that occur at testator's death.[23]

Although the UPC's drafters attempted to include *all* non-probate transfers, states have no ability to control donative transfers that are governed by federal law. According to the Supreme Court, non-probate vehicles that are provided by testator's employer and governed by ERISA (the Employee Retirement Income Security Act of 1974) cannot be revoked by operation of state law, because federal law preempts state law. And ERISA, the applicable federal statute, directs that non-probate assets should be distributed to those named as beneficiaries in the testator's contract, and contains no provision for revocation of the beneficiary designation in the event of divorce.[24]

B.   Revival

Revival problems occur in a very limited set of circumstances: a testator executes a second will that revokes a prior will; subsequently, the testator revokes the second will by physical act. In so doing, the testator may believe that will number one will be probated at his death. After all, will one was never destroyed, and testator knows that it is the only will that will be found after his death. Testator may therefore assume that will one was "revived" by the destruction of will two. On the other hand, a different testator might assume that the first will remained revoked. How should the law deal with this problem?

At common law, will one could not be revived unless it was re-executed with testamentary formalities. The drafters of the Uniform

---

[23]   *See* UPC § 2–804.

[24]   Egelhoff v. Egelhoff, 532 U.S. 141 (2001).

Probate Code tried to fine tune the common law rule so that it is less likely to frustrate the intentions of testators who intended to revive will one. Section 2–509(a) creates a presumption that will one remains revoked. The presumption applies only if will two completely revoked will one. The presumption against revival can be overcome if evidence shows that the testator intended to revive will one. Relevant evidence includes facts about the revocation, including testator's contemporaneous or subsequent statements.

If will two is an amendment ("codicil") to will one, and therefore only partially revokes it, then the testator destroys will two by physical act, the presumption is reversed; will one is presumed to be revived in its entirety, unless the circumstances and/or testator's statements show that the testator intended that will one remain revoked.[25]

C.   Dependent Relative Revocation

Dependent Relative Revocation can be a confusing doctrine. Courts created the doctrine as another tool to effectuate testator's intent when testator's attempt to revoke a will leads to unforeseen results. To be more specific, courts apply the doctrine when *testator's revocation of a will is conditioned on a mistake of law or fact.* In other words, had testator known the truth, she might not have revoked the will. **If evidence shows that ignoring testator's revocation would better serve testator's intent than validating the revocation, the court will probate the revoked will.**

The most common factual scenario giving rise to the application of the doctrine occurs when testator revokes a will that revoked a prior will, assuming that revocation of the second will revives the first one. Suppose, for instance, testator's first will left "my painting of grandma to my cousin Charlotte," and the remainder of her estate to her sister, Sue (leaving nothing to her estranged brother, Bill). Testator's second will leaves her entire estate to her sister, Sue. Testator later reconsiders, and revokes the second will, expecting that she has reinstated the first will. In revoking will two, testator is *mistaken about the common law,* because will one cannot be revived absent re-execution in compliance with testamentary formalities. At common law, then, testator died intestate, because will two revoked will one, and testator revoked will two. As a result, Sue and Bill would share the estate equally, assuming testator died without issue. The doctrine of dependent relative revocation allowed the court to disregard the revocation of the second will *if probating the second will would better effectuate testator's intent than allowing testator to die intestate.* In the example, probating the second will would leave

---

[25]   *See* UPC § 2–509(b).

the entire estate to Sue—a result testator would clearly prefer to intestacy.

The confusing aspect of the doctrine is this: if the court is really concerned with effectuating testator's intent, why doesn't the court simply give effect to will one, and give the painting to Charlotte? In other words, why not ignore the revocation of will one? To the common law mind, this result was not tenable. When testator revoked will one, she did so intentionally, and common law courts could not conceive of undoing that revocation. But the revocation of the second will was not "intentional" in the true sense, since testator was mistaken about the consequences of revocation. This is why DRR is sometimes referred to as "the law of the second best": testator doesn't get what she wants, but what she gets is better than intestacy.

D.   Limits on the Power to Revoke: Joint Wills and Will Contracts

Married couples often have similar, if not identical, estate plans. For example, many couples want the entire estate of the first spouse to die to pass to the surviving spouse, and the survivor's estate to pass to the couple's children. Some of these couples execute *reciprocal wills:* each spouse's separate will has provisions that mirror the other's. Some (poorly advised) couples go a step farther and execute a *joint will*: one will executed by both of them. Because people are poor predictors of the future, it may not occur to couples at the time of execution that one spouse may later have legitimate reasons for wanting to change his or her will. Consequently, spouses sometimes restrict each other's right to revoke or amend the reciprocal or joint will.

When couples contract not to revoke their wills, problems inevitably arise. For example, years can pass between the death of the first and second spouse. During those years, the surviving spouse may remarry, have additional children, or accumulate significant assets. The estate plan to which the surviving spouse originally agreed may no longer make much sense. This often leads to litigation over whether the surviving spouse has the right to revoke the original will.

If the couple executed reciprocal wills, the surviving spouse has the right to revoke his or her will unless the court finds sufficient evidence that each spouse contracted *not to revoke his or her will.*

In other words, the fact that the couple executed reciprocal wills is not, by itself, sufficient evidence of a contract not to revoke. Courts will find such a contract only in the face of explicit language of contract. Uniform Probate Code section 2–514 agrees that reciprocal wills alone are not evidence that a couple contracted not to revoke, and provides that such a contract can be established only if 1) the will contains provisions stating the material terms of such a contract, 2) the will refers to such a contract and the terms of the contract can be proven by extrinsic evidence, or 3) the decedent signed a separate contract.

The question is much more complicated if the married couple executes one joint will. Although some joint wills clearly state the couple's agreement that neither spouse can revoke the joint will, other wills are less clear. For example, in *Estate of Wiggins*, a couple's joint will stated that "it is the mutual wish and desire of each of us that the survivor of us shall have the full use and power to consume the principal of the decedent's estate during his or her lifetime, except the right to dispose of the same by Will."[26] Does that language provide sufficient evidence of a contract not to revoke? On this language, the Surrogate Court found insufficient evidence of a contract not to revoke. On appeal, the majority of the court found that the language *did* create a contract, and that the surviving spouse was bound to die with the will in place. A strong dissenting opinion agreed that the parties had contracted not to revoke, but argued that the contract had a limited scope. In the view of the dissent, the surviving spouse had agreed only to distribute the couple's *marital property* in accordance with the joint will, and was therefore free to distribute property acquired after his wife's death as he saw fit. Because joint wills have the potential to generate significant litigation costs, a good lawyer will not recommend them.

If a court does find a contract to make a will, and the surviving testator breaches by executing a new will, the new will—not the old one—is entitled to probate. The probate court's job in that circumstance is to determine which will is the last to be properly executed by the testator; so long as the new will is executed in accordance with testamentary formalities, it is entitled to probate. But the beneficiaries of the old will have a breach of contract claim against the survivor's estate. And, because creditor claims enjoy priority over the claims of estate beneficiaries, the beneficiaries of the old will are entitled to the benefits provided them by that will before any money is distributed in accordance with the provisions of the new will. If, by the terms of the first will, the testator has contracted to leave her entire estate to particular beneficiaries, there will be no estate left for the beneficiaries of the subsequent will.

---

[26] Estate of Wiggins, 45 A.D.2d 604, 360 N.Y.S.2d 129 (1974).

Problems

1.   In 2009, Tomasina Testator validly executed a will (hereafter "Will 1"). At the time of the will execution, Testator had a daughter Sue Ellen, and a son, Lance. Years before, Testator had objected to Sue Ellen's marriage, and Testator and Sue Ellen became estranged and remained so at the date of the execution of Will 1. Will 1 devised testator's entire estate to Lance.

In 2010, Lance ran up $300,000 worth of debt, including debt owed to some unsavory characters who tended to be rather aggressive in showing their displeasure when debtors defaulted. Deeply ashamed, Lance faked his own death by staging a boating accident. He then fled the country. Sue Ellen attended Lance's funeral, and in an emotional scene, she and her mother forgave each other for the mistakes of the past.

At a family dinner on Sept. 1, 2011, (attended by Sue Ellen, Lance's family, and Testator's best friend, Martha), Testator produced Will 1, crumpled it into a ball, tossed it on the floor and announced, "I'd like you all to watch me execute my new will!" Just then, a notary arrived. Testator produced a new will (hereafter "Will 2"). Will 2 made significant bequests to Lance's family, but gave the bulk of Testator's estate to her daughter, Sue Ellen. Testator signed Will 2 at the end of the document. She then directed Martha to sign the will as a witness, which Martha did. Testator had intended to have Sue Ellen sign as the second witness, but the notary pointed out that because Sue Ellen was a beneficiary under the will, it might be a bad idea. Testator agreed to find a second witness at some later date (although she never did get around to finding one). Martha then signed the self-proving affidavit, and the notary acknowledged her signature on the affidavit.

In January of 2016, Testator died, survived by Sue Ellen and, as it turned out, Lance, who showed up at the funeral, much to everyone's shock. The day after Testator's funeral, Lance offered Will 1 for probate (he had found the crumpled will among his mother's possessions and flattened it out with an iron). Sue Ellen offered Will 2 for probate, and contested the probate of Will 1. If the Uniform Probate Code has been adopted in Testator's state, which will, if any, should the court admit to probate?

2.   Same problem as above, but change the facts as follows: Suppose Testator never crumpled Will 1 into a ball. Suppose also that Lance resurfaced in November of 2015, before Testator's death. Testator was overcome with joy. She invited her best friend Martha over, and in front of Lance, ripped up will 2 saying, "I'm so happy to know you'll be taken care of after my death." Soon after, Testator died. Lance offers will 1 for probate.

a. What arguments can Sue Ellen offer if she wants to object to the probate of will 1?

b. What arguments can Sue Ellen advance in favor of probating will 2?

3. Robert Jones married Eugenia Patrick in 1977. They had two daughters, Kitty and Lisa. Robert divorced Eugenia in 1988. In 2008, Robert executed a will leaving his entire estate to Kitty and Lisa. Robert married Marilyn Smith in 2015. Before the marriage, Marilyn signed a prenuptial agreement limiting her rights to Robert's assets on divorce or his death.

On May 14, 2016, Marilyn called her attorney, Lola McGuigan, and requested that she draft a will for Robert, leaving everything to her (Robert had become ill with cancer). McGuigan prepared the will and the next day, May 15, came to Marilyn's house. Marilyn had arranged for her friend, Diana White, to be present as a witness. Robert was in bed and weak. Marilyn, McGuigan and Diana went into Robert's room. McGuigan asked Robert questions to ensure that he had capacity, and she informed Robert that the will left everything to Marilyn. McGuigan then placed the will on a magazine and handed it and a pen to Robert. Robert had difficulty grasping the pen, and it slipped out of his hand at least five times. Finally, Diana grasped Robert's wrist and the pen and guided Robert in signing his name. Diana and Marilyn then signed as witnesses. Robert entered the hospital the next day, and died there eleven days later.

Kitty and Lisa contest the probate of the 2016 will. Should the court admit the will to probate?

4. Terrence Testator died in 2016. While searching Testator's house for a will, Testator's son Wilbur found several pieces of paper. The first was titled "Last Will and Testament of Terrence Testator". It consisted of a form that Terrence apparently had purchased at a drug store. Terrence had filled in the blanks. The document looked like this:

> Last Will and Testament of
> *Terrence Testator*
>
> On this day of *March 31, 2005*, I,
> *Terrence Testator*, being of
> sound mind and memory hereby
> bequeath my estate as follows:
>
> *All of my property, of whatever
> kind and nature, I hereby give to
> my son, Wilbur, whom I dearly
> love.*
>
> Signed,
>   *Terrence Testator*
> Witnessed,
>   *Hannah Epstein*
>   *Elizabeth Leslie*

Wilbur, being an honest fellow, also admitted to finding a second piece of paper. That document, typed on Terrence's computer, printed out, and signed in Testator's hand, looked like this:

> More on my will:
>
> I want my girlfriend Laura
> Cunningham to have my most
> precious object, my 52 inch flat-
> screen television.
>
> Signed:
>   *Terrence Testator*

Terrence Testator's entire estate is worth $4,000, including the flat-screen television, which is valued at $1,000. Wilbur has offered the first document for probate. Laura argues that the second document should be admitted to probate along with the first, and construed as part of Terrence's will. Should the court admit the second document?

5.   Same as four, except that suppose that the second document had an attestation clause and was signed by two witnesses. If Laura argues that only will 2 should be admitted to probate, should she prevail on that argument?

6.   Testator's will dated July 4, 2009, provides in relevant part:

Article Four: My home, located at 55 Morningside Drive, I
devise as directed in a letter that I will write and deliver to
my daughter, Blanche.

Article Five: The rest of my estate I hereby devise to my
daughter Samantha.

At Testator's death in January of 2016, Blanche produces a
sealed envelope with a signature in testator's hand across the seal.
When the envelope is opened, the following letter, written entirely in
testator's hand, is found inside:

> *December 10, 2009*
>
> *To Whom It May Concern:*
>
> *It is my wish that my home,
> located at 55 Morningside Drive, be
> given to my dear daughter Blanche,
> in appreciation for the loving care
> that she lavished on me during my
> final illness.*
> *Teresa Testator*

Should the court admit the December 10th letter to probate and
distribute the house to Blanche?

7.   Which of the following will provisions are valid under the
doctrine of facts of independent significance?

   a.   I devise $100.00 to each member of my household staff.

   b.   I leave the funds in my mutual fund accounts to my
         sister, Louise.

   c.   In my right desk drawer are located monthly
         statements of several of my mutual account funds. I
         leave the funds in those accounts to my cousin Darla.

   d.   My residuary estate shall be distributed as the last will
         and testament of my husband directs.

8.   Dan DeCedant just died, survived by his three children, Lou,
Joan and Hope. Dan's wife, the mother of his children, predeceased
Dan some thirty years ago. Dan's valid will provided, in relevant
part, as follows:

Article Three: I devise my yacht, Marigold, to my friend
Peter Jones.

Article Four: I devise $1,000,000 to my daughter Hope.

Article Five: I devise $1,000,000 to my son Lou.

Article Six: I devise $1,000,000 to my daughter Joan.

Article Eight: All the rest, residue and remainder of my estate I hereby devise to my dear friend Theresa Lore, in appreciation for her love and companionship.

When Dan executed the will in 1995, he had assets totaling more than $8,000,000. When Dan died in 2015, his probate estate (after payment of all taxes and expenses) was valued at $600,000 ($300,000 in cash, and Marigold, which is now worth $300,000). Both Peter Jones and Theresa Lore are alive at Dan's death. How would Marigold and the $300,000 cash in Dan's probate estate be distributed in a majority of states? Please give dollar amounts where appropriate.

9.   Same facts as Problem 8, above, but suppose that Marigold was destroyed in 2013 when one-hundred-year-old Dan took her out for a sail during a squall. The insurance company sent Dan a check for $300,000 to cover the loss. When Dan died in 2015, his assets total $300,000. To what is Peter entitled, if anything?

10. Would your answer be different if Dan destroyed Marigold shortly before his death in 2015, and the insurance company had not yet sent the money?

11. Trina Testator's validly executed will, dated March 2, 2005, provided in relevant part:

Article Three: I bequeath my china and silver to my friend Allison Smith.

Article Four: My remaining personal property shall be distributed in accordance with a list that is in the drawer of my bedside table.

Article Five: The rest of my estate I hereby devise to my daughters, Elizabeth Ann and Hannah Kate, in equal shares.

Two years later, Trina sold her china and silver for $3,000. Then, in 2009, Trina inherited a grand piano from her Aunt Mildred. At Trina Testator's death in 2015, her estate was valued at $25,000 (including the piano, valued at approximately $5,000). At Testator's death, Hannah Kate discovered a memo in the drawer of Testator's bedside table. It looked like this:

```
Dated: February 1, 2010
By: Trina Testator

1. My Andy Warhol
painting to Louise Gold.
2. My Jimmy Choos to
Marla Johnson.
3. My grand piano to Stella
Martins.
```

How should Trina Testator's estate, including the grand piano, be distributed?

12. Wanda Wealthy died in 2016 with an estate consisting of a $200,000 painting and $7.8 million in stocks and bonds. Wanda's will devised the painting to her sister, Neva, $1,000,000 to her brother, Bob, and the rest of her estate to her daughter, Dana.

Assume Neva, Bob, and Dana all survived Wanda, and assume further that the estate tax on Wanda's $8,000,000 estate is $1,000,000.

    a.   How should Wanda's executor distribute the $7,000,000 remaining in Wanda's estate (after taxes)?

    b.   How, if at all, would your answer change if Wanda's will had provided "I direct that all estate and inheritance taxes on my estate be treated as an expense of the estate."?

13. Consider the following family tree: (dotted lines indicate marriage; underlines indicate that the underlined individuals are deceased).

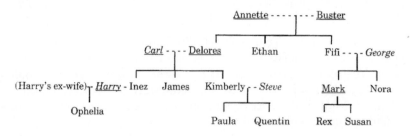

a.   Suppose Inez's validly executed will left her entire estate to her husband Harry. Harry died in 2011. Inez died in 2016. How should Inez's estate be distributed?

b.   Suppose Inez's validly executed will leaves her entire estate to Kimberly. If Kimberly predeceases Inez, leaving a will that leaves everything to her husband Steve, to whom will Inez's estate be distributed?

c.   Suppose Inez's validly executed will bequeaths "$200,000 to be divided among my siblings". Inez devises her residuary estate "to my step-daughter, Ophelia, and my wonderful Aunt Fifi, equally."

     (1)   If Kimberly predeceased Inez, how would the $200,000 bequest to Inez's siblings be distributed under the UPC?

     (2)   If Ophelia also predeceased Inez, how would Inez's residuary estate be distributed?

     (3)   If Ophelia survived Inez, but Aunt Fifi predeceased Inez, how would Inez's residuary estate be distributed?

d.   Suppose Inez's will left her residuary estate "to my wonderful Aunt Fifi, if she survives me." If Aunt Fifi predeceases Inez, how should Inez's estate be distributed?

e.   Would your answer to (d) be different if Inez's residuary clause read as follows:

> "I leave my residuary estate to my wonderful Aunt Fifi, if she survives me. If she does not survive me, I direct that my residuary estate be distributed to my sister Kimberly."

14.   Testator's will, executed in 2011, directs that "$6,000,000 shall be distributed among my grandchildren living at the time of my death." Testator had two children, Adam and Brooke. Brooke had two children, who are still living. In 1995, Adam was married to Eileen. While Adam was serving in the armed forces, Eileen became pregnant. She gave birth to a son, Charles, in 1996, and Adam was named as Charles's father on the birth certificate. Shortly after, Eileen and Adam were divorced. Adam never contested Charles's paternity, and he paid child support. He never visited Charles or developed a relationship with him, however. Charles now claims that he is entitled to $2,000,000 because he is one of testator's grandchildren. Brooke moves to admit extrinsic evidence that Testator never believed Charles was his grandchild, and that he

never developed a relationship with him. Should the court admit extrinsic evidence?

15. Eve Peterson's will devised "my home at 4 Brookdale Lane, which I purchased prior to my marriage, to my husband, Tom, and at his death to our daughters, Willa and Grace." Eve also appointed Tom executor of her estate. After Eve's death, Tom sought to sell the Brookdale Lane house, and his daughters objected, claiming that the will gave Tom only a life estate in the home, with a remainder in them. Tom offered the testimony of Eve's attorney, who would testify that he omitted the words "if the house has not been sold", so that the bequest should have read, "my home at 4 Brookdale Lane, which I purchased prior to our marriage, to my husband, Tom, and, *if the house has not been sold* at his death, to our daughters Willa and Grace." Will the court admit the testimony of Eve's attorney?

16. On February 10, 1980, John and Theresa Hopper, husband and wife, together executed a joint and mutual will. The will provided, in relevant part,

> *It is our wish and desire that our property be distributed in accordance with the plan provided herein, and each of us agrees to be bound by the following provisions.*

> *Clause One: at the death of the first to die, all property shall pass to the surviving spouse.*

> *Clause Two: at the death of the survivor of us, our property shall be distributed as follows:*

> *a)* *Theresa's piano shall be given to her daughter Scarlett.*

> *b)* *All the rest, residue and remainder of our estate shall be distributed to our two lovely children, Ava and Maude.*

In 1980, Ava and Maude were in their early twenties, and Maude had one child, age 3. John and Theresa had assets valued at $300,000. When Theresa died in 1985, the couple's assets were valued at approximately $350,000. In 1990, John married Margarite, a woman twenty years his junior. John and Margarite had two children. At John's death in 2016, John had assets totaling $5,000,000. He also left a will that revoked all prior wills made by him, devised $500,000 to each of his four children, nothing to his grandchildren, and the remainder of his estate to Margarite.

Ava and Maude have filed a breach of contract claim against John's estate, claiming that he was bound by his contract with his first wife to keep the 1980 will in effect. They seek as damages the residuary of his estate. Evaluate their argument.

17. Robin and Jake Lompoc were married in 2000. After the birth of their first child, Robin executed a will naming Jake as executor, and devising small amounts to Jake's sister's children, and giving the residue of her estate to Jake. Robin and Jake were divorced in 2014, but Robin never contacted her lawyer to revoke her will and draft a new one. Robin died in a car accident in 2016. Will a court applying the UPC give effect to her will?

Chapter Five

CONTESTING THE WILL

I. Capacity

To make a valid will, a testator must possess testamentary capacity. Testamentary capacity is a legal standard, not a medical one. Therefore, the question is not whether testator is ill, or feeble, or mentally healthy. A typical formulation requires testator to understand the nature and extent of her property, the natural objects of her bounty, and that she is engaged in the enterprise of making a will. A few courts have found that testators possessed the requisite capacity even though guardians had been appointed to manage their affairs. The justice or wisdom of testator's disposition is of no importance to the capacity determination, at least in theory.

In practice, however, courts and juries sometimes invalidate wills even when the evidence of capacity is very strong. For example, in *Barnes v. Marshall,*[1] the testator, Dr. Marshall, suffered from untreated bipolar disorder. Dr. Marshall's will left a mere $5.00/month to his only surviving daughter, but made detailed bequests in trust to various individuals, charities and religious and fraternal organizations. There was no evidence that Marshall was unaware of the nature and extent of his property, the identity of his family members, or that he did not understand what he was doing when he made his will. There was evidence that he was frequently, perhaps unfairly, angry with his daughter, and that he was cruel to his wife. In upholding the jury's determination that Dr. Marshall lacked capacity, the appellate court focused on Dr. Marshall's bizarre actions (including his claims that he had direct conversations with God), fiery temper, delusions, and extremely unconventional religious beliefs.

The Marshall case raises an interesting question. Should testator's mental illness, peculiarities, or just plain mean-spiritedness to those who stood by him during his life be a sufficient basis for invalidating his will? In exploring this question, it helps to explore why the law requires testamentary capacity at all. Why not simply admit all validly executed wills? After all, a will is unlike a contract in that testator cannot hurt himself by executing a will. As long as testator had the ability to amass property and articulate a coherent plan for its distribution, why not give the will effect?

---

[1] 467 S.W.2d 70 (Mo. 1971).

One justification that is offered for requiring testamentary capacity is that the law should enforce only the true intentions of the testator. The capacity doctrine serves a protective function, ensuring people that only their true, rational desires will be taken seriously after their deaths. Surely, most people would be happy to know that the law would not enforce a will that they might make while suffering from advanced stages of Alzheimer's disease. On this rationale, the Marshall case can be understood as giving effect to what Dr. Marshall would have wanted had he not suffered from mental illness. But it leaves one to wonder whether a person can be separated from his thought processes and mental states.

The capacity requirement serves another function, albeit one not generally articulated in judicial opinions: it protects "deserving" family members. When testator's only will is denied probate because testator lacked capacity, testator's estate is distributed to his or her closest kin. Although the United States is perhaps more committed to the principle of testamentary freedom than any other jurisdiction, there is nonetheless a strong sense among many people that family members should provide for one another, at least as long as the family is functioning as a mutually supportive unit. Perhaps the capacity doctrine owes its existence in part to the idea that family members should not be disinherited unless disinheritance is "rational."

Although courts reject this idea in principle, juries often decide capacity questions. If a jury determines that a testator lacked capacity, the question for the court on appeal is whether there is *any* evidence in the record to support the jury's determination. As a result, findings of incapacity are generally upheld on appeal. Moreover, even judges, including appellate judges, seem vulnerable to the idea that deserving family members should not easily be disinherited.

A.   Challenging the Will: Proving Incapacity

Jurisdictions take no consistent approach to the question of which party bears the burden of proof on the capacity issue. In many states, the burden of proof lies squarely on the party contesting the will. This is especially true if the testator's will includes an attestation clause, which in some states creates a presumption that the will was duly executed. In other states, a self-proving affidavit creates a presumption of due execution. In a minority of states, the will's proponent has the burden of establishing capacity, even if the testator executed a self-proving affidavit.

Because incapacity is a legal, not a medical, standard, it is not essential that one trying to prove capacity or lack of it introduce expert testimony on the testator's mental state. Lay witnesses may offer evidence relevant to whether testator's mental state met the capacity standard. Lay witnesses may not state a conclusion that the testator had or lacked capacity without testifying about the facts on which the conclusion is based. Because some testators have periods of lucidity alternating with periods of confusion, the best evidence comes from witnesses who observed the testator at or close to the moment of will execution.

Often, contestants or will proponents offer expert testimony on the capacity issue. An expert can testify regardless of whether she examined, or even met, the testator. An expert who has not examined the testator can give an expert opinion that is based on the evidence offered by other witnesses at the trial. The expert may also give a "hypothetical opinion". An attorney elicits a hypothetical opinion by presenting the testifying expert with a long list of symptoms and/or behaviors, and then asking the expert to draw a conclusion about whether a person exhibiting those traits would possess testamentary capacity. In at least one case, however, the court held that a hypothetical opinion that the testator lacked capacity was not, by itself, sufficient evidence to create a triable issue of fact on the capacity issue.[2]

Should the very fact that testator disinherited her closest relatives be considered evidence of lack of capacity? Emphasizing this fact could cause the jury to disregard the capacity standard out of strong sympathy for the testator's unfairly disinherited heir. On the other hand, evidence that testator disinherited family members with whom she had a close relationship is relevant to the capacity question, because it is evidence that testator did not know the "natural objects of her bounty."

B.   Insane Delusion

Sometimes, will contestants argue that the testator lacked capacity because he or she held an **insane delusion** that prevented testator from knowing the true objects of his or her bounty. To prove insane delusion, a contestant need not show that testator was literally insane, but just that testator clung to a belief that was not true, despite being presented with all contrary evidence, and that his erroneous belief influenced the dispositions made in his will. If a court concludes that an insane delusion led testator to disinherit one or more close family members, the entire will is generally denied probate, which usually results in distribution by intestacy (unless there is a prior, valid will). If there are any facts that support testator's belief, however, a court will treat testator's misimpression as a mistake of fact, and will probate the will. Typical claims of

---

[2]   Estate of Van Patten, 215 A.D.2d 947, 627 N.Y.S.2d 141 (1995).

insane delusion involve male testators who disinherited their children in the belief that they were fathered by other men, and testators who disinherited spouses under the belief that the spouse was having an adulterous affair.

II. Undue Influence

A will is not entitled to probate if a contestant can show that the will is a product of **undue influence**. Of course, will beneficiaries influence testators all of the time: a child might be extra thoughtful to her father to obtain a larger share of his estate; a second wife might convince her spouse that she should take more of his estate than his children from a previous marriage; an elderly person might agree to leave a significant portion of her estate to her niece in exchange for care in her old age. The trick is in determining when influence is *undue*. If the will is a product of testator's free agency, then the influence is not undue.

Undue influence claims are of two types. The first occurs when testator's free will is overcome by pressure from another. The testator believes she has no real choice other than to succumb to the influence. In other words, the influence or pressure amounts to coercion; testator acts out of fear, not out of a natural desire to leave her property to the designated beneficiaries. When the will is a product of coercion, it represents the intent of someone other than the testator, and will not be admitted to probate.

The second type of undue influence is more subtle, arising when a close relative or trusted advisor, acting out of self-interest, manipulates the testator into believing that the will advances the testator's own testamentary agenda, while in fact, the will advances the advisor's agenda. When testator enjoys a relationship of trust or confidence with a relative or advisor, testator may expect that advice will be offered in the testator's interest. This expectation gives the advisor significant power to influence testator's will. When the advisor abuses that power, courts invalidate the will for undue influence, even when testator has not acted out of fear.

Both forms of undue influence typically arise when a **confidential relationship** existed between a will beneficiary and the testator. A confidential relationship is a relationship of trust and intimacy, where parties might assume that each has the other's best interests in mind. Of course, a confidential relationship alone is not evidence of undue influence, because almost every testator leaves bequests to those with whom she has a confidential relationship. It makes sense that a wife would leave her estate to her husband, a mother to her child. But if will contestants establish that the testator had a confidential relationship with a beneficiary and that **suspicious circumstances** exist, those two factors together create a presumption of undue influence in most states. Once the presumption is established, the burden of proof shifts to the will beneficiary to establish that he did not exercise undue influence.

It is impossible to draft a comprehensive list of suspicious circumstances. The objective is to find instances of behavior that indicate that *the beneficiary abused the confidential relationship* he or she enjoyed with the testator. For example, suppose testator's previous wills consistently set forth the same dispositive scheme, but that her distribution plan changed radically after she entered into the confidential relationship. Or, suppose the beneficiary was actively involved in the drafting or execution of the will. Perhaps beneficiary selected the drafting attorney, and had a prior relationship with that attorney. Or, perhaps the beneficiary drove the testator to all of the appointments with the drafting attorney, was always present when testator communicated her testamentary wishes to the attorney, and was present at the will execution.

Another common suspicious circumstance is that beneficiary had strong control over the testator, so that testator was emotionally and physically dependent on the beneficiary. Perhaps testator was physically and/or mentally weak, or emotionally vulnerable (some courts require this showing as a requisite to proving undue influence). Perhaps beneficiary lived with and took care of testator, limited testator's contact with close family members and friends, or assumed control of testator's finances. In general, courts are likely to regard a will that cuts out all close family members as a suspicious circumstance.

Once the burden of proof shifts to the will proponent, the proponent must prove a lack of undue influence by a preponderance of the evidence. At least one court has held, however, that if the drafting attorney had a conflict of interest stemming from a preexisting relationship with the beneficiary who exercised undue influence, then the will proponent must overcome the presumption of undue influence by *clear and convincing evidence.*[3]

When a will leaves a significant bequest to testator's lawyer, a court will be very reluctant to validate it. Because the lawyer is a fiduciary for his or her client, a confidential relationship exists between lawyer and testator. To many courts, the very fact that the lawyer receives a bequest is a suspicious circumstance. The lawyer will have a very difficult time overcoming the presumption of undue influence, even if the lawyer was not the attorney who drafted the will. For instance, in *Estate of Burren,*[4] the court upset a will leaving

---

[3]   *See* Haynes v. First National Bank of New Jersey, 87 N.J. 163, 432 A.2d 890 (1981).

[4]   994 N.E.2d 1022 (Ill. App. 2013).

two-fifths of testator's estate to the children of testator's lawyer, even though testator had a relationship with the lawyer's mother, and the lawyer called testator "Pops." There was no direct testimony that the lawyer had drafted the will, but the court concluded that the lawyer had participated in the will's execution. In the rare case where a will devising testator's estate to testator's lawyer is admitted to probate, it is usually because testator had a strong personal, as well as professional, relationship with the attorney, and the attorney played absolutely no role in the drafting process.[5]

California has addressed these problems by enacting a statute invalidating (subject to narrow exceptions) any donative transfer to the drafter of an instrument making the transfer, or to a care custodian of the transferor. If a testator wants to make a transfer to the drafter or a care custodian, the testator must submit the instrument to an independent attorney for counseling and review.[6] The independent attorney must then prepare a certificate for the transfer to be valid. Although the statute should cut down both on undue influence and on undue influence claims, it appears that a certificate of independent review does not preclude disappointed heirs from bringing undue influence claims contending that the independent attorney did not provide adequate counseling.[7]

Undue influence doctrine is designed to protect testators from overreaching by unscrupulous beneficiaries. But, as with the capacity doctrine, courts and juries sometimes seem to apply it to invalidate wills that fail to conform to social norms. If a will makes an unorthodox disposition, devising testator's estate to a lover, same-sex partner or care taker instead of testator's closest relatives, there is a real risk that a court or jury will invalidate it on grounds of undue influence, even in the face of clear evidence that the will represents testator's intent.

Medical advances now make it possible for the elderly to live for many years in weakened or compromised states, often dependent upon care givers or nursing homes for basic care. We predict that undue influence cases will increase in number.

III. The No-Contest Clause

Testators who fear that heirs will contest the will after testator's death might choose to include a **"no-contest"** or **"in terrorem"** clause in their will or trust. A no-contest clause directs that any beneficiary who contests the will shall be deprived of his or her bequest. A typical no-contest clause follows:

---

[5]   Vaupel v. Barr, 194 W.Va. 296, 460 S.E.2d 431 (1995).

[6]   *See* Cal. Prob. Code §§ 21350–51.

[7]   *See* Winans v. Timar, 183 Cal.App.4th 102, 107 Cal.Rptr.3d 147 (2010).

If any beneficiary under this will (or trust) shall contest the validity of, or object to this instrument, or seek to alter or change the provisions hereof, such person shall thereby be deprived of all beneficial interest to which they would be entitled hereunder.

A no-contest clause serves two functions. Its first (and most obvious) function is to deprive an unsuccessful contestant of any benefit under testator's will. Its second (and more important) function is to deter will contests: a beneficiary will be reluctant to contest a will if an unsuccessful contest deprives the beneficiary of any share in testator's estate. As a result, a no-contest clause will only be effective if the testator has left the potential contestant with a significant bequest in the will. If the amount that a beneficiary is to receive under the will is small in comparison to the amount she stands to gain from a successful will contest, then a no-contest clause will do little to deter a challenge. One other point bears emphasis: A no-contest clause does not bar a contestant from sharing in testator's estate if the contest proves successful. In that case, the will is invalid, and the no-contest clause falls with the will, leaving the contestant free to take under the terms of a prior will, or by intestacy.

Some jurisdictions will not enforce no-contest clauses if the challenging beneficiary had *probable cause* to bring the contest. The Uniform Probate Code (section 3–905) codifies this approach. As you can imagine, the *probable cause* standard is fuzzy, and it is difficult for a beneficiary to predict whether a court will find that probable cause exists in any given case. UPC § 3–905 reduces the risk involved in contesting a will, and is therefore good for disgruntled beneficiaries and litigators. To be fair, it also acknowledges that anyone who is scheming enough to exercise undue influence might also be smart enough to include a no-contest clause in the will. Section 3–905 thus protects coerced testators even from smart "undue influencers." On the other hand, section 3–905 makes it harder for competent testators to protect their estates from the costs of contests by spoiled or litigious beneficiaries.

IV. Fraud

Another ground for contesting a will is that the words or actions of a beneficiary fraudulently induced testator into making a particular bequest. Fraud claims are much less common than contests based on lack of capacity or undue influence. To succeed on a fraud claim, the contestant must show that someone (usually a will beneficiary): 1) knowingly made false statements of material fact to the testator, 2) made those statements intending to deceive the testator, 3) the testator was in fact deceived, and 4) that the testator relied on those false beliefs in making his or her will.

Note that fraud claims require proof of the defrauding party's mindset: the speaker must have *known* that the statement was false, and the speaker must have *intended* to deceive the testator. These requirements make it difficult to prove fraud. But eliminating the *mens rea* requirements would cause other problems. A rule that required only that the contestant prove that a speaker made a false statement on which testator relied in making his or her will would probably increase litigation. The claim would essentially be a mistake of fact claim. As you recall, courts do not recognize mistake allegations unless the mistake and the disposition that the testator would have made but for the mistake are apparent on the will's face. The justification for these stringent limitations is to avoid opening the floodgates to rampant allegations that testator's will is premised on a false belief.

At least one court has held that *failure to disclose* a material fact can be the basis for a fraud claim.[8] In that case, a rapidly declining testator falsely believed that her son was trying to steal her jewelry. Testator's daughter knew that testator was mistaken, and she assured her brother that she would set things straight with their mother. Instead, she said nothing, and stood by while her mother changed her will to leave everything to her daughter. The court noted that, as a general matter, *failure to disclose* cannot be the basis for a fraud claim. In this case, however, the daughter and testator enjoyed a *confidential relationship*. The daughter, therefore, had a *duty* to correct the testator's mistaken belief. Because the daughter breached that duty, the appellate court upheld the probate court's invalidation of certain bequests to testator's daughter.

V. Tortious Interference with Inheritance

In the last two decades, disgruntled would-be will beneficiaries have devised a new strategy. Instead of challenging the will as invalid, these beneficiaries have sued third parties for **tortious interference with inheritance**.

Tortious interference claims are particularly useful in two circumstances. First, consider the would-be beneficiary who claims that someone has prevented decedent from executing a will. *Beckwith v. Dahl*[9] is illustrative. Decedent, in the hospital awaiting surgery, asked his life partner to prepare a will dividing decedent's estate between his sister and the life partner. The life partner prepared a draft, and emailed the sister, who advised him not to have decedent execute the will because she would have lawyer friends prepare trusts instead. The sister knew decedent's surgery was risky, but the

---

8   Rood v. Newberg, 48 Mass.App.Ct. 185, 718 N.E.2d 886 (1999).
9   205 Cal.App.4th 1039, 141 Cal.Rptr.3d 142 (2012).

life partner did not. The sister did not have either the trust documents or the will executed before surgery. Decedent died, intestate. A will contest would not have helped the life partner because he was neither the beneficiary of a prior will nor an intestate heir. On those facts, a California appeals court held that the life partner had stated a claim for tortious interference (or, as the court called it, intentional interference with an expected inheritance).

Second, consider the situation in which someone induces decedent to make lifetime dispositions that denude the estate of assets. For instance, in *Wellin v. Wellin*,[10] decedent's fourth wife allegedly persuaded decedent to replace his financial advisors with new ones of her choosing, to have decedent revoke powers of attorney given to his children, and to have decedent amend his revocable trust and take other steps that would result in the transfer of tens of millions of dollars of transfers to the wife. Even a successful will contest would not, by itself, have enabled the children to recover the assets they had lost as a result of the wife's allegedly wrongful actions. On these facts, a South Carolina federal court held that the children had stated a claim for tortious interference.

Not every state has yet recognized a claim for tortious interference, but the vast majority of states to consider the issue now recognize the claim. The Restatement (Second) of Torts provides, in § 774B, that "[o]ne who by fraud, duress or other tortious means intentionally prevents another from receiving from a third person an inheritance or gift that he would otherwise have received is subject to liability to the other for loss of the inheritance or gift." To prove tortious interference, the plaintiff must generally show that 1) she had a reasonable expectation of inheritance, and 2) she would have received the inheritance but for the defendant's exertion of intentional and tortious behavior amounting to fraud, duress or undue influence.[11] A plaintiff who can prove these elements can recover compensatory and punitive damages from the tortfeasor (*not* the testator's estate).

Some courts strictly limit the tort to plaintiffs who cannot be made whole in probate proceedings. The scope of this limitation, however, remains unclear. For instance, in one federal case, the court held that when an alleged tortfeasor strips decedent of assets during decedent's lifetime, an heir or will beneficiary may not bring a tortious interference claim because the personal representative would be entitled to recover the assets in the probate process.[12] If all

---

[10] 2015 WL 5781266 (U.S. Dist. Ct., D. S.C. 2015).

[11] *See* Diane J. Klein, *Revenge of the Disappointed Heir: Tortious Interference with Expectation of Inheritance—A Survey With Analysis of State Approaches in the Fourth Circuit*, 104 W.VA. L. REV. 259 (2002).

[12] *See* McDonald v. Copperthwaite, 2015 WL 519290 (D.N.J. 2015).

courts embraced that approach, many tortious interference claims like the one in *Wellin v. Wellin* would be dismissed.

Problems

1.   Testator's will, executed when he was 85 and bedridden with cancer, left all of his assets to the American Cancer Society. His two daughters, who had been the beneficiaries of his prior will, executed 15 years earlier, contested the will on the ground that Testator lacked capacity.

At trial, the American Cancer Society offered the self-proving affidavits of the two witnesses, both secretaries from the office of the lawyer summoned by the hospital staff. The daughters offered testimony from a neighbor who had indicated that he had visited Testator three times during the week in which he prepared his will, and that conversations with Testator were incoherent on each occasion. The daughters also offered testimony from a former co-worker of Testator, who testified that Testator had told her that his daughters were dead, and that Testator continued to insist that they were dead even when the co-worker called them on the telephone and had them speak to Testator.

  a.   If a jury were to find that Testator lacked capacity, would there be grounds on which a trial or appellate court could overturn the jury verdict?

  b.   If a jury were to find that Testator had capacity, would there be grounds on which a trial or appellate court could overturn the jury verdict?

  c.   Suppose instead that the neighbor and the co-worker had testified that, in their opinion, Testator lacked capacity, but they could not recall particular events or statements that had led them to that conclusion. If the jury were to find that Testator lacked capacity, would there be grounds on which a trial or appellate court could overturn the jury verdict?

2.   Testator was survived by a son and a daughter and a will that left her entire estate to her daughter. Testator moved into her daughter's home a week before she executed her will, and lived with her daughter for her final five years. When she moved into her daughter's home, the daughter made it clear to Testator that she was only permitting Testator to move in on condition that Testator changed her will to leave her entire estate to her daughter. Testator's son does not dispute this account of the facts.

  a.   If the son contests the will on undue influence grounds, and the jury concludes that the will was the product of undue influence, should the trial court or an appellate court overturn the jury's verdict?

b.   If the jury concludes that the will was not the product of undue influence, should the trial court or an appellate court overturn the jury's verdict?

3.   Testator's will leaves $1,000,000 to his minister and the residue to be divided equally between his two sons. Testator's probate estate is valued at $1,250,000. The sons can produce testimony at trial to demonstrate that the minister had frequently told Testator that those who give generously to the church's agents increase their chances of salvation. The minister would concede making these representations, which he would assert that he believes to be true. The sons can also produce testimony from one of Testator's close friends in which Testator indicated that he wanted to give his property to his sons, but couldn't "take the chance."

On what grounds, if any, could the sons contest the will? Evaluate the likelihood of their success.

4.   Assume that the will in Problem 3 also includes a provision that provides "I leave to any person who contests this will the sum of $10,000, and I direct that any such person forfeit any further share in my estate." Assume each son has a child of his own at Testator's death. If Testator's estate is valued at $1,250,000, is the provision likely to be an effective deterrent for will contests by Testator's sons? Explain why or why not.

5.   Testator executes a will devising all of his property to his son. Testator thereafter falls in love with a woman 50 years his junior and marries her. He then instructs his lawyer to write a new will leaving the bulk of his property to his new wife. When testator informs his son that he has asked the lawyer to draft a new will, the son calls the lawyer and instructs the lawyer not to draft the will because testator is "not thinking straight." The lawyer does not draft the will, and testator dies 18 months after his marriage.

Can the wife contest the will? If not, what recourse, if any, is available to the wife?

Chapter Six

TRUSTS

I. What Is a Trust?

The trust can be traced at least as far back as the 13th century. To avoid feudal taxes and creditors, and to evade the prohibition on devising land, a landowner would transfer title to real property to a "feoffee." This arrangement, called a "use", was based on the understanding that the transferor could continue to use the property, and that the feoffee would later transfer the property to a beneficiary of the transferor's choosing. The transfer to the feoffee was in writing, but the underlying understanding was not. As a result, uses were unenforceable at law. Contract law required a written covenant as a basis for recovery and awarded only damages to the prevailing party. Rigid pleading requirements barred any other claim that might have proven useful. Thus, the transferor had to "trust" the feoffee to honor the arrangement. Over time, the "use" became known as the "trust", and the feoffee the "trustee".

Notwithstanding the law's failure to enforce them, uses grew in popularity. In the late 14th and early 15th centuries, disgruntled beneficiaries began to appeal to courts of equity when the trustee proved faithless. With increasing frequency, the Chancellor granted relief on the theory that he was "compelling the trustee to act upon the dictates of his conscience."[1] By mid-15th century, the Chancellor routinely enforced trusts.

Although early trusts were used to transfer title to real property, today any interest in property can be held in trust. The property owner who creates a trust is called the **settlor**, the **transferor**, or the **trustor**. Ownership is divided between the trustee, who holds "legal title" to the property, and the beneficiaries, who hold "equitable title." The trustee has all of the responsibility, and none of the fun, of ownership. The trustee must maintain and invest the property, must keep accounts, and must manage and distribute the trust assets in the best interests of the beneficiaries. The trustee is entitled to collect a set fee for its trouble, but cannot benefit in any other way from its position as trustee.

A settlor may appoint more than one trustee to serve concurrently. This practice has become increasingly common as investing has become more complex. A settlor who desires both an expert level of investment services and someone with intimate

---

[1]   Scott on Trusts, § 1, at 5.

knowledge of the beneficiaries might appoint both a professional trustee (such as a bank) and a non-professional (such as Aunt Louise).

Beneficiaries have none of the obligation and most of the fun of ownership. They have the right to benefit from the trust in accordance with the settlor's directives. Generally speaking, beneficiary interests are split up over time. One or more beneficiaries will have the right to receive income, profits and other distributions from the trust for the duration of their lives. These beneficiaries are usually referred to as the "income beneficiaries" or "life beneficiaries." At the expiration of the life interests, the settlor may (or may not) name a second order of income beneficiaries (to the extent that interest does not violate the Rule Against Perpetuities, if applicable). Finally, **remainder beneficiaries** (or "remaindermen") are those to whom the trustee distributes the trust principal at the expiration of the income beneficiaries' interests. Once the trustee distributes all the trust assets to the remainder beneficiaries, the trust terminates.

How do beneficiaries ensure that trustees do not abuse the privilege of having legal title? The trustee owes the beneficiary **fiduciary duties**. The two basic fiduciary duties are the **duty of care** and the **duty of loyalty**, although there are many others. The subject of trustee fiduciary duties is explored at length elsewhere in this book. For now, a brief explanation of the basic concepts should suffice. The duty of care requires the trustee to use care in investing, managing and distributing trust assets. The duty of loyalty prohibits the trustee from engaging in business with the trust in its personal capacity or from profiting (aside from trustee commissions) from its position of trust. The beneficiaries' ability to bring a legal action for breach of fiduciary duty is the primary enforcement mechanism.

Trusts are more popular today than ever before, for a variety of reasons. Trusts allow settlors to provide for successive generations of beneficiaries over time and to provide special protection for irresponsible or incapacitated beneficiaries. Trusts maximize flexibility in an estate plan because trustees can adapt as circumstances change over time. Trusts can be used to minimize estate taxes or to avoid probate.

Trust law has historically been a common law discipline. Many states have enacted states clarifying or altering those common law rules, but until 2000, there had been no significant move to codify the trust law. The Uniform Trust Code (UTC), initially promulgated in 2000 and subsequently amended, has now been adopted by more than half of the 50 states.

II. Types of Trusts

A.   Private Express Trusts vs. Charitable Trusts

There are two types of trusts: the **private express** trust, and the **charitable trust**.

The private express trust is a trust created by a settlor to benefit specific individuals or to carry out particular, non-charitable purposes. A private trust can be created in a testator's will (a **testamentary trust**) or by declaration or transfer during settlor's life (an *inter vivos* **trust**). A charitable trust, which can be testamentary or inter vivos, benefits a segment of the public at large, and is intended to advance the public good in some way. Private express trusts historically have been subject to the Rule Against Perpetuities, and are limited in duration (although this is changing). Charitable trusts can endure forever. This chapter focuses mostly on the private express trust. Charitable trusts are separately considered toward the end of the chapter.

B.   Irrevocable Trusts vs. Revocable Trusts

A settlor who creates a trust may make the trust either irrevocable or revocable. All testamentary trusts are irrevocable; once the settlor has died, the settlor is not in a position to revoke. Historically, most settlors who created *inter vivos* trusts also made them irrevocable, and the presumption in most jurisdictions has been that trusts are irrevocable unless the trust instrument specifies otherwise.

Over the last several decades, revocable trusts have become popular as a probate avoidance device. Revocable trusts raise a number of special problems that they share in common with other nonprobate transfers. We address those problems in greater detail in Chapter Eight.

The popularity of revocable trusts has led a number of jurisdictions to reverse the common law presumption that trusts are irrevocable unless the instrument specifies otherwise. Section 602(a) of the Uniform Trust Code takes this approach. A comment to section 602(a) explains that when a trust instrument is silent about revocability, "the instrument was likely drafted by a nonprofessional, who intended the trust as a will substitute."

C.   "Trusts" That Are Not "Trusts": Constructive and Resulting Trusts

Despite their names, neither Constructive Trusts nor Resulting Trusts are actually trusts. Both devices are judicially created remedies. The law of trusts applies to neither.

A resulting trust is a remedy a court imposes when a settlor or testator attempts to create a trust but fails. The court will hold that the trustee holds the trust assets in a "resulting trust" for testator's heirs. This means simply that the trustee will distribute the assets to testator's heirs. It does not mean that the trustee will hold on to the trust assets for any length of time.

For example, suppose the residuary clause in testator's will creates a trust, names a trustee, and directs the trustee to manage the assets for the benefit of testator's "friends." As you will learn later, a trust for testator's friends is generally unenforceable. Because the trust fails, trustee holds the trust assets in a resulting trust for testator's heirs. This is a fancy way of saying that testator's heirs take the money.

A constructive trust is a remedy that a court imposes to avoid unjust enrichment. As Judge Cardozo put it,

> A constructive trust is the formula through which the conscience of equity finds expression. When property has been acquired in such circumstances that the holder of legal title may not in good conscience retain the beneficial interest, equity converts him into a trustee.[2]

Courts have imposed a constructive trust when property has been obtained by fraud or fraudulent misrepresentation. The defrauding property owner is deemed to hold title as "trustee" for the person who would have had ownership but for the fraud. The "trustee" must transfer legal title to the beneficiary immediately.

III. Trust Requisites

It is often said that a trust must have three elements to be valid: a trustee, property, and beneficiaries. The rules pertaining to each element are explored below.

A. The Trustee

As we have explained, the trustee holds legal title, and is responsible for managing and distributing the trust assets. There are a few age-old maxims pertaining to trustee appointment. These maxims, which seem to find their way into hornbooks and bar exam review courses, are not of terrible importance to most practitioners. Nonetheless, we identify them here, and include a short explanation for each.

1. A trust will not fail for want of a trustee.

Any well-drafted trust instrument appoints and clearly identifies a trustee, as well as a series of successor trustees who shall

---

[2]　Beatty v. Guggenheim Exploration Co., 225 N.Y. 380, 122 N.E. 378, 380 (1919).

serve if the trustee dies, becomes incapacitated or is unwilling to serve. *If, however, the settlor has failed to appoint a trustee, or if the trustee dies or refuses to serve, the trust will not fail. Instead, a court will simply appoint a trustee.*

2.   If the same person holds sole legal and equitable title, legal and equitable title will "merge," and the trust will terminate.

A trustee can also be a trust beneficiary. For example, a settlor may name his wife trustee and income beneficiary, and name their three children as remainder beneficiaries. Or, the settlor may name his wife and one or more of his children as co-trustees of the same trust. The rule that a trustee can also be a beneficiary is subject to one limitation: *the sole trustee cannot also be the sole beneficiary. See* Uniform Trust Code, § 402(a)(5). In that circumstance, legal and equitable title "merge", and the trust terminates. The beneficiary holds the property free of any trust.

This limitation, called **the merger doctrine**, does not come into play often, because no informed settlor would name the sole trustee as sole beneficiary. Merger does not occur as long as there is at least one beneficiary other than the trustee, no matter how contingent that beneficiary's interest. Merger issues do, however, occasionally arise inadvertently. For instance, if a settlor names her husband sole trustee and life beneficiary, with a remainder in their only child, but the child dies before the husband, leaving her father as her only heir, then the husband is the sole trustee and sole beneficiary. At that point, the legal and equitable title would merge, and the husband would hold the property free of trust.

3.   "Passive" trusts are invalid.

It is often said that passive trusts—trusts which do not impose any management duties involving the exercise of trustee discretion— are invalid. The Uniform Trust Code embraces the rule, providing that "[a] trust is created only if . . . the trustee has duties to perform." Uniform Trust Code § 402(a)(4). If a trust is invalidated as "passive," both legal and equitable title vest in the beneficiaries. This rule, a remnant of the common law, is now rarely invoked as a ground for invalidating a trust. The maxim can be traced back to 1535 and the Statute of Uses. Prior to that time, people used trusts, then called "uses", to avoid paying taxes. It worked like this: landowner would transfer only legal title to his real property to another, but would retain equitable title. The landowner would then continue to possess and enjoy the land, but could claim that he owed no taxes because he did not "own" the property. The King enacted the Statute of Uses to frustrate this tax avoidance scheme. Although courts ultimately construed the statute not to apply to "active" uses—the precursors of the modern trust—courts could not avoid the conclusion that the Statute invalidated passive trusts.

American courts followed the passive trust rule, and extended it to apply to trusts of both real and personal property. Although courts still occasionally invoke the passive trust rule to invalidate a trust (usually because the trust should be invalidated for some other good reason, for instance to avoid having the remainder violate the Rule Against Perpetuities), the exceptions to the rule have soundly gutted it. For example, "standby trusts" (discussed later in this chapter), which hold no property at creation and impose no duties on trustee until the trust is funded at settlor's death, are valid in all states.

B. Beneficiaries

The traditional rule is that if a settlor attempts to create a private (as opposed to charitable) trust, but neglects to identify specific beneficiaries, the trust will fail. *See* Uniform Trust Code § 402(a)(3). In that case, a court will direct the purported trustee to hold the assets in a "resulting trust" for the benefit of the settlor or the settlor's estate.

The beneficiary requirement ensures (at least in theory) that someone has the power to enforce the trustee's fiduciary duties. If beneficiaries are the only monitors of trustee behavior, why would any settlor fail to identify one? Settlors might have one of several motivations:

— Settlor wants the trustee to name the beneficiary or beneficiaries at some later time;

— Settlor creates the trust to accomplish a particular objective, rather than to benefit a particular person;

— Settlor wants the beneficiaries' identity to remain secret for as long as possible.

Courts have struggled to reconcile these settlor objectives with traditional trust law doctrine. Both the Uniform Trust Code and the Restatement of Trusts have provisions designed to deal with the issues raised by these settlor objectives. We now turn to the issues.

1. Identification of Beneficiaries

A poorly counseled testator might name a testamentary trustee and attempt to give that trustee the responsibility for identifying the beneficiary some time after testator's death, in light of existing circumstances. For example, testator might transfer property "to Carol, as trustee, to distribute the property to the person who took the best care of me during my final illness." Or, testator might direct Carol to distribute certain property "among my close friends as my trustee selects." Because circumstances might change between will execution and testator's death, the testator in each case would prefer that the trustee identify the beneficiaries at some later time.

Historically, courts have been willing to uphold a trust that fails to identify beneficiaries specifically if *extrinsic evidence clearly establishes the beneficiary's identity.* For example, courts would sustain a testamentary trust to benefit the person who best cared for testator during her final illness if extrinsic evidence proved that one person clearly fit the description. Similarly, courts tended to uphold trusts for "relatives," because courts can look to intestacy statutes for a definition of the term, and extrinsic evidence will clearly establish the identity of settlor's heirs.

By contrast, courts had more difficulty enforcing a trust to benefit testator's "friends," because the term "friends" has no clear definition and the identity of those who fit the description may be difficult to establish, even considering extrinsic evidence. In such a case, courts were more likely to hold the trust invalid, leaving the assets in a resulting trust for testator's heirs.

Note that when a court invalidates a trust for failure to identify beneficiaries, the resulting distribution to testator's heirs usually violates testator's intent. For this reason, section 402(c) of the Uniform Trust Code provides that "[a] power in a trustee to select a beneficiary from an indefinite class is valid." The trustee has the *power, but not the duty,* to identify the trust beneficiaries when the testator names an indefinite group of people as beneficiaries and their identity cannot be clearly proven by extrinsic evidence. In other words, the trustee would act as the holder of a power of appointment,[3] with the *discretion,* but not the *obligation,* to act. The power is valid as long as there is one person who fits testator's beneficiary description. If the trustee fails to exercise the power within a reasonable time, he or she holds the property in a resulting trust for the persons who would take if the settlor had never made the disposition—often the testator's heirs. Restatement (Third) of Trusts § 4 dictates a similar result.

2. *Trusts for Purposes*

Sometimes, a testator designates funds to be held in a private trust to accomplish a purpose other than to benefit particular people. A common example of this problem is the testator who creates a trust to be used to maintain his burial plot. Until recently, courts did not enforce these so-called "purpose trusts" because there was no beneficiary to hold the trustee accountable. The trust would fail, and

---

[3]   *See* Chapter Nine for more on powers of appointment.

the "trustee" would hold the assets in a resulting trust for the testator's heirs at law.

Here again, the Restatement and the UTC have been more hospitable to effectuating the wishes of the settlor—although their approaches differ. Section 47 of the Restatement (Third) of Trusts echoes section 46, recommending that when a transferor transfers property in trust to achieve a specific purpose, *the trustee has the power, but not the duty, to distribute or apply the property to that purpose.* If the trust is not a charitable trust, section 47(2) provides that the trust shall endure "for a reasonable period of time, normally not to exceed twenty-one years."

Section 409(1) of the Uniform Trust Code goes further, and simply directs that "[a] trust may be created for a noncharitable purpose without a definite or definitely ascertainable beneficiary or for a noncharitable but otherwise valid purpose to be selected by the trustee." That is, the trustee has a duty, not merely a power, to use trust funds to accomplish the settlor's objective. Section 409(b) provides that the trust shall be enforced either by an individual appointed by the trust's terms, or, if the trust does not appoint anyone, by a person appointed by the court for that purpose.

3. Pet Trusts

Perhaps the most common example of a "purpose trust" is a trust for the care of a pet. Historically, these trusts were not enforceable, because a pet could not enforce the trustee's duties. Nevertheless, some courts sanctioned these trusts as "honorary" trusts, which operate like powers or conditional gifts. The trustee would be entitled to take the trust funds as long as she used them to care for the pet. If the trustee failed to use the funds to care for the pet, or if the pet died, the assets would be distributed to testator's estate. The concept assumes that testator's estate beneficiaries would have some incentive to make sure that the "trustee" took good care of the pet.

Today, statutes in most states authorize enforceable pet trusts. UTC § 408(a) authorizes a settlor to create a trust to provide for care of an animal or animals alive during the settlor's lifetime, and provides that the trust terminates upon the death of the last surviving animal. The settlor may designate an individual with power to enforce trust obligations. If the settlor fails to designate such an individual, then the court may do so. Finally, property not required for the intended use must be distributed to the settlor if the settlor is living, otherwise to the settlor's successors in interest. UTC § 408(c). The Restatement, by contrast, treats pet trusts along with other "purpose" trusts, and provides that the trustee has the power, but not the duty, to apply trust funds for the care of the pet or pets. *See* Restatement (Third) of Trusts § 47, Illustration 8.

4.   *Secret Trusts*

Sometimes, a testator wishes to keep the trust beneficiaries' identity a secret from everyone but the trustee. In that case, the trust document or will might identify the trustee and set forth the trust terms, but the settlor might orally communicate the beneficiaries' identity to the trustee. For example, suppose testator's will leaves a sum of money "to my friend Heather, to be distributed in accordance with my wishes that I have made known to her." Historically, courts refused to allow extrinsic evidence to establish the identity of the beneficiary, and would decline to enforce this "semi-secret" trust, holding that Heather held the assets in a resulting trust for testator's heirs.[4]

This formalistic stance was hard to justify. First, it was inconsistent with the courts' validation of oral trusts. Second, it seemed inconsistent with courts' approach to the question of "secret" trusts. A secret trust exists when testator's will bequeaths property to someone outright, without using any language to suggest that the beneficiary is to act as a trustee. For example, testator leaves "$100,000 to my friend Jane." If testator's residuary legatees have evidence that Jane and testator had an oral agreement that Jane would distribute the $10,000 to testator's companion, Robert, courts would admit that evidence. Courts justified this departure from the "no extrinsic evidence rule" as necessary to prevent Jane from becoming unjustly enriched. But they could not justify allowing extrinsic evidence to identify a beneficiary when the intent to create a trust was clear on the face of the will (the "semi-secret trust"), because the trustee would not be unjustly enriched if the trust failed: instead, the trustee would be required to distribute the trust assets to testator's residuary legatees or intestate heirs.

Consistent with the general trend in wills and trusts law toward admitting extrinsic evidence to effectuate testator's intent, the Third Restatement of Trusts[5] would admit extrinsic evidence to establish beneficiary identity in both the secret and semi-secret trust situations.

C.   **Trust Property**

To create a valid trust, the settlor must transfer property (or title to property) to the trustee. The definition of "property" for this purpose is broad: *any current and identifiable interest in property* can be trust property. So, settlor can direct the trustee to hold in trust "all proceeds of my life insurance policies paid out at my death" and the trust will be valid. Even though settlor's policies may lapse, or he

---

[4]   *See, e.g.,* Olliffe v. Wells, 130 Mass. 221 (1881).

[5]   Restatement (Third) of Trusts § 18 cmt. c (2003).

might later change his beneficiary designation, the trust will be held valid if someone later challenges it as lacking property. All matter of contingent interests can be trust property.

A mere expectancy, however, does not qualify as trust property. Thus, if O transfers in trust "all of the inheritance that I will receive from my mother's estate," and O's mother is still living, O has not yet created a valid trust. O has no currently identifiable property interest in his mother's assets. At most, he *expects* to obtain an interest in the future. Suppose, however, that O's mother dies, leaving O the bulk of her estate, after O has declared the trust. Is the trust valid now? Only if O again *manifests an intention* to treat the property as trust property. The determination whether O has sufficiently manifested such an intention is fact specific.

IV. Trust Creation

There are three elements of trust formation. First, the settlor must have the **capacity** to execute the will or trust document. Second, the settlor must **intend** to create a trust. Third, the testator must follow the applicable **formalities** (if any!). Although these elements are similar to those necessary to execute a will, their substantive content is much different.

A. Capacity

The settlor of a trust must have capacity to create the trust. Uniform Trust Code § 402(a)(1). If the trust is testamentary, or if the trust is revocable, the settlor must have testamentary capacity (he must comprehend the nature and extent of his assets, know the objects of his bounty, and understand that he is making a will). The standard for creating a valid irrevocable trust is higher, and varies depending on the settlor's reason for creating the trust. If the settlor's irrevocable trust is a gift, then the settlor must have testamentary capacity and must also understand the effect that the gift might have on the settlor's future financial security and on the security of settlor's dependents. If the settlor creates the irrevocable trust as part of a negotiated settlement or adversarial transaction, then the settlor must possess the capacity to contract.

Like wills, trusts may be challenged not only for incapacity, but also on grounds of undue influence, and fraud. *See* Uniform Trust Code § 406. A relative may, however, be reluctant to challenge an *inter vivos* trust during settlor's lifetime, for fear that the challenge will displease the settlor and lead to outright disinheritance. Challenges after settlor's death also present obstacles: if a settlor creates and funds an *inter vivos* trust, and the trust remains in existence during settlor's lifetime, the statute of limitations, among other defenses, may bar claims of incapacity, undue influence, and fraud.

B.　Intent to Create a Trust

The Uniform Trust Code, like the common law, requires that settlor indicate an intention to create a trust. Uniform Trust Code § 402(a)(2). In most cases of trust creation, settlor's intent to create a trust is clearly established because settlor drafts and executes a trust document (or a will that creates a testamentary trust). Occasionally, however, uncounseled settlors use what are called "precatory words" to describe a gift or bequest, and inadvertently cause confusion about the character of the gift. Precatory words are words that express a desire or request. When a settlor or a testator uses precatory words to describe a gift, confusion often arises about whether the settlor is expressing a preference, or whether she intends to impose a mandatory duty on the beneficiary.

Suppose for example, that testator's will bequeaths "$2,000,000 to my son, Jeff, with the desire that he use some of this money to pay the rent, every month, for my sister Lisa's apartment for the rest of her life." Is testator expressing a desire, and giving Jeff the *option* of complying with it? Or, is she *requiring* Jeff to pay the monthly rent for Lisa's apartment? If the request is optional, then Jeff can choose to comply or simply pocket the money. If testator's directive is mandatory, Jeff holds at least some of the money as trustee, to be used to make Lisa's rent payments.

In determining whether testator intended to impose an enforceable obligation, courts examine intrinsic and extrinsic evidence of intent, and the degree of specificity with which the testator expresses her desires. The more specific the directive, the more likely testator intended it to be mandatory. Also relevant is the identity of the recipient and his or her relationship to the testator. For example, a court is more likely to conclude that precatory language imposes a mandatory obligation when the bequest is to testator's lawyer than when the bequest is to testator's daughter. Few testators intend outright bequests to their lawyers, and a court will therefore be likely to conclude that loosely worded instructions to the lawyer create a binding obligation.

C.　Trust Formalities

We have seen that testators must satisfy the applicable will formalities statute to create a valid will, and that will formalities statutes can be complicated. When a testator creates a testamentary trust, the trust is validly executed if the will was validly executed. But it may be bewildering to learn that, in most states, a settlor can create an inter vivos trust simply by declaring that she holds particular property in trust! Although trusts are subject to the statute of frauds, which may require a writing to transfer title to real property to a trustee, courts have upheld oral trusts of personal property, provided that there is evidence (a preponderance or clear and convincing) of testator's intent to create a trust. Needless to say, a judicial proceeding to determine whether testator created an oral trust is time-consuming and fraught with difficulty and expense. A few state legislatures recently have enacted trust formalities statutes that mirror or approximate will formalities statutes.[6]

Even if a state does not require a written document and other formalities for trust creation, no competent lawyer would create an oral trust. A written trust document is called a **"declaration of trust"** if the settlor is also named as trustee, and a **"deed" or "instrument of trust"** if the trustee is someone different than the settlor.

One formality that is required to establish a trust is **delivery** of the trust assets to the trustee. The objective of the delivery requirement is to ensure that settlor truly intended to make the transfer. But the acts that are sufficient to constitute delivery may vary depending on the state. In some states, attaching a description of titled assets or real property to the trust instrument suffices. In others, delivery occurs only if the settlor actually transfers title to titled assets to the trustee as trustee. When the settlor is also the trustee, most states do not require delivery of trust property, on the theory that a settlor cannot deliver property to himself. A few states, however, require the settlor to transfer title of titled assets from himself individually to himself as trustee.

V.   The Functions of the Trust

A.   Maximizing Flexibility

1.   *The Trust vs. the Legal Life Estate*

No doubt you studied the legal life estate and future interests in your real property course. You therefore know that a property owner who wishes to divide up ownership interests over time can simply create a life estate with remainder interests. Thus, "I devise Blackacre to my husband, Herb, for life, remainder at his death to our children in equal shares." The smart estate planner, however, would not use a legal life estate and remainder. Instead, she would create a trust, giving Herb a life interest with the remainder to the couple's children.

Why is the trust mechanism preferable to the legal life estate and remainder? Because the latter severely limits transferor's ability

---

[6]   *See* Fla. Stat. § 737.111; N.Y. E.P.T.L. § 7–1.17.

to accomplish particular objectives, and provides few tools to cope with problems created by changed circumstances that the transferor failed to anticipate.

For example, suppose that O transfers Blackacre, a working farm, to her daughter A, age 21, for life, with a remainder to O's grandchildren in equal shares. Further suppose that *O's primary objective is to provide A with enough to support and educate A during her life,* and that her *secondary objective* is to prevent A from transferring title to A's husband or someone other than A's children. At the time of transfer, Blackacre generates sufficient income to accomplish O's first objective. Twenty years after the transfer, however, the farm is no longer generating sufficient income to support A (although Blackacre's value for commercial development has tripled). In addition, A would like to return to school to earn a nursing degree, but the profits from farming are insufficient to pay for A's education.

Because circumstances have changed in a way that O failed to anticipate, O's primary objective, to support A, cannot be realized. But A alone cannot sell all or part of Blackacre to obtain support or finance her education; because A and the remaindermen share legal title, A must obtain the agreement of all of the remaindermen in order to sell. This may be difficult, if not impossible. The remaindermen may not wish to sell the property, believing that the market will improve if they sell at a later time. Or a remainderman might exploit her bargaining position, holding out for an unreasonable share of the profits as a condition for consenting to the sale. Finally, the remaindermen may be minors or not yet born.

Moreover, A has no power to lease or otherwise alienate the property for a period beyond the expiration of the life estate. This will make it difficult for A to attract tenants, because prospective tenants might reasonably fear that the life tenant could die prior to the lease's expiration. In addition, A cannot use Blackacre as collateral to obtain a loan, because in the event of A's default, the lender's only recourse would be to foreclose on the life tenant's interest, the life estate. As a result, banks are not likely to make loans on the security of a life estate.

Suppose A wants to sell minerals or oil located underneath Blackacre. A, wanting to maximize profits in the short term, may try to extract as much profit from Blackacre as possible, while the remaindermen will not want A to deplete resources before the remaindermen have a right to possession. The doctrine of **waste** deals with these issues, but not well; the murky rules provide little guidance to the life tenant.

Finally, the division of legal title between life tenants and remaindermen creates legal issues about the parties' respective obligations. Suppose, for instance, that buildings are destroyed in a hail storm, and the cost of necessary repairs will exceed the return that A would realize on the expenditures.

Now, explore how the trust mechanism minimizes or eliminates these problems. Suppose instead that O had transferred Blackacre "to First National Bank as trustee" and had directed that the trustee should manage the trust assets "to provide for the support, education and maintenance of my daughter A for her life, with a remainder to my grandchildren in equal shares." If the profits generated by Blackacre for farming became inadequate to support A, the trustee could sell all or part of Blackacre as the trustee deemed necessary to provide reasonable support, because the trustee has sole legal title. The proceeds from the sale would become trust property, and the trustee would use the income generated from investing the assets to support A. If the trust instrument so provided, the trustee could, if necessary, distribute some of the trust principal to A as well. Or, the trustee could lease the property, exploit some or all of its natural resources, or mortgage the property to finance A's education or necessary repairs. The trustee need not obtain beneficiaries' consent prior to acting. As long as trustee's acts are consistent with trustee's fiduciary duties, it may act unilaterally.

Trusts are more flexible because trust documents are contracts; settlor can customize trusts to give the trustee the powers and duties that settlor thinks appropriate, such as the power to sell, lease or mortgage trust assets, or to benefit particular beneficiaries more than others. When the trust instrument fails to offer sufficient guidance to the trustee, trust law's extensive default rules step in to fill the gap and give guidance to trustees.

2. *Increasing Flexibility: Discretionary and Support Trusts*

If Samantha Settlor wishes to divide benefits over time, she can create a trust that names one or more life beneficiaries who are entitled to all of the income generated by the investment of trust assets, and one or more remainder beneficiaries to receive the trust principal when the life beneficiaries are dead. This basic structure, however, does not give the trustee sufficient flexibility to respond to a later change of circumstances that might frustrate Settlor's intent. Some examples follow.

First, Settlor may desire and assume that the trust income will be the income beneficiary's sole means of support. After Settlor's death, however, rising costs of living or unanticipated medical expenses could render the trust income inadequate to care for the income beneficiary's basic needs. But the trustee can do no more than pay out income, even if trustee believes that Settlor would have wanted the income beneficiary supported. If the trustee makes a payment from the principal to the ailing income beneficiary, the act will constitute a breach of the fiduciary duty trustee owes to the remainder beneficiaries.

Or, suppose Settlor names several income beneficiaries, and wants the trustee to have the ability to vary the amount that each beneficiary receives depending on the beneficiaries' respective needs. A mandatory trust term that requires the trustee to distribute income in fixed shares does not allow for that. If trustee distributes more income to one beneficiary than the trust document allows, the other income beneficiaries can sue the trustee for failing to be impartial, a breach of fiduciary duty.

Third, suppose Settlor is concerned about the pronounced fiscal irresponsibility of one of the beneficiaries. If Settlor creates the "plain vanilla" trust described above, the beneficiary's creditors can (except in New York) attach the trust assets to satisfy their claims, leaving the beneficiary with no source of income.

Practitioners have developed mechanisms to give trustees greater flexibility in dealing with changing circumstances. These mechanisms are **support trusts** and **discretionary trusts**. Support trusts and discretionary trusts also provide beneficiary with protection from his or her creditors.

The settlor who wants to ensure that a beneficiary is supported can *require* the trustee to pay out amounts of income and/or principal as necessary for support. To ensure that a beneficiary will be supported by the trust, the trust should direct that the trustee *must* pay out principal as necessary *to provide for beneficiary's comfortable support, education, health and maintenance.* Language of this nature creates a **support trust**. The trustee's duty to support the beneficiary is mandatory, not optional. Generally, the trustee's duty is to support the beneficiary in a style consistent with the standard of living the beneficiary enjoyed immediately prior to trust creation. If the trustee fails to ascertain what the beneficiary needs for support or to invade principal to make necessary payments, trustee has committed a breach of the fiduciary duty of care owed to the income beneficiary. Conversely, if the trustee makes payments without ascertaining whether the beneficiary needs money for support, the trustee breaches a duty of care to the remainder beneficiaries.

On the other hand, the settlor may style the trustee's ability to distribute income or invade principal as a *discretionary power, rather than a mandatory duty.* A settlor who wishes to maximize trustee's discretion to make payments of income or principal can create a **discretionary trust**. Typical language creating a discretionary trust is "the trustee may pay to the income beneficiaries such amounts of income or principal as the trustee, in its absolute and uncontrolled discretion, deems advisable." When the trust is a pure discretionary trust, it is very difficult for beneficiaries to establish that the trustee breached the duty of care by making or failing to make a distribution. It might be tempting to think that trustee can never breach that duty; after all, the scope of his discretion is "absolute" and "uncontrolled." Yet, as the Restatement (Third) of Trusts,[7] indicates, it makes no sense to assume that settlor intended to relieve the trustee of all accountability for its distribution decisions. So, the trustee must act honestly, and "in the state of mind contemplated by the settlor." Generally speaking, if a trustee of a discretionary trust acts in good faith and exercises reasonable care in the decision making process, it will generally be immune from liability for making or failing to make a distribution.

Many trusts are **hybrids, or discretionary support trusts** (now often referred to as "**discretionary trust with standards**"). That is, the trustees' distribution duties have both mandatory and discretionary components. For example, a trust document may direct that the trustee distribute "so much of the income and principal as the trustee, in its sole discretion, deems necessary for the comfortable support and maintenance of my wife." Here, the settlor makes clear his intent that his wife should be supported, but also indicates that the trustee should have considerable discretion in determining what payments are necessary to satisfy that objective. The trustee has a mandatory duty to make good faith, reasonable determinations about what is necessary to support settlor's wife. The trustee breaches its duty to the income beneficiary if it fails to keep abreast of beneficiary's financial situation, or makes decisions that are *inconsistent with the settlor's objectives,* such as failing to make any payments to a beneficiary who cannot provide for his basic needs.

One issue that frequently arises is whether the trustee, in determining whether to make a distribution, can or should take into account a beneficiary's other assets or sources of income. For instance, suppose the income beneficiary also works, or has other assets that could be used for her support. Can the trustee decline to make a distribution on the grounds that the beneficiary already has enough money?

It depends on whether the trust is a support trust, a discretionary trust, or a hybrid of the two. If the trust is purely a support trust, then most courts will presume that the settlor intended the trust to be the primary means of beneficiary's support. That means that the trustee must make distribution decisions

---

[7]   Restatement (Third) of Trusts, § 50(1), cmt. c (T.D. 2, 1999).

without considering the other assets that are available to the beneficiary. Of course, the settlor who wants the trustee to take into account other assets can draft that instruction into the trust document.

If the trust is a pure discretionary trust, then the trustee can consider beneficiary's other assets if trustee is inclined to do so, but trustee is not obligated to consider them. If the trust is a hybrid, the answer is more complicated. The Restatement creates a presumption that the trustee is to consider other resources available to the beneficiary unless the settlor has directed otherwise. Some courts, however, have held that the failure to consider other resources is not an abuse of discretion. Much depends on the particular language in the trust setting forth the standard for the scope of trustee's discretion.

B.   Protecting Beneficiaries from Their Creditors

When a debtor fails to pay a debt, her creditor can sue for payment and obtain a judgment. The judgment gives the creditor a lien on debtor's assets. If debtor fails to pay the judgment, the creditors can garnish debtor's wages or attach and sell debtor's other assets to the extent necessary to pay the judgment in full.

Suppose the debtor is a trust beneficiary, but has few other assets. Can the creditor attach the trust assets once the trustee has distributed them to the beneficiary? Of course. In practice, however, trying to capture those assets is like trying to catch a fish with a fork—time consuming and frustrating. Insolvent beneficiaries are very good at spending or hiding assets. For this reason, creditors would prefer to attach the beneficiary's interest in the trust, so that the trustee is required to distribute trust assets directly to the creditor as necessary to satisfy the debt. The extent to which the creditor can do this varies depending on the terms of the trust and the relevant law.

If the trust instrument provides for mandatory payments to trust beneficiaries, and includes no spendthrift provision, a trust creditor can generally attach the beneficiary's interest in the hands of the trustee, requiring the trustee to make the mandatory payments to the creditor instead of the trust beneficiary. Section 501 of the Uniform Trust Code codifies this result by providing that, "to the extent a beneficiary's interest is not subject to a spendthrift provision, the court may authorize a creditor or assignee of the beneficiary to reach the beneficiary's interest by attachment of present or future distributions . . . or other means."

If, however, the trust is a support trust, a discretionary trust, or a spendthrift trust, the rights of creditors may be more limited.

1.   Support and Discretionary Trusts

Ironically, prior to the promulgation of the Uniform Trust Code, the legal rules with respect to creditors' rights in support and discretionary trusts were fairly uniform across states. The UTC, however, gives creditors fewer rights than they enjoyed at common law. Because the UTC has been adopted in a significant number of states, states now vary in their approach to creditors rights in trusts. The following paragraphs first explain the common law rules. We then explain how the UTC limits creditors' common law rights.

First, consider the common law approach. To determine what interests creditors can attach, focus on the nature of the debt. A creditor who seeks to attach trust assets "steps into the shoes" of the beneficiary. The creditor has no greater or lesser rights than the beneficiary herself possesses. If the beneficiary had demanded payment for the underlying item or service, would trustee have a *duty* to pay it? If so, the trustee must pay the creditor. If not, then ask whether the trustee *may* pay for the item: if the trustee paid for the underlying item or service even though it was not required to, would trustee be in breach of its fiduciary duty to the remainder beneficiaries? If yes, then trustee cannot pay the debt. If not, then trustee can choose whether to pay it.

Consider some examples. Suppose a University obtains a judgment for unpaid tuition against a beneficiary of a support trust. Does the trustee of a support trust have a *duty* to pay for beneficiary's education? Yes. Therefore, because the creditor steps into the shoes of the beneficiary, the creditor has the same right to payment. Suppose instead that the beneficiary incurred the debt by defaulting on payments for a private jet. Must the trustee of a support trust pay for beneficiary's private jet? No. So trustee is not *required* to pay the creditor. But *may* the trustee pay the creditor? Again, the answer is probably no. If the trustee of a pure support trust paid for the income beneficiary's private jet, the remainder beneficiaries would probably have a strong claim that the jet is not necessary for support and so the payment was a breach of the trustee's fiduciary duty to the remainder beneficiaries. The upshot is that trustees of pure support trusts must pay all creditors whose claims are related to the provision of necessities to the beneficiary. The trustee cannot pay creditors whose claims rest on goods or services not necessary for the beneficiary's support, maintenance, health or education.

Next, let us consider creditor claims against beneficiaries' interests in pure discretionary trusts. Suppose a creditor's debt is for unpaid college tuition. Does the trustee of a purely discretionary trust have a *duty* to pay the debt? Probably not, because the trust document allows trustee broad discretion over distributions. So the trustee is not *required* to pay the creditor. But *may* the trustee pay the creditor? In other words, would trustee's payment of income beneficiary's college tuition be a breach of trustee's duty to the remainder beneficiaries? Because the trustee has broad discretion, he may pay the creditor as long as he acted in good faith and payment represents a reasonable attempt to carry out the settlor's objectives. The analysis is much the same if the debt is related to the beneficiary's failed attempt to purchase a private jet. The trustee may pay the debt, but only if it is consistent with settlor's objectives. Trustee is free to decline to pay the debt as long as declining is consistent with settlor's objectives.

Because the trustee of a discretionary trust is always free to decline to pay beneficiary's debts (as long as doing so is consistent with settlor's objectives), a discretionary trust might appear to provide very strong protection against the claims of a beneficiary's creditors. However, that is not necessarily the case. Remember, when a creditor attaches a beneficiary's interest in a trust, it steps into the shoes of the beneficiary. If the beneficiary has a right to receive payment when the trustee decides to make a payment, then the creditor obtains the same right. Once the creditor has attached beneficiary's trust interest, any payments the trustee decides to make to the beneficiary must instead be delivered to the creditor until the debt is satisfied. If the trustee ignores the lien and makes a payment directly to the beneficiary instead of the creditor, the trustee will be held personally liable to that creditor. The creditor's ability to prevent the beneficiary from receiving payments from the trust creates a very strong incentive for the trustee to pay the creditor or settle the debt.

The UTC changes the traditional approach to creditor's rights in trusts. Although section 501 reaffirms the common law rule allowing creditors to attach beneficiaries' interests in trusts, section 504 appears to undermine that rule by providing that a creditor "may not compel a distribution that is subject to the trustee's discretion", even if the scope of trustee's discretion is limited by an ascertainable standard, and even if the trustee actively abuses its discretion in failing to make a distribution. In addition, the comments to section 504 indicate that the rule "eliminates the distinction between discretionary and support trusts." Building on the insight that even "pure" support trusts require trustees to exercise some discretion, the drafters conclude that support trusts should be treated no differently from discretionary trusts. On its face, then, section 504 appears to eliminate creditors' rights to compel distributions from support and hybrid trusts, even if those creditors' claims stem from provision of necessities.

Whether the UTC alters the common law rule that holds a trustee of a discretionary trust personally liable for making distributions to the debtor/beneficiary after trustee has been served with a garnishment order is unclear.

The UTC does, in section 504(c), protect creditors who are children or former spouses of trust beneficiaries whose claims stem from beneficiaries' failure to make child support or maintenance payments. These creditors have the right to compel payments from the trustee. However, the trustee must pay such claims only if the child or spouse can show that failure to pay would constitute noncompliance with the standard articulated in the trust instrument, or an abuse of discretion under the trust document.

2. Spendthrift Trusts

Support and discretionary trusts offer only limited protection from beneficiary's creditors. To truly protect a beneficiary's interest in trust, it is necessary to include a "spendthrift provision" in the trust document. A spendthrift provision is a trust term inserted by the settlor that prohibits voluntary and involuntary alienation of the beneficiary's interest in the trust. A typical spendthrift provision might read: "the interests of the trust beneficiaries shall not be capable of assignment or seizure by legal process." The provision can be added to any trust, including a support trust, a discretionary trust or a discretionary support trust.

Spendthrift trusts caused much controversy when they were first introduced in the late nineteenth century. Courts justified enforcing them by reasoning that the trust property belonged to the settlor, and holding that the settlor should be free to impose conditions on a transfer of "his" property, including a condition that would insulate the transfer from the beneficiary's creditors. To many people, there is something disturbing about allowing a person to escape responsibility for debts simply because he had the good fortune to be born into a family with sufficient assets to provide children with spendthrift trusts. Nonetheless, at this point spendthrift trusts are here to stay, and are explicitly recognized in section 502 of the Uniform Trust Code.

Many jurisdictions allow creditors who have provided necessities to a beneficiary to reach the trust assets, notwithstanding a spendthrift provision. This limited ability to pierce spendthrift protection is necessary to encourage creditors to provide necessities to trust beneficiaries. Moreover, in most jurisdictions, specified classes of creditors—for instances, spouses with alimony claims or children with support claims—are entitled to reach spendthrift trust assets. The Uniform Trust Code codified protection for these claimants in section 503(b).

3.   Asset Protection Trusts

Until quite recently, it was firmly established that spendthrift provisions in self-settled trusts were unenforceable. In other words, a settlor could not create a spendthrift trust to benefit herself. Courts unanimously agreed that allowing settlors to have free access to their funds while insulating themselves from creditor claims was against public policy.

In recent years, however, a few states have enacted legislation that validates self-settled spendthrift trusts. In 1997, Alaska, in a move to attract more business to Alaskan trust companies and banks, became the first state to authorize self-settled spendthrift trusts. In recent years, Delaware, Rhode Island, Nevada, Hawaii, Wyoming, South Dakota, Oklahoma, Tennessee, New Hampshire, Missouri and Utah have enacted statutes that allow asset protection trusts in various forms. These statutes allow residents and non-residents to create trusts that purport to shield assets from creditor claims.

Because states' principal objective in enacting asset protection statutes is to attract trust business to state banking institutions, asset protection statutes direct that the trustee must either be an individual resident of the particular state, or a qualified trust or banking institution doing business in the state. The statutes require that the trustee have some administrative duties, such as keeping records or filing tax returns, and the settlor must physically locate some of the trust assets in the state.

The key feature of the asset protection trust is the settlor's ostensible surrender of control over the trust assets. To qualify as an asset protection trust, the trust must be irrevocable (or, in some states, such as Alaska and Utah, revocable only with the consent of a person having a substantial adverse interest in the trust). In several states, the trustee must be given complete discretion over distribution decisions. Other states do not go quite so far; some allow settlor to retain the right to receive mandatory income distributions, while others (such as Delaware) grant asset protection trust status to support *and* discretionary trusts.

The irrevocability of the asset transfer and discretionary nature of the trustee's duties to distribute principal may create the impression that the settlor has given up control over and access to trust principal (thus justifying the frustration of creditor's claims). Yet asset protection statutes allow settlors to use various tools to control trustee decision-making and distribution of assets. No statute goes so far as to permit settlor to serve as a trustee with power to make distribution decisions. But the statutes allow settlor to name a trusted friend or relative "trust advisor." The advisor can have the power to "advise" the trustee about investment and distribution decisions. Statutes also allow settlors to have the power to remove and replace the trustee. The trustee who fails to follow the advisor's "advice" about distributions might quickly find itself replaced by settlor.

Economic forces also work to ensure that the trustee cooperates with settlors' preferences concerning distribution decisions. If a bank trustee regularly rejects a settlor's demands for distributions, word is likely to spread, and that bank will lose asset protection business. Moreover, the state legislature's goal of attracting capital to the state will be frustrated.

In all states, asset protection trusts are subject to fraudulent transfer law. If an insolvent or potentially insolvent settlor transfers assets to an asset protection trust to avoid creditor claims, creditors can bring an action to set aside the transfer as fraudulent. Because it is unethical for an attorney to assist a client in violating the law, an attorney who creates an asset protection trust should ensure that she is not facilitating a fraudulent transfer.

That aside, whether courts will actually enforce asset protection trusts remains to be seen. It seems likely that courts in states without asset protection statutes will be hostile to asset protection trusts. If the creditor can bring suit in a state other than the one in which the trust is located, there is a strong chance that the court will decline to apply the asset-protection state's law.

C.   Using Trusts to Plan for the Costs of Institutional Care

Another reason that the trust has become popular is that it greatly facilitates planning for old age or incapacity. The life-span of the average American continues to increase, and the post-retirement period of life can last well more than twenty years. Sadly, many people will spend some of those years in declining mental and/or physical health. Health care costs, which may include the costs of hospitalization or institutionalization, can deplete a family's assets.

The Medicaid program exists to provide some basic level of medical insurance to elderly and disabled persons who cannot afford health care (Medicaid should not be confused with Medicare, which provides various benefits to U.S. citizens regardless of income level). The Medicaid program is a creation of the federal government, but is administered by the states, which must comply with federal Medicaid statutes and regulations to qualify for federal funding. Each state has its own rules governing qualification for benefits, and those rules vary greatly from state to state, making easy generalization impossible. Our modest goal is to introduce you to the basic legal issues that arise when people use (or attempt to use) trusts to keep assets while qualifying for Medicaid.

When a person is or becomes incapacitated and requires institutionalized care, the costs of care are usually greater than the individual or her family can afford. At some point, the institutionalized person will have to apply for Medicaid. To qualify, an applicant must establish that the value of his or her assets is equal to or below the state statutory maximum allowed. Most states characterize an applicant's interest in a trust as an "available" resource that is included in the eligibility calculation, although there are a variety of exceptions to this rule.

When an applicant is married, Medicaid regulations require the state to consider the assets of both spouses to determine whether the applicant qualifies. If one spouse is institutionalized (in Medicaid parlance, the "institutionalized spouse"), the Medicaid statute provides some limited protection to the non-institutionalized spouse ("the community spouse"). Specifically, the statute prohibits the state from placing a lien on the married couple's home, and provides that the community spouse's income shall not be deemed "available" to the institutionalized spouse for Medicaid purposes. More importantly for our purposes, if the community spouse, but not the institutionalized spouse, is entitled to receive distributions from a trust, the trust property is not counted as "available" to the institutionalized spouse. Most states allow the community spouse to keep a certain amount of marital property as well, but the variation between states on this point is sufficiently great to preclude easy generalization.

Many states have "reimbursement" statutes that allow the state to obtain from the incapacitated person's estate amounts paid on his or her behalf during life. States often define "estate" for this purpose as including the beneficiary's interest in support or hybrid trusts.

If carefully constructed, however, a trust can be used to provide an incapacitated person with comforts and additional medical support that he or she would not be entitled to have if she depended entirely on government assistance. The assets in a **"supplemental needs trust"** will not be counted as an "available" resource for Medicaid, social security and other government benefits, and the state will not be entitled to seek reimbursement from the trust assets at the beneficiary's death. To qualify as a valid supplemental needs trust, the trust instrument must be funded with assets of someone other than the beneficiary herself. The trust document should prevent the trustee from paying for the beneficiary's basic support needs, and must expressly state that the trust's purpose is to provide care that supplements specific government benefits to which the beneficiary is entitled. The trust instrument should give the trustee complete discretion to make distributions, and it should direct that the trust be administered to ensure that the beneficiary does not lose his or her eligibility for benefits.

Often, individuals worry that the health care costs of age-related incapacity will use up their savings, depriving their spouses and/or descendants of support and an inheritance. But if a married couple retains all of their assets in the hope that the community spouse can maintain his or her standard of living, the institutionalized spouse might not qualify for Medicaid, and the costs of institutional care might deplete their savings, leaving little or nothing for the community spouse or for the couple's descendants. If, on the other hand, the couple "spends down" (spends or gives away sufficient assets) to qualify for Medicaid, the non-institutionalized spouse will suffer a significantly reduced standard of living.

Estate planners have addressed client concerns by stretching the boundaries of the trust mechanism in an effort to enable the institutionalized spouse to qualify for Medicaid without depleting the assets available to the community spouse. Planners created *self-settled* discretionary trusts and claimed that assets in such trusts should not be deemed "available" to the settlor/beneficiary. These trusts are referred to as **"Medicaid Qualifying Trusts."** This strategy, while it worked, enabled the settlor/beneficiary to qualify for Medicaid while continuing to enjoy payouts from the trust.

In response, Congress set out to make it clear that people could not qualify for Medicaid by using Medicaid Qualifying Trusts. As the law currently stands, the assets in a revocable self-settled discretionary trust created after 1993 will be counted toward settlor's eligibility in accordance with the following formulation: if, "under any circumstances any amount of money might be paid to the beneficiary, the maximum of such amount is deemed to be available to the beneficiary."[8] Thus, if a trust allows trustee to make payments to the settlor/applicant under any circumstances, but provides that "the trustee shall have no authority whatsoever to make any payments to or for the benefit of the beneficiary when the making of such a payment shall result in the beneficiary losing her eligibility for Medicaid", the entire amount that the trustee *could pay under any circumstances* will be deemed available to the applicant.

In a number of cases, disabled people have received tort judgments or settlements and people acting on their behalf have attempted to create trusts and place the recovery in trust to supplement the disabled person's receipt of public assistance. Courts see no distinction between these supplemental needs trusts and

---

[8]   Cohen v. Commissioner, 423 Mass. 399, 668 N.E.2d 769 (1996).

Medicaid Qualifying Trusts, because they view the money as belonging to the disabled person.

Under two circumstances, however, disabled individuals can retain the benefit of an interest in trust without having the trust corpus count as an asset that could disqualify the individual from obtaining Medicaid benefits. First, Congress has authorized so-called **"payback" trusts**—supplemental needs trusts created by a family member or guardian of a disabled person under age 65 with the disabled person's assets. Trust assets can be used to supplement Medicaid, but the funds remaining in the trust after the disabled person's death must be used to repay the state for all amounts spent on the Medicaid recipient's behalf. Second, disabled people, or their family members or guardians, can participate in **"pooled" trusts**, which are created and managed by nonprofit agencies. With this arrangement, assets of a number of disabled individuals are pooled together for investment purposes, though the trustee maintains separate accounts for each beneficiary. Upon the incapacitated person's death, the trustee transfers the assets remaining in his or her account to the accounts of the other trust beneficiaries.

D.   Providing for Minor Children

A major concern for testators with small children is making sure that their wills, or revocable living trusts, provide for care in the event that the children are left parentless before reaching the age of majority. In a two-parent family, each parent's plan should provide for two contingencies; the death of the testator prior to the partner, and the death of the testator after (or concurrently with) the partner. For the single parent, a well-drafted document providing for the care of minor children is especially important. Divorced parents might wish to devise assets to minor children without involving former spouses in the management or distribution of these assets. The trust does important work for all of these families.

Trusts for minor children can be drafted as part of a parent's will (a testamentary trust) or as part of a revocable living trust that will continue as an irrevocable trust after the settlor's death. A well-drafted will or trust provision to provide for minor children should contain two key provisions: the first should nominate a custodial guardian who will assume primary care for the orphaned children. The second should name a trustee to hold, manage and distribute the children's assets.

The testator may want the trust to hold non-probate assets, such as life insurance proceeds, in addition to probate assets. If so, the documents governing the non-probate assets should be amended to name the trustee of the minor children's trust as the contingent beneficiary in the event that the child is orphaned.

The guardian and the trustee can be the same person, which gives that person maximum flexibility and ease in caring for the child. If the testator believes that those who would best care for the child are not those who are best suited to manage assets, then testator may name different people to serve each function.

VI. Trust Modification and Termination

Once a trust has been established, can the trust be modified or terminated before it naturally ends? If the trust is revocable, the clear answer is yes, and we have seen that UTC § 602 creates a presumption that trusts are revocable in the absence of language to the contrary. (Many states, however, continue to abide by the common law rule that trusts are irrevocable unless expressly made revocable).

Even irrevocable trusts can be modified or terminated in a number of circumstances. The first circumstance occurs when the settlor is living. A court will permit modification or termination of a trust if the settlor and all of the beneficiaries consent. In that event, all of the parties with an interest in the trust have agreed to the modification or the termination, so there is no good reason to continue the trust.

Once the settlor has died, it is no longer possible to know for sure whether settlor would have wanted the trust to terminate before the time specified in the trust instrument. As a result, courts are more cautious about permitting termination. Nevertheless, judicial modification or termination is available in at least three circumstances: a court will revoke a trust (1) if all the beneficiaries consent to termination and early termination will not frustrate a material purpose of the settlor (*see* Uniform Trust Code § 411(b)); (2) if modification is necessary to correct a drafting error that would otherwise result in the frustration of settlor's intent (*see* Uniform Trust Code § 415); or (3) if changed circumstances, unforeseen by the settlor, threaten to frustrate settlor's objectives (*see* Uniform Trust Code § 412(a)).

In addition to judicial termination, a growing number of states have authorized trustees to make changes to discretionary trusts, without judicial approval, by "decanting" the trust assets into a new trust.

A. Consent of the Beneficiaries

When beneficiaries are unborn, minors or contingent, it may be difficult or impossible to obtain the consent of all the trust beneficiaries. When beneficiaries are minors, some courts will appoint a guardian *ad litem* to represent the minor beneficiaries' interests. And some states have enacted legislation to allow termination when all *living* beneficiaries consent.[9]

Although some cases are straightforward, determining the settlor's material purpose is not always an easy matter. First, examine a fairly simple case. Suppose a testator creates a trust for the "health, support and education of my son Dilbert for the duration of his life." If Dilbert seeks early termination (which would enable him to receive a fractional share of the trust principal outright) most courts would refuse to terminate the trust before Dilbert's death, even if all the remainder beneficiaries agree. There is no guarantee that Dilbert would use the lump sum for support, health care and education expenses; he could spend the entire amount on a drug binge or a trip around the world, probably the very scenarios that the testator sought to prevent.

Posit a more difficult case: suppose the testator gives the trustee complete discretion over whether to make any payments of income or principal to Dilbert. Would early termination frustrate a material purpose of the settlor? The answer would depend on whether a court believed that settlor had some protective purpose in mind in giving the trustee complete discretion. The Restatement (Third) suggests that a pure discretionary trust may represent "nothing more than a settlor's plan for allocating benefits . . . flexibly among various beneficiaries . . . " and thus would not represent a material purpose that would be frustrated by early termination.

Suppose that the settlor imposes a mandatory duty on trustee to pay out all income to the income beneficiary for the duration of the beneficiary's life? Some courts have viewed this as evidence that a material purpose of the settlor was to provide a steady income to that beneficiary for life. But if the settlor did not restrict the income beneficiary's ability to alienate his or her interest, then finding a material purpose in settlor's designation of an income beneficiary seems misguided. Consequently, courts are split over this question. The Uniform Trust Code endorses the Restatement (Third)'s position that "[m]aterial purposes are not readily to be inferred."

If the settlor did create a spendthrift trust, most, but not all, courts have interpreted the spendthrift provision as evidence that settlor intended to ensure continuous support for the beneficiary throughout her lifetime, which means that the trust cannot be prematurely terminated. Section 411(c) of the Uniform Trust Code initially attempted to reverse this position, providing that "[a] spendthrift provision in the terms of the trust is not presumed to constitute a material purpose of the trust." The UTC provision, building on comment d to Section 65 of the Restatement (Third) of

---

[9]   N.Y. E.P.T.L. § 7–1.9.

Trusts, rests on the premise that a spendthrift clause may simply be boilerplate or merely expressive of the settlor's desire to facilitate beneficiaries' successive enjoyment of trust property. As a result, the drafters concluded that a spendthrift provision alone does not signal that termination would frustrate a material purpose of the trust.

State legislatures, however, resisted the UTC's position, and the drafters of the code "bracketed" the provision, suggesting that it was "optional" for states considering adoption of the Code. Most states, then, continue to adhere to the common law rule that a spendthrift clause bars early termination of the trust.

B. Correcting Mistakes

Although courts have been extremely hesitant to reform wills for mistake, they have been more receptive to requests to reform trusts for mistake. Section 415 of the Uniform Trust Code provides that parties seeking reformation must prove the existence of the mistake by clear and convincing evidence.

Sometimes, the trust instrument was designed to achieve tax advantages, but the trust instrument as drafted does not accomplish that objective. In that instance, courts have been willing to admit extrinsic evidence (such as a lawyer's affidavit) to establish that there has been a mistake. Section 416 of the Uniform Trust Code goes further, and permits judicial modification to achieve settlor's tax objectives even in the absence of evidence that the provisions resulted from a drafting mistake.

C. Unforeseen Circumstances

Like all people, settlors have limited ability to predict the future. Sometimes changed circumstances frustrate the trust's purpose. For example, the trust assets may decline in value so that administrative costs approach the costs of trust administration, preventing the income beneficiary from receiving any funds from the trust. Or, a settlor's assumption that the trust income would be more than sufficient to provide for the income beneficiary's living expenses proves unfounded. Courts will terminate a trust if it is no longer able to accomplish settlor's purpose, or modify it as necessary to achieve settlor's objectives.

The Uniform Trust Code codifies this common law doctrine in two separate sections. Section 412(a) authorizes modification or termination because of unanticipated circumstances, while section 414(b) permits judicial modification (or appointment of a different and presumably less expensive trustee) if a court determines that the value of the trust property does not justify the cost of administering the trust. Section 414(a) also permits the *trustee* to terminate or modify a trust that has diminished in value to less than $50,000 if the trustee concludes that the value of trust property is insufficient to justify administrative costs.

D. Trust Decanting

Termination of a trust for mistake or changed circumstances requires judicial approval, which can be both time-consuming and expensive. In recent years, a number of states have authorized a *trustee* to modify the terms of a trust, without judicial approval, by "decanting" the trust assets from one vessel (the original trust) into a new one (the new or "decanted" trust).

In general, a trustee has decanting power only when the original trust conferred on the trustee discretion to make outright distributions to a trust beneficiary. The theory behind decanting is that if a trustee had power to make outright distributions to a beneficiary, the trustee must also have the power to make a distribution to another trust for that beneficiary.

By using the decanting power, a trustee may be able to extend the duration of a trust to provide for a beneficiary who, in the trustee's judgment, is not capable of managing trust assets at the time for termination specified in the trust instrument. In some cases, decanting may also enable the trustee to ensure that trust assets will not disqualify the beneficiary from public assistance benefits.

The availability of decanting varies from state to state, as does the scope of the power to decant. Decanting's popularity, however, appears to be growing.

VII. Charitable Trusts

A. What Is a Charitable Trust?

Charitable trusts are created to benefit some subset of the public at large by relieving poverty, advancing education, science or health, promoting religion or supplementing governmental activities. *See* Uniform Trust Code § 405(a). Charitable trusts differ from private express trusts in two important ways. First, charitable trusts cannot benefit particular individuals. A trust to provide scholarships to needy children in a particular community would be a charitable trust. A trust to provide for the education of three particular children would not be. Because charitable trusts have no clearly identifiable beneficiary to enforce the trust, the attorney general in each state is charged with the responsibility.

Second, unlike private express trusts, charitable trusts can endure forever. States that ascribe to the Rule Against Perpetuities, USRAP, or other limitations on the duration of trusts exempt charitable trusts from those limitations. Courts are often called upon to determine whether a trust truly serves a charitable purpose, or whether it is simply a private express trust masquerading as a charitable trust to avoid the rule. One infamous case that illustrates this issue concerns a testator who created a testamentary trust to benefit schoolchildren in his town. The will required trustee to pay the trust income twice a year, prior to Easter and Christmas vacations, to the children for "the furtherance of his or her obtainment of an education."[10] Testator's heirs, his collateral relatives, argued that the trust was not a valid charitable trust, that it failed as an express trust because it violated the Rule Against Perpetuities, and that therefore testator's residuary estate should be distributed to them in accordance with the intestacy statute.

The court found that the testator's motives were "benevolent" but not charitable, because testator created no mechanism for ensuring that the school children would use the funds for educational purposes. Moreover, the court viewed the timing of the gifts as evidence that the testator sought only to make the children happy by giving them money to use on their school vacations. Although the court acknowledged that the gifts would give the children pleasure, that impact was not enough to constitute a charitable purpose. The court added that the result might have been different had the testator directed the trustee to distribute the money to children who were poor or in need.

B.   Cy Pres

Recall that a court can amend a private trust when necessary to avoid frustration of settlor's material purpose due to changed circumstances. Similarly, the doctrine of *Cy Pres* ("as near as possible") allows a court to modify charitable trusts when settlor's specific purpose can no longer be effectuated. Because charitable trusts can endure forever, this problem occurs with some frequency.

For instance, suppose testator's will creates a charitable trust to benefit a private college, but years later the college goes bankrupt and closes. Or, suppose the charitable trust exists to fund research to cure a particular disease, but that the cure is eventually found. Often in such cases, testators' heirs argue that the trust should be terminated since its purpose can no longer be carried out, and that the court should distribute the balance of the trust funds to them. The *cy pres* doctrine, however, allows a court to redirect the benefits of the trust fund to a cause that best approximates settlor's objectives. *Cy pres* means, roughly "as near as possible".

---

[10] Shenandoah Valley National Bank v. Taylor, 192 Va. 135, 63 S.E.2d 786 (1951).

At common law, the *cy pres* doctrine is available only when a court determines that the settlor had a general charitable intent. The key to *cy pres*, then, is to determine whether settlor's intent was *specific* (in which case *cy pres* cannot apply and the trust should be terminated) or *general* (in which case the court can apply *cy pres* and redirect the trust benefits). A specific intent is an intent to benefit just the specific charity named. If settlor's intent was specific, courts assume that the settlor would have preferred the money to be distributed to his heirs once the trust's purpose was accomplished or frustrated. A general intent exists when settlor wants the funds to be placed toward charitable objectives not necessarily limited to the specific purpose or charity named. Relevant factors include whether the charitable bequest was a residuary bequest, the extent to which testator imposed limitations on the charitable bequest, whether the bulk of testator's estate was devised to charity, and whether testator made gifts to those who would take if the trust were to fail.

The Uniform Trust Code significantly expands the availability of *cy pres*. Section 413 presumes that settlor had a general charitable intent, and then leaves it to a court to determine how best to accomplish settlor's charitable purposes. Trust property would be distributed to non-charitable beneficiaries only if the settlor includes an express provision in the trust instrument overriding the statutory presumption in favor of *cy pres*. Moreover, even if the trust instrument does include an express provision, the statute permits enforcement of that express provision only if fewer than 21 years have passed since the trust's creation, or if the trust property would revert to the settlor and the settlor is still living. Otherwise the statutory presumption in favor of *cy pres* would prevail even over the settlor's express instructions to the contrary.

Problems

1. In March of 2015, Trina Thompson was diagnosed with Alzheimer's disease. Trina's illness was in its early stages, and she had significant lucid intervals. However, because it was clear that Trina's mind was deteriorating, Trina and her daughter Blanche, with whom she lived, agreed that Trina should move to a nearby nursing home. On the day Trina moved, she handed Blanche an envelope and said, "this is my gift to you in appreciation for all you've done for me." The handwritten letter inside the envelope read:

4/20/15

My Dear, Dear Blanche,

I am deeply indebted to you for the constant love, support and care that you have shown me. Therefore, I hereby transfer my home to you. You shall have the right to live in

*the house for life, and to determine who shall receive the
house at your death, although I'd prefer that your daughter
Allison receive the house if at all possible.*

I love you, Mom.

Trina transferred title to the house to Blanche, and Blanche
continued to reside in the house. Blanche's daughter, Allison, moved
to California. Blanche has fallen on hard times, and has put the
house up for sale. She intends to use the proceeds to buy a small
apartment, and plans to use the remaining money for living
expenses. Allison has sued to stop her. Should she prevail?

2.   Marvin Greenblat's will provides as follows:

> "I devise my entire estate for the benefit of my dog, Herbert,
> who has been my faithful and loving companion throughout
> the last years of my life. He shall live with my butler, Klaus,
> who has graciously agreed to care for him. Klaus shall be
> the trustee, and shall be authorized and required to spend
> the income and as much of the principal as reasonably
> necessary to ensure that Herbert is happy, stimulated and
> well provided for."

Is Marvin's trust enforceable?

3.   On May 30, 2009, Sam Settlor executed an irrevocable trust
document titled "the Sam Settlor Irrevocable Trust" pursuant to
which he transferred $2,000,000 to:

> . . . my brother, Bob, as trustee, to hold in trust to benefit
> my son Adam for as long as he lives. The trustee shall make
> payments to, or on behalf of, Adam of as much income and
> principal as necessary to provide for Adam's health, support
> and maintenance, without regard for the needs of the
> remainder beneficiaries. At Adam's death, the trustee shall
> distribute the remainder to my grandchildren equally.

> a.   Adam is a compulsive partier and a free spender. A
>   local nightclub recently sued him for failing to pay a
> $50,000 debt he incurred when he hosted a party there.
>   The club obtained a judgment against Adam in that
>   amount. Can the club obtain an order of garnishment
>   compelling Bob to pay the judgment from trust
>   proceeds? If the club does not obtain a garnishment
>   order, may Bob pay the judgment?

> b.   Adam has requested that Bob make a distribution from
>   the trust to finance a business opportunity that he is
>   interested in pursuing. Specifically, Adam wants to
>   start a clothing company. Adam figures that $500,000

would be sufficient capital to enable him to launch his venture. May Bob make the distribution? Must he?

c.   Adam is also several months behind on the rent payments for his luxury apartment. If Adam asks Bob for a trust distribution to bring him current on those payments, must Bob make that distribution? May Bob make that distribution? If Adam's landlord sues the trustee to force Bob to cure the rent default, will the trustee prevail?

4.   Would your answer to either 3(a), 3(b) or 3(c) change if the trust also contained the following provision:

"Adam's interest in this trust shall not be assignable or subject to seizure by legal process."

5.   Would your answer to either 3(a), 3(b) or 3(c), above, change if the trust document read,

"My brother, Bob, as trustee, shall hold these funds in trust to benefit my son Adam for as long as he lives. The trustee shall pay all income generated by the trust assets to my son Adam on a quarterly basis. The trustee may, in his absolute and uncontrolled discretion, make payments of principal to Adam as he deems appropriate. At Adam's death, the trustee shall distribute the remainder to my grandchildren equally."

6.   Refer again to the facts in Problem 3. Suppose when Adam reaches the age of sixty, he enters into an agreement with the three children of his deceased brother, Ronald, to terminate the trust. Adam has never had any children, and never intends to have any. Ronald's children are the only remainder beneficiaries. The trust principal is currently worth $3,000,000. Pursuant to their agreement, Adam will be paid $1,000,000, and the three remainder beneficiaries will divide $2,000,000. If Adam sues to terminate the trust, will the court order termination?

7.   Refer again to the facts in Problem 6, and assume Adam did not seek to terminate the $3,000,000 trust. Over the following two years, Adam had significant health issues that led Bob to make significant payments for Adam's medical care. As a result, the trust principal is now $60,000. Adam and the remainder beneficiaries agree to terminate the trust, and to have the $50,000 distributed to Adam. Will a court order termination? Would your answer be different if one of the remainder beneficiaries objected to termination?

8.   Again refer to the facts in Problem 3. Suppose when Adam is seventy, he suffers serious and debilitating health problems that require him to reside in a nursing home. If Adam applies for

Medicaid, will the state view the trust as "available" to Adam in determining his eligibility for Medicaid?

9. Would your answer to Problem 8 be different if the trust were as provided in Problem 5?

10. Tom Testator's will includes the following dispositive provisions:

> *One. I leave $100,000, in trust, to the Metropolis Museum of Art for establishment of a collection of Yugoslav naive art, to be exhibited year-round in the museum's main building.*

> *Two. I leave $100,000, in trust, to the Illyrian Refugee Fund, to assist in providing relief to victims of ethnic violence in the former Yugoslavia.*

> *Three. I leave the remainder of my estate to my daughter, Alice.*

Testator was a native of the former Yugoslavia. At Tom's death, the Museum concludes that the $100,000 is inadequate to fund a collection of Yugoslav naive art, and seeks permission to use the money to add to its collection of Russian art. Alice Testator, who wants the $100,000, opposes the modification. Will a court grant the museum's request?

11. How, if at all, would your answer be different if Testator were a New Yorker of Hispanic descent, and if, after including paragraph one, Testator's will left the balance of his estate "to the three largest art museums in upstate New York, in equal shares?"

Chapter Seven

FIDUCIARY DUTIES

Although personal representatives hold legal title to estate property and trustees hold legal title to trust property, personal representatives and trustees hold that title for the benefit of estate and trust beneficiaries. An extensive set of legally enforceable duties have developed to insure that trustees and executors act in the interest of trust beneficiaries. These duties vary somewhat depending on context. For instance, the investment responsibilities of trustees differ somewhat from the investment responsibilities of personal representatives, because the trustee's objective is to maximize value of the trust corpus over the long term, while the personal representative's objective is to distribute estate assets as expeditiously as possible. Nevertheless, with some allowances for differences in context, the fiduciary duties of personal representatives and those of trustees are remarkably similar. Although the discussion below focuses on trustees, similar principles govern personal representatives, except where indicated.

I.   The Duty of Loyalty

Perhaps the most basic fiduciary duty is the duty of loyalty, which requires the trustee to act in the interest of the trust beneficiaries, not in self-interest. The trustee is entitled to compensation for his efforts on behalf of the beneficiaries; he is not entitled to obtain financial advantage from transactions made in a fiduciary capacity.

At its core, the duty of loyalty involves a prohibition on self-dealing by the trustee. The prohibition on self-dealing rests on the premise that the fiduciary's temptation to advance his own interests might cause him to shortchange beneficiaries in transactions involving the fiduciary's personal interests. A transaction that advances the fiduciary's personal interests need not be bad for the beneficiary. Indeed, most contracts contemplate benefit to both parties; if they did not, parties would not make them. Each party can protect himself against bad bargains; courts need not review each transaction for fairness to all parties. Ordinary contracts, however, do not find the same party on both sides. By contrast, if a trustee deals with himself in his individual capacity, there is no good way to assure that he is acting in the interest of the trust beneficiaries. Consider an example. Suppose it is in the interest of the trust beneficiaries to sell real property owned by the trust. The trustee is willing to pay $200,000 to the trust. Is the sale in the interest of trust beneficiaries? The property can't be worth less than $200,000, because the trustee would not then be willing to pay $200,000. But if the property is worth more than $200,000, the trustee is benefitting personally from the transaction with the trust. That is, the trustee might well be willing to pay more than $200,000 if forced to do so. When the trustee also represents the seller, it is too easy for the trustee to take advantage of his position on both sides of the transaction to buy the property for a reasonable price rather than the highest price the trust could obtain. The prohibition on self-dealing is designed to avoid this dilemma.

A.   The No Further Inquiry Rule

When a trustee engages in prohibited self-dealing, fairness of the transaction is not a defense to an action for breach of the duty of loyalty. The beneficiary can meet his burden of proof simply by establishing that the trustee, in its personal capacity, transacted with the trust. The trustee who self-deals is strictly liable. Section 802(b) of the Uniform Trust Code codifies the "no-further-inquiry" rule, which holds that the transaction constitutes a breach without regard to its underlying fairness. The statute provides that a "transaction involving the investment or management of trust property entered into by the trustee for the trustee's own personal account or which is otherwise affected by a conflict between the trustee's fiduciary and personal interests is voidable by a beneficiary affected by the transaction . . . " Beneficiaries are not required to prove that trustee's self-dealing was unfair to the trust. Instead, a court can order the trustee to pay to the trust all of the profits that the trustee realized as a result of self-dealing.

B.   The Advance Approval Doctrine

There are occasions when a transaction between the trustee and the trust is in the interest of the trust beneficiaries. The trustee might value particular trust property more than any other potential buyers. In these circumstances, the trustee can seek judicial authorization of the transaction. *See, e.g.*, Uniform Trust Code § 802(b)(2) (codifying the rule). So long as the trustee persuades a court that the transaction serves the interest of the trust beneficiaries, the court is likely to approve the transaction.

Judicial authorization of self-dealing transactions can be time-consuming and expensive. A trustee might, therefore, prefer to obtain the consent of the beneficiaries. A release signed by all of the trust's beneficiaries is sufficient to absolve the trustee from liability for self-dealing, so long as the trustee can establish that the beneficiaries have been fully apprised of all of the rights they are signing away. *See, e.g.*, Uniform Trust Code § 802(b)(4). But, because many beneficiaries are dependent on the trustee, and are unlikely to object to any document proposed by the trustee, courts often want concrete evidence that the beneficiaries understood the nature of the transaction to which they gave consent. As a result, courts typically construe against the trustee agreements consenting to trustee self-dealing.

Thus, if the trustee seeks beneficiary consent to a particular transaction, but does not advise the beneficiaries that the transaction involves a personal benefit to the trustee, the consent is not likely to insulate the trustee against subsequent claims by the beneficiaries. And courts virtually never find consent by implication.

Another problem with beneficiary consent arises when some of the trust beneficiaries are unborn, or lack capacity. Consent of some of the beneficiaries will usually be insufficient to shield the trustee from liability to those beneficiaries who were incapable of giving consent.

C.   Authorization by the Trust Settlor

When the trust instrument explicitly authorizes the trustee to engage in particular self-dealing transactions, the trustee is not liable to the beneficiaries for engaging in those transactions. *See, e.g.,* Uniform Trust Code § 802(b)(1). For example, the trust instrument may authorize a trustee to invest in companies in which the trustee has a significant interest.

Moreover, courts will sometimes imply an authorization of self-dealing from the circumstances existing at the time the trust is created. For instance, if the settlor names as trustee a person who is a principal in a company owned in part by the trust, the settlor knows that the trustee will inevitably engage in self-dealing: the trustee must decide whether to sell or to retain the trust's interest in the company's assets.

Courts, however, are reluctant to enforce trust provisions exculpating the trustee from all liability for self-dealing. A blanket immunity from liability for self-dealing essentially gives the trustee power to treat the trust property as his own, which is inconsistent with the premises of the trust: that settlor intended the trustee to act for the benefit of the trust beneficiaries.

D.   Transactions Between the Trustee and Related Parties

Traditionally, the prohibition against transactions involving a conflict-of-interest included transactions between the trust and close family members of the trustee. There is some basis in the case law for relaxing the standard for nonprofessional trustees acting with good faith but an inadequate understanding of the rules. If, in such a case, the trustee's act did not damage the trust, a court might decline to apply the no-further inquiry rule. This approach is understandable; when a settlor names as trustee a family member or close friend (as opposed to an institution), it seems likely that the settlor would not want the trustee to be held liable for acts taken in good faith that do not damage the trust beneficiaries, especially when the trustee is uncompensated.

Uniform Trust Code section 802(c) embraces this approach, but then relaxes the rule even further, directing that transactions between the trustee and a relative, an agent or attorney of the trustee, or "a corporation or other person or enterprise in which the trustee, or a person that owns a significant interest in the trustee, has an interest that might affect the trustee's best judgment" are only presumptively void. The trustee can rebut the presumption by proving that the transaction was not affected by the conflict. Factors to be considered are the "fairness" of the transaction and generally whether the transaction is similar to one that would have been made with an independent party.

It is hard to defend the UTC's exemption from the no-further-inquiry rule for transactions between professional trustees and related individuals or entities. Because the no-further inquiry rule forces the trustee to disclose to beneficiaries the nature of the conflict and the terms of the deal, it affords protection to trust beneficiaries that the UTC does not.

E. Typical Self-Dealing Transactions

1. *Sales and Loans Between Trustee and Trust*

A trustee may not sell property to the trust or estate, nor may the trustee purchase property from the trust or estate, without securing judicial permission. Purchases by the trustee are most often challenged when the trustee has paid less than market value for estate or trust assets. There is, of course, little incentive for beneficiaries to challenge purchases made at fair market value unless there have been significant price fluctuations after the self-dealing transaction. Where there have been price fluctuations, and where the fluctuations have favored the trustee rather than the trust, the trustee is subject to liability because courts infer that the trustee used his best business judgment to further his own interests rather than the interests of the trust beneficiaries.

The prohibition against sales between the trust and the trustee extends beyond transactions with the trustee personally. If the trustee sells trust property to entities in which the trustee has a significant pecuniary or professional interest, a presumption arises that the transaction is affected by a conflict of interest. *See, e.g.,* Uniform Trust Code § 802(c)(4). As a result, the trustee is liable for breach of the duty of loyalty. *Matter of Rothko*[1] furnishes the most notorious modern illustration. Decedent, an internationally known abstract painter, left an estate consisting primarily of his own paintings. Of the three executors named in decedent's will, one was an officer and director of a gallery and another was a struggling artist. The executors contracted with the gallery to sell estate paintings at a 50% commission, when, before his death, decedent had contracted with the same gallery to sell at a 10% commission. The court held that the gallery director had breached his duty of loyalty both because of his position as director and officer of the gallery, and because of his incentive to curry favor with the gallery to encourage sales by the gallery of items from his family's extensive private art collection. The struggling artist breached his duty of loyalty because he too had reason to favor the gallery's interests over those of the trust; the gallery could be, and indeed was, useful to the artist in promoting his own painting. Hence, both of these directors had engaged in prohibited self-dealing.

2.   *Purchase or Retention of Stock in Corporate Trustee*

A corporate trustee in need of capital might want the trust to purchase stock in the trustee-corporation. Moreover, purchases by the trust, even if made from individual shareholders, and not from the trustee-corporation itself, might maintain or drive up the price of corporate stock, benefitting the corporate shareholders. The prohibition against self-dealing forbids a corporate trustee from using trust proceeds to purchase corporate stock for these or other purposes.

3.   *Using Trust Assets to Secure Control, Salary, or Position in a Corporation Owned in Part by the Trust*

As legal titleholder of trust or estate property, the trustee has the power to vote shares of corporate stock owned by the trust. Especially when the trust holds a large percentage of the shares in a corporation, the trustee's voting power may make him an influential figure in the corporate structure. The trustee's duty of loyalty, however, limits his right to use his influence for personal benefit.

A trustee may not use power to vote trust stock to secure a salaried position with a corporation owned in part by the trust. There is, however, an exception to this rule: when the trust owns too little corporate stock to significantly influence hiring decisions, or where the trustee held the salaried position before becoming a trustee,

---

[1]   43 N.Y.2d 305, 401 N.Y.S.2d 449, 372 N.E.2d 291 (1977).

courts have found no impropriety in retaining both the salaried position and the fiduciary office.

Salary is not the only personal benefit a trustee might secure through use of his power over trust assets. The prohibition on self-dealing also prohibits use of the trust's voting power to obtain corporate control, which might be of substantial benefit to the trustee if the trustee also owns corporate stock in his individual capacity.

II. The Duty of Care: Portfolio Management

A trustee must not only be loyal; a trustee must also be prudent. Trust beneficiaries are entitled to a trustee who diligently safeguards their interests, and avoids unnecessary losses. By the same token, the trustee need not be clairvoyant; not all losses suffered by the beneficiaries are the product of trustee negligence, and the trustee is not an insurer of the value of the trust.

Although the duty of care extends to prudence in the management of trust property that requires active management, in most cases, the question is whether trustee has prudently selected and reviewed the trust's investment portfolio.

A. The Traditional Approach

Historically, trust law regarded the trustee's primary objective as preservation of the trust principal. The trustee's secondary objective was to generate income, but the trustee was not permitted to seek higher income at the cost of risking trust principal. These objectives were incorporated into fiduciary duty law in one of two ways. First, a number of states adopted a "legal list" approach to trust investments. In these states, trustees were permitted to invest only in a list of fixed-income securities (with a focus on real estate mortgages); investments in other assets were imprudent *per se* for trust funds. Second, other states adopted a somewhat more flexible "prudent man rule," later known as a "prudent investor rule." These states did not codify a list of permissible investments, but instead permitted more choice to the trustee—always subject to the premise that the trustee's primary objective was preservation of trust principal. As a result, the prudent investor rule required the trustee to invest conservatively.

This requirement of conservatism was rooted in the presumed intent of most trust settlors. The assumption underlying the traditional prudent man rule was that the settlor of the trust expected—and wanted—the ultimate beneficiaries of the trust principal to receive assets of value comparable to the assets settlor had initially placed in trust. The trustee was not, therefore, supposed to maximize trust income in the abstract, but instead to maximize trust income subject to a primary obligation to preserve principal. Courts and scholars, therefore, differentiated sharply between investments prudent for individual investors and investments prudent for trustees. As the drafters of the Second Restatement of Trusts explained:

> "Where ... the risk is not out of proportion, a man of intelligence may make a disposition which is speculative in character with a view to increasing his property instead of merely preserving it. Such a disposition is not a proper trust investment, because it is not a disposition which makes the preservation of the fund a primary consideration."[2]

Of course, a particular trust settlor was free to authorize his or her trustee to make investments that would otherwise conflict with the statutory "legal list" or the "prudent investor rule," but the conservative investment requirement remained the default rule for trust investments.

This approach worked reasonably well in a time of no inflation or low inflation. But as inflation became a more common phenomenon, the legal list approach, and, to a lesser extent, the conservative prudent man rule, significantly advantaged income beneficiaries and disadvantaged trust remaindermen. The conservative approaches focused on maintaining constant dollar value of the trust principal. Inflation, however, reduced the purchasing power of those dollars. Legislatures and courts responded to these changes by authorizing trust investments in common stocks, but only when those common stocks constituted "prudent" investments; a trustee was not generally entitled to purchase securities for the purpose of "speculation."

Under the traditional "prudent investor rule," courts evaluated each trust investment independently. The trustee was not authorized to invest even a small portion of the trust's portfolio in speculative stocks. If, therefore, the trustee did invest some assets in a speculative enterprise, and the trust lost money on that investment, the beneficiaries were entitled to recover for breach of the duty of care even if the trustee's investment had, in the aggregate, generated an impressive return.

B. Modern Portfolio Theory

Since the early 1990s, modern portfolio theory has revolutionized trust investment practices. Trustees remain subject to a "prudent investor rule," but the content of that rule has changed dramatically in several respects. The new prudent investor rule has

---

[2]   Restatement (Second) of Trusts, Section 227 (cmt. e).

now been codified in many states in the Uniform Prudent Investor Act, and is also reflected in the Restatement (Third) of Trusts.

The most important change is that the prudent investor standard that governs trustee investments is applied not to individual investments, but to the trust portfolio as a whole. Under the traditional approach, a court reviewing trustee behavior would ask, with respect to each individual investment, whether the investment was suitable for a trust. If the answer to that question was yes, the trustee had not breached its fiduciary duty even if the trustee had invested the entire trust portfolio in that investment. If the answer to the question was no, then the trustee could not avoid liability, no matter what the composition of the remainder of the trust portfolio. The modern prudent investor rule rejects that approach. In the words of the Restatement (Third) of Trusts, the prudent investor standard

> "requires the exercise of reasonable care, skill, and caution, and is to be applied to investments not in isolation but in the context of the trust portfolio and as a part of an overall investment strategy, which should incorporate risk and return objectives reasonably suitable to the trust."[3]

In rejecting the traditional focus on the individual investment, the modern prudent investor rule considers not whether the individual investment was a prudent investment, but whether the trustee included that investment as part of an appropriately diversified portfolio. That is, no individual investment is, per se, too risky for the trust, so long as the risk associated with the investment is adequately diversified.

The modern prudent investor rule rests in considerable measure on the efficient markets hypothesis, which holds that no individual investor (and hence no trustee) has better insight into the future performance of a particular investment than does the market as a whole. That is, the market price of any publicly-traded investment incorporates all of the best information available to each individual and institutional investor. Because no individual investor has as much information as the market as a whole, no individual investor can expect to perform better than the market on a regular basis.

The efficient market hypothesis generates two corollaries that are critical for trust investment purposes. The first corollary is that no investment is, *per se*, a bad investment. Each investment's market price will reflect the investment's future prospects, so that an investment in any publicly-traded security can be prudent as part of a properly diversified portfolio. The second corollary is that an

---

[3]   Restatement (Third) of Trusts (Prudent Investor Rule), Section 227.

investment in a single security will always be less prudent than an investment in a portfolio of securities. Because market price is the best estimate of future performance of all securities, an investment in a particular security generates the same expected return as an investment in any other security of comparable risk. Investment in a portfolio of securities, then, does not reduce expected return, but does reduce overall risk. As a result, prudent investing requires diversification.

Modern portfolio theory distinguishes between two components of risk in any investment. The first component is "unique" or "diversifiable" risk. This component represents the chance that the particular investment will perform less well than other investments with comparable overall risk. Consider, for instance, an investment in the common stock of a company with natural gas reserves and an investment in the common stock of an airline company. If worldwide oil prices increase, the natural gas stock is likely to increase in price, while the airline stock is likely to decrease. Conversely, if oil prices decrease, the natural gas stock is likely to decrease in price, while the airline stock is likely to increase. Assume that at the time of purchase, the investment in the airline stock had the same expected return as an investment in the natural gas stock, and that the two stocks presented comparable risks. By dividing a portfolio between the two stocks, an investor maintains the same expected return, but reduces overall risk, because changes in oil prices are less likely to have a significant impact on the overall value of the portfolio. The investor can reduce risk even further by dividing the portfolio among a broad range of investments. Hence, the risk of each investment is "diversifiable". A trustee who does not diversify breaches the duty of care by increasing the trust's overall risk without increasing the trust's expected return.

The second component of risk is "market" or "nondiversifiable" or "compensated" risk. Certain investments are inherently more volatile than others. In general, common stocks are more subject to market fluctuations than are corporate bonds or real estate mortgages, and some common stocks (perhaps technology stocks) are inherently more subject to fluctuation than others (perhaps public utilities). The now conventional wisdom is that because investors are generally risk averse, more volatile investments typically have to offer a higher expected return than stable investments. That is, investors in volatile stocks are "compensated" for the risk they take. A trustee cannot diversify away this sort of "market" risk; by definition, the risk is dependent on the general state of the market.

The modern prudent investor rule does not prohibit a trustee from taking market risks, because, according to modern portfolio theory, those market risks are generally accompanied by higher expected return. Significant stock market declines in 2000 and 2008 have generated some questions about the general theory, but have not yet had any impact on the amount of risk a trustee may lawfully take. But in choosing how much market risk to take, the trustee must consider the risk tolerance of the trust. For instance, if the trust instrument requires the trustee to distribute trust principal at periodic intervals, the trustee may be obligated to avoid market risks that would be tolerable if the trustee were concerned principally about long-term performance. Typically the trustee has considerable discretion, and courts are likely to hold the trustee liable for investment decisions only when the trustee has abused that discretion.

C. The Effect of Settlor's Instructions

The modern prudent investor rule is a "default rule" for trust investments. That is, the rule applies unless the settlor provides different instructions to the trustee. The settlor can, however, authorize the trustee to keep the bulk of trust assets invested in a closely-held family corporation, or can require the trustee to avoid investments in common stocks, or can otherwise structure the trustee's investment decisions.

The extent to which the settlor can exculpate the trustee from liability for investment decisions remains a controversial question. Section 1008 of the Uniform Trust Code would hold exculpatory clauses unenforceable in limited circumstances: when the clause relieves the trustee of liability for bad faith breaches or when the trustee abused a confidential relationship to induce the settlor to include the exculpatory clauses.

D. Inception Assets

Many trusts are funded with an inadequately diversified portfolio. Many settlors hold investments that do not conform to the ideals of modern portfolio theory. A settlor might have held a substantial portion of her assets in stock of a single Fortune 500 corporation—perhaps settlor's employer—or might have funded the trust with the family farm or stock in a closely-held business. Much litigation has arisen over the trustee's obligation to dispose of these "inception assets"—assets held by the trust at the time of its creation.

In the absence of express or implied authorization from the settlor, the trustee breaches the duty of care if the trustee permanently retains inception assets when the inception portfolio is inconsistent with the prudent investor rule. That is, the trustee must convert the inception portfolio into one that complies with the prudent investor rule.

The difficult question is determining how quickly the trustee must sell some or all of the inception assets to bring the portfolio into compliance with the prudent investor rule. When the inception assets include too heavy a concentration of a publicly-held security, the trustee generally has an obligation to reduce that concentration within a reasonable time. Because buyers are readily available at market price, the "reasonable" time will typically be short, unless tax considerations associated with the trust or its beneficiaries make it imprudent to sell the security too quickly.

When inception assets are less marketable—the family farm or the family business—the trustee still has an obligation to dispose of those assets within a reasonable time, but the trustee must balance the trust's interest in immediate diversification against the need to avoid a sacrifice of the assets at a price below their long-term value. Just as the trustee might be liable for breach of duty by holding the assets for too long, the trustee might also be liable for selling at too low a price.

When the trust instrument authorizes the trustee to retain inception assets, the trustee is less likely to be held liable for retaining those assets. This is especially true when the trust instrument authorizes the trustee to operate the settlor's business. An authorization in the trust instrument, however, does not insulate the trustee entirely, especially if changed circumstances make it imprudent to retain inception assets.

III. The Duty of Care: Other Management Responsibilities

A. In General

When the trustee succeeds to assets other than cash or publicly traded securities, the trustee's management responsibilities extend considerably beyond portfolio management. If the settlor transferred real estate or an unincorporated business into the trust, the trustee bears responsibility for managing those assets. The trustee must act as a prudent person would act, and failure to do so constitutes breach of a duty of care.

A principal area of dispute concerns a trustee's sale or transfer of trust assets. Although statutes and the trust instrument will generally give the trustee power to sell, that power alone does not excuse the trustee from responsibility to obtain the best possible price for the trust. If, for instance, the trustee sells trust property other than publicly traded securities, the trustee takes a significant risk if the trustee arranges a private sale without first testing the market or having the property appraised. The beneficiaries may subsequently assert that the property could have been sold for a higher price, and they may contend that the trustee's sale at a lower price, without having the property appraised, constituted a breach of the duty of care.

B. Employment of Advisors

Few individual trustees possess the expertise to perform every function expected of a trustee. Depending on the nature of the trust, the trustee may need to employ accountants, lawyers, appraisers, and other professionals to assist the trustee in preparing tax returns, selling assets, and distributing trust property. When the trust property includes an active business, the trustee may have even greater need for expert advice.

Trust law has long permitted trustees to hire advisors to assist in trust management. At one time, courts questioned whether trustees could compensate these advisors out of the trust principal, suggesting instead that compensation should come from the trustee's commissions, on the theory that the trust beneficiaries should not have to pay twice for trust management services. Today, however, it is well established that employment of experts to assist in trust management is a legitimate trust expense, and the trustee may pay those expenses out of trust proceeds.

When the trustee seeks and receives expert advice, the trustee must exercise judgment in evaluating the advice provided by the expert. Of course, the trustee cannot be expected to second-guess every detail of an accountant's tax return or a lawyer's litigation strategy; if the trustee had the expertise to do so, the trustee would not have needed the expert. At the same time, however, the trustee cannot simply hide behind the expert's advice when the trustee knows or should know that the advice is suspect. For instance, courts have rejected an "advice of counsel" defense when the trustee knows of a legal requirement that the trustee's lawyer advises him to ignore. In that instance, failure to comply with the requirement constitutes a breach of trust, even if the trustee relied on his lawyer's advice.

C. Delegation of Fiduciary Duties

Many trustees are chosen not for their investment acumen, but for their trustworthiness or close relationship to the settlor and the settlor's family. A trustee with limited investment experience is likely to want to hire an investment professional to manage the trust's portfolio, or at the very least, to purchase mutual funds, effectively allowing the fund manager to manage the trust portfolio. Suppose the trustee delegates the investment function to a professional, and the professional makes bad investment decisions, or simply steals the trust's money. What liability does the trustee bear for the loss?

The traditional rule was that a trustee who delegates investment functions breaches the duty of care. Although a trustee was entitled to delegate ministerial functions, the trustee was required to perform personally all of the critical discretionary functions associated with trust administration—including, especially, selection of trust investments. The Second Restatement of Trusts provided expressly that a trustee could not properly delegate power to select investments.

As modern portfolio theory expanded the range of permissible trust investments, generating more choices for trustees, criticism of the traditional rule intensified. First, it was not clear that the traditional rule permitted investment in mutual funds, because purchase of a mutual fund effectively delegated to the trust manager a portion of the investment selection function. And under modern portfolio theory, mutual funds were an ideal investment because they made it easier to achieve the diversification demanded by modern portfolio theory. Second, the traditional rule appeared unfair to trustees without investment expertise; if such trustees were liable for breach whenever they delegated investment functions, they might become reluctant to accept appointment, although they were particularly well suited to many of the trustee functions contemplated by the settlor.

The modern rule, embodied in section 807 of the Uniform Trust Code and section 80 of the Restatement (Third) of Trusts, authorizes a trustee to delegate the responsibilities of trusteeship whenever a "prudent person of comparable skill" would delegate those responsibilities. Thus, because a person of limited investment skill would naturally delegate investment responsibilities to someone with greater skill, if such a person were named as a trustee, that person would be acting prudently if he delegated investment responsibilities. The trustee who delegates responsibility for management of the trust portfolio breaches the duty of care only if the trustee fails to act prudently in selecting a person to exercise management functions, of if the trustee fails to monitor the performance of the chosen delegate. That is, the trustee has an obligation to investigate the past performance of an investment advisor before delegating responsibilities to that advisor, has a responsibility to outline investment objectives with the chosen advisor, and has a responsibility to supervise the advisor's performance. If the trustee's capacity is so limited that the trustee cannot perform even these limited functions, the trustee should not agree to serve as the trustee.

The implications of these modern rules are that if the trustee's delegate makes imprudent investment decisions, the beneficiaries have recourse against the delegate, not against the trustee. The modern rule holds that the person to whom a trustee has delegated trustee responsibilities owes fiduciary duties to the beneficiaries. But the trustee cannot avoid all liability by abdicating fully his trust responsibilities; the trustee always remains liable for imprudence in selecting and monitoring delegates.

D. Accountings and the Duty to Inform Trust Beneficiaries

Historically, trustees and personal representatives have been required to report to trust beneficiaries on information relevant to the trust or estate. Without information, beneficiaries are in a poor position to monitor the trustee's actions. In most jurisdictions, trustees and other fiduciaries must report to beneficiaries at specified intervals (often once a year) and when the trustee takes particular actions that might affect the interests of beneficiaries. These reports have often been labeled "accountings," because the trustee is "accounting" to the beneficiaries for its actions. These accountings are often in the trustee's self-interest. If the beneficiaries or a court approve the trustee's accounting, the trustee may be protected from future claims of breach of fiduciary duty.

In recent years, however, some wealthy trust settlors have pushed to change prevailing law to permit them to create "quiet trusts": trusts in which the beneficiaries are not informed about their interests in the trust, or even about the existence of the trust. Those settlors are concerned that the beneficiaries will become slothful or complacent if they learn that the trust will provide for all of their needs.

The Uniform Trust Code has generally imposed on trustees a mandatory duty to inform trust beneficiaries of the nature of their interest in trust. At the behest of lawyers for wealthy settlors, however, the drafters of the Code have enabled states to adopt much of the Code while still giving settlors the option to override the duty to provide information. Many states have taken advantage of these provisions and watered down the Code's notification provisions in one way or another.

IV. Multiple Trustees

A trust settlor will often choose to appoint more than one trustee. A settlor, for instance, might want to give several children equal control over trust assets, or might want to combine a close family member with a professional trustee in order to assure that judgments are made both with knowledge of the family situation and with expertise in trust administration.

When the settlor appoints multiple trustees, the default rule is that a majority of the trustees must join in any action taken on behalf of the trust. A single trustee cannot act on his or her own. The settlor, however, can alter the default rule by express language in the trust instrument. For instance, the settlor can allocate to one trustee the power to make investment decisions, while giving another trustee power to make decisions about distribution of trust assets.

Even in the absence of express language in the trust instrument, one or more trustees can delegate certain trust responsibilities to a particular trustee, so long as it would be prudent to do so. Thus, family members who serve as trustee could delegate investment responsibilities to one of their number, or to a professional co-trustee. Delegation, however, does not relieve a trustee from monitoring the performance of co-trustees.

A trustee is not generally liable for a co-trustee's breach of fiduciary duty. For instance, if one co-trustee engages in a self-dealing transaction which results in a loss to the trust, the other trustees are not automatically liable for that loss. But the other trustees are liable if they knew of the self-dealing and took no steps to avoid it, or if they failed to learn of the self-dealing because of improper monitoring of the co-trustee who committed the breach. The same framework typically applies to a single co-trustee's breach of the duty of care: the other co-trustees are not liable *per se*, but they are liable if their own improper actions enabled the breaching co-trustee to commit the breach.

V. Multiple Beneficiaries

A. The General Duty of Impartiality

When a trust has more than one beneficiary, the trustee has a duty to treat the trust beneficiaries impartially. This duty is not a duty to treat beneficiaries equally, because the different needs and circumstances of the various beneficiaries might make equality inappropriate, even if it were possible to treat the beneficiaries equally. The trustee's duty is to balance the competing interests of the trust beneficiaries in a way that advances the settlor's preferences and priorities, to the extent those preferences can be discerned from the terms of the trust instrument.

The duty of impartiality has both a substantive and a procedural aspect. Procedural breaches are often easier to identify. Thus, if the trustee shares information with some trust beneficiaries, but not others, the trustee is likely to have breached the duty of impartiality unless the trustee can offer a strong reason for discriminating among beneficiaries. Precise delineation of the substantive duty to treat beneficiaries impartially is more difficult. But the trustee may be called upon to articulate reasons for disparate treatment among the beneficiaries—especially when the trustee is himself one of the trust beneficiaries.

B. Impartiality Among Successive Beneficiaries: Principal and Income

The trustee's duty to treat beneficiaries impartially arises most frequently when disputes arise between holders of present and future interests in the trust. Consider a traditional trust in which the settlor provides that her husband is entitled to trust income during the husband's life, and the principal is to be divided among the settlor's children after the husband's death. The trustee must determine what sorts of investments fairly treat both the husband and the children.

At a time of low inflation, when trustees were largely restricted to a small number of stable investments, the trustee's problem was generally not a serious one. The trustee could invest in a fixed-principal security, for instance, a real estate mortgage, distributing mortgage interest to the income beneficiary while keeping the trust principal intact for the holders of the remainder interest.

As the range of permissible trust investments expanded, however, trustees had to deal with a significant fact: some investments are better for income beneficiaries, while others favor remaindermen. For example, some common stocks generate no dividends at all; the company reinvests all profits in order to maximize capital appreciation. Investments in stocks like these are terrific for remaindermen, but terrible for income beneficiaries: if the investment generates no dividends, there is no traditional "income" to distribute. Conversely, in a time of inflation, an investment in a real estate mortgage with a high interest rate may be beneficial for the income beneficiary, but devastating for the remaindermen: the real value of the mortgage principal declines each year, while the income beneficiaries reap benefits in the form of higher income.

In recognition of these problems, courts have held, first, that a trustee has a duty to income beneficiaries to exercise care to assure that the trust estate produces a reasonable amount of income. Second, courts have held that the trustee has a duty to preserve the value of the trust corpus for the benefit of the remaindermen. An investment policy that generates no income, or a policy that erodes the value of the interest of the remaindermen, violate the trustee's duty of impartiality.

This duty, however, applies only when the trust entitles one set of beneficiaries to "income" and another to "principal." If the trustee has discretion to make payments to lifetime beneficiaries, or if lifetime beneficiaries are entitled to periodic payments not tied to the "income" generated by the trust, then the trustee need not worry about whether the investments generate adequate income. The trustee can focus solely on risk and return without worrying about what segment of the investment's return should be treated as "income."

The Uniform Principal and Income Act, now enacted in most states, goes one step further. Even when the trust instrument distinguishes between income and principal, the trust confers on trustees a power to adjust ordinary definitions of income and principal. The adjustment power arises when the trustee invests as a prudent investor and deems such adjustments necessary to effectuate the purposes of the trust. Thus, in defined circumstances, the statute would permit the trustee to invest in assets that would historically be considered unproductive, and then to allocate to income beneficiaries a portion of the trust's capital.

Problems

1.   Decedent's will divides his estate equally between his son and his daughter. The estate consists entirely of stock in a closely-held corporation which has, in recent years, been managed by decedent's daughter, who is also the personal representative of decedent's estate. Decedent's son has no relationship to the corporation.

Decedent's daughter plans to offer her brother the option to purchase her shares for $200,000; if the brother chooses not to purchase, the daughter will pay her brother $200,000, and distribute the shares to herself. Would the daughter's proposed course of action subject her to a claim by her brother?

What course of action would you recommend to the daughter?

2.   Decedent created a trust that requires the trustee to distribute trust income quarterly to decedent's husband, and to distribute principal at the husband's death to decedent's children in equal shares. At the time of the trust's creation, trust assets consisted of decedent's closely held business, which had a market value of $1,000,000. The trustee sold the business, and invested one percent of the trust's portfolio in shares of common stock in each of 100 companies that are among the S & P 500.

After five years, the trust has generated income of two percent per year, which the trustee has distributed to the husband. The value of the trust principal has declined by 25% (reflecting a comparable decline in the S & P 500 generally, and in other common stocks). During the five-year period, the interest rate on real estate mortgages has averaged six percent. Meanwhile, the business owned by the decedent at his death has tripled in value.

Does anyone have a breach of fiduciary duty claim against the trustee? For how much?

How, if at all, would your answers be different if the value of trust principal (and of the S & P 500) had increased by 25% during the five-year period, while all other facts remained the same?

3. Assume the same facts as in question 5 (including all variations), except that the trustee hired an investment advisor, at a cost of $10,000, to make all investment decisions for the trust. The trustee turned the trust funds over to the advisor, who arranged the investments.

Does anyone have a breach of fiduciary duty claim against the trustee? Against the investment advisor?

Chapter Eight

REVOCABLE TRUSTS AND OTHER NON-PROBATE ASSETS

The probate process can be lengthy and expensive. It has long been possible to avoid probate by making lifetime gifts or by creating irrevocable trusts. Those devices, however, do not enable an owner of property to achieve, simultaneously, the two objectives of retaining complete control over property during her lifetime while disposing of her property at death without the need to involve a court. Over the last half century or so, lawyers have adapted the trust to enable a property owner to achieve both objectives.

Although the revocable trust has become enormously popular as a probate avoidance device, it is not the only device that enables the property owner to retain control over property while avoiding probate. The bank account trust, also known as the Totten Trust, has been around for more than a century. Retirement accounts are a more recent phenomenon, but an increasing fraction of wealth is now held in IRAs and 401(k) accounts, which typically pass outside of probate through beneficiary designation forms executed during the account holder's lifetime.

The explosion in non-probate assets has generated one set of problems that didn't exist when all of a decedent's property passed through her probate estate: what happens when the decedent has executed multiple documents—each of them valid, if taken in isolation—that provide conflicting directions about how particular property should be distributed? Litigation on this issue is on the rise, and courts and legislatures have struggled to resolve the issue.

Clients typically do not appreciate the distinction between probate and non-probate assets. A client who has $100,000 in a "Totten Trust" bank account, $300,000 in a brokerage account, $200,000 in an IRA, and $400,000 in a 401(k) retirement plan may think of herself as having $1,000,000 in assets. If she seeks the help of a lawyer in preparing a will or a revocable trust instrument, she may assume that the will or trust instrument will dispose of all of her assets. That assumption, however, would be incorrect, and the instrument drafted by the lawyer could frustrate the client's wishes unless the lawyer is careful to ask the right questions.

This chapter starts by exploring the most significant devices for avoiding probate, and focuses on the difficulties generated by the need to co-ordinate these devices with each other, and with the probate estate.

163

I.   The Revocable Living Trust

A.   The Basics

In the typical revocable trust, the trust instrument names the settlor as the trustee and the sole beneficiary for settlor's lifetime. The settlor retains the right to revoke the trust at any time, and to receive distributions of income and/or principal as the trustee deems appropriate or as the settlor demands. The trust also designates a successor trustee to take over at settlor's death, and one or more remainder beneficiaries who are entitled to the trust principal, if any, that remains in trust at settlor's death. The successor trustee will distribute the trust principal to the remainder beneficiaries without need for a court order or any need to engage in the probate process.

The trust instrument also includes a schedule of trust property, and the settlor declares that settlor holds that property subject to the terms of the trust. This declaration of trust does not significantly constrain the settlor's ability to transfer or consume the property. Because the settlor has power to revoke the trust, the settlor can also transfer any of the property in the trust—so long as the settlor complies with the procedures set forth in the trust instrument.

At first, the use of the revocable living trust to avoid probate met with fierce resistance from courts. Because settlor was the sole trustee and beneficiary during settlor's lifetime, the trustee owed no fiduciary duties to anyone other than himself. Because he could revoke the trust at any time and for any reason, trustee/settlor owed no duties to the remainder beneficiaries (because if the remainder beneficiaries sued trustee to protest any decision trustee made, settlor would simply revoke the trust). The trust document, then, was simply a will, which was invalid unless it complied with the relevant will formality statute (which it invariably did not).

Ultimately, however, courts realized that allowing people to avoid probate made a certain amount of sense. Now, revocable living trusts are enforceable in every state, and regularly used by estate planners. Certainly where a trust document is well drafted, signed by the settlor and notarized, there seems to be little reason not to validate it. Yet the judicial acceptance of revocable living trusts has caused some problems. Because in most states there are no formal requirements for trust creation, poor planning leads to questions about which pages are part of the trust document, which assets settlor intended to transfer into the trust, or other similar problems. In response, Florida and New York have enacted formalities statutes for trust creation. It remains to be seen whether other states will follow suit. The Uniform Trust Code, for instance, includes no provisions requiring formalities for creating revocable trusts; section

401 provides that a trust may be created by a settlor's declaration that he holds property as trustee.

Although revocable living trusts enable settlors to distribute assets at death without court involvement, living trusts do not completely eliminate the need for a will. Inevitably, some items of settlor's property are not transferred to the trust, and a will is necessary to dispose of those assets at settlor's death. Typically, a revocable living trust document is accompanied by a "pour over will", which directs that the residuary of testator's estate be distributed to the trustee of testator's revocable living trust. This enables all of testator's assets, both probate and non-probate, to be consolidated and managed as a whole.

B.   Modification or Termination

If a trust is revocable, the settlor may revoke or modify the trust by following the procedures established in the document. Occasionally, issues arise concerning whether settlor properly followed his own instructions for revoking or amending. For example, the trust instrument might direct that any revocation or modification must be in writing, and that the writing must be delivered to the trustee. If the instrument includes this type of language, Uniform Trust Code § 602(c)(1) provides that the settlor may revoke or amend "by substantial compliance with a method provided in the terms of the trust." Courts generally hold that an oral declaration of revocation or a provision in the settlor's will purporting to revoke the trust is ineffective for failure to comply with the terms of the trust.

Of course, revocation powers can be drafted broadly to allow settlor to revoke freely, for example without the need for a writing or delivery. In that instance, the Restatement (Third) of Trusts and the Uniform Trust Code provide that the settlor may revoke by any method that provides clear and convincing evidence of an intent to revoke. *See* Uniform Trust Code § 602(c)(2). The Restatement and the UTC also provide that settlor may revoke by executing a subsequent will or trust instrument that refers to the trust or that disposes of property that would otherwise have passed through the trust. A number of courts, however, have been reluctant to permit revocation by will, on the theory that a living trust can be revoked only during the settlor's life.

Although broadly drafted provisions make it easier for settlor to revoke, they can also cause problems for trustees. First, trustees might not receive notice of the revocation or modification. Second, tenuous evidence of revocation or modification might give rise, after settlor's death, to questions about settlor's intent. For these reasons, drafters frequently include more stringent revocation procedures in the trust document, often at the trustee's insistence.

C.   Co-Ordination with Probate Assets: Pour Over Wills and "Standby" Trusts

Suppose Sally Settlor has $1,000,000 in assets to which she has sole title, and also holds an insurance policy payable to her daughter, and retirement benefits that can be paid to her daughter in the event of testator's death. Sally would like all of the assets to be consolidated into one trust at her death, to be managed for the benefit of her daughter until her daughter reaches the age of 35, at which time the trustee can pay out the principal directly to the daughter.

Sally can accomplish this in one of two ways. The first option is to transfer her $1,000,000 in assets to a revocable living trust that will become irrevocable at her death and continue with the above terms. She can make the life insurance policy payable to the trustee of the trust, rather than to her daughter directly. She can also name the trustee the contingent beneficiary of her retirement benefits. At Sally's death, none of her significant assets will pass through probate, and the trust will continue with a successor trustee to manage the assets for the benefit of Sally's daughter. But Sally might well acquire some assets that she neglected to transfer to the trust. To make sure those constitute part of the trust after her death, she would typically execute a **"pour over will"** that leaves all of her remaining assets to her revocable living trust.

Sally's other option is to vary the above steps in a significant way: she can create a revocable trust but not fund it during her life. Her pour over will should devise her probate assets to the trustee of the trust. Again, her retirement funds and insurance proceeds should be payable to the trust. When a revocable living trust remains unfunded during the settlor's lifetime, it is often referred to as a **"standby trust,"** because the trust simply stands by during the settlor's lifetime waiting to receive assets at settlor's death. Because this design does not avoid probate of Sally's $1,000,000 in assets, it is a less desirable course. On the other hand, the design is helpful for those who do not want to place their assets in trust during their lifetime.

Originally, heirs sought to invalidate standby trusts and pour over wills. Attacks took two forms: first, heirs often argued that standby trusts were not valid trusts because they contained no property until after settlor's death, thus failing to meet the requirement that a valid trust must contain trust property.

Second, heirs challenged pour over wills as invalid testamentary dispositions. The argument went as follows: if a residuary clause of a will devises probate assets to a revocable trust, then the trust document, too, must satisfy testamentary formalities. If it does not, then the pour over provision is invalid, and testator's residuary estate must be distributed to testator's heirs.

Trust proponents had two counter arguments. First, they argued that the trust document could be **incorporated by reference** into the will. This strategy worked so long as the elements of incorporation by reference were met: the will had to clearly identify the trust, and the trust had to be in existence when the will was executed. This last requirement often proved to be the stumbling block, because if the settlor had amended the trust document after the will's execution, then those amendments could not be incorporated by reference.

Second, trust proponents could argue that the doctrine of **facts of independent significance** validated the trust. If the trust had a purpose during settlor's lifetime other than to direct distribution of settlor's assets at death, then the trust was valid. This argument worked only if settlor transferred at least some assets to the trust during settlor's life. If so, then the trust's independent purpose was to hold those assets, and the pour over to the trust was valid. If the settlor had not funded the trust during life, however, then the trust had no independent function during settlor's life, and facts of independent significance doctrine could not be used to validate the pour over provision.

These problems were solved by the Uniform Testamentary Additions to Trusts Act, a version of which is now enacted in almost all of the states. That statute validates pour over wills. It also provides that trusts are valid even if they are unfunded during settlor's lifetime and their sole function is to receive property at settlor's death. In the few states where pour over will provisions are not authorized by statute, courts continue to struggle to validate those provisions by stretching the doctrines of incorporation by reference or facts of independent significance.[1]

II. Totten Trusts and POD and TOD Accounts

The Uniform Probate Code (and comparable provisions in many states that have not adopted the UPC) permits a person to open a bank account or a brokerage account with a provision that makes the account payable or transferable to designated beneficiaries upon the death of the account holder. POD and TOD accounts build on the widespread acceptance of "Totten Trusts," under the terms of which a depositor opened a bank account "in trust for" a designated beneficiary. Courts recognized that Totten Trusts were not real trusts, and conferred no rights on the beneficiary until the depositor's

---

[1]   *See, e.g.,* In re Estate of Phelan, 375 Ill.App.3d 875, 314 Ill. Dec. 275, 874 N.E.2d 185 (2007), app. denied, 226 Ill.2d 615, 317 Ill. Dec. 503, 882 N.E.2d 77 (2008).

death, but nevertheless rejected arguments that these designations were invalid testamentary transfers. Instead, they upheld the right of the designated beneficiaries to take the funds.

Totten Trusts, POD accounts, and TOD accounts have often been conceptualized as "will substitutes," permitting the account holder to direct the disposition of the account without writing a will. In many ways, modern law treats these documents like wills. For instance, many of the rules for construing wills—including the UPC's requirement that a beneficiary survive the decedent by 120 hours in order to be eligible to take—apply to these accounts. Similarly, UPC § 2–804, which provides that divorce revokes a will bequest to a former spouse, applies to these accounts.

Difficulties arise, however, when the account holder writes a will, and when the beneficiaries under the will are different from the beneficiaries named on the POD or TOD account. That is, suppose a depositor opens a POD account at a local bank, naming her son as the account beneficiary. The depositor then writes a will directing that all of her property be divided equally between her son and her daughter. How are the two documents—the POD designation and the will—to be reconciled?

There is general agreement that a will disposing of all of testator's property or a residuary clause disposing of the "remainder of testator's property" will not, in general, dispose of property held by testator in a Totten Trust, POD account, or TOD account. The assumption is that the will disposes of all of testator's *probate* property, but not property disposed of outside of probate.

By contrast, there is sharp disagreement about the effect of a will provision expressly revoking a designation in a Totten Trust, POD account, or TOD account. Section 2–613 of the Uniform Probate Code provides that "[a] right of survivorship arising from the express terms of the account . . . or a POD designation, may not be altered by will." By contrast, the Restatement (Third) of Trusts takes the opposite position, that a Totten Trust "may be revoked in whole or in part by the depositor's will, either by express provision or by necessary implication."[2] California, by statute, adopts the UPC position,[3] while New York has a statute endorsing the Restatement approach.[4]

The approach embodied in the UPC and the California statute protects financial institutions who make payments in reliance on the designations filed by their depositors. If banks were liable for making

---

[2] Restatement (Third) of Trusts, § 26, cmt. c; *see also* Restatement (Third) of Property (Wills and Other Donative Transfers, § 7.2, cmt. e).

[3] Cal. Prob. Code, § 5302(e).

[4] N.Y. E.P.T.L § 7–5.2(2).

payments that turn out to be inconsistent with the depositor's will, banks would have an incentive to delay making any payments to designated beneficiaries until after probate of the depositor's will— removing one of the primary incentives for creating a POD account in the first place. On the other hand, the UPC and California approach removes the incentive for delay at the cost of frustrating the wishes of a testator whose will makes it clear that testator no longer wants the designated beneficiary to take the property in the POD or Totten Trust account.

An intermediate approach (discussed in passing in the Restatement[5]) would absolve the bank or other financial institution from liability for paying the designated beneficiary, but would give the will beneficiary a restitution claim against the designated beneficiary in cases where the will expressly revoked the beneficiary designation. Case law has not yet developed to support this intermediate approach.

The doctrinal uncertainty makes it imperative that a lawyer consulted about estate planning ask about any accounts the client may have, and that the lawyer check the beneficiary designations for those accounts. Only by asking the right questions can the lawyer insure that the client's property will be distributed in accordance with the client's wishes.

III. Retirement Plan Assets

Many Americans have a large percentage of their savings in retirement plan assets of one sort or another. Most companies have replaced traditional "defined benefit" pension plans, which guarantee retirees a certain annual benefit for each year after retirement, with "defined contribution" plans, by the terms of which the employer and/or the employee make annual contributions to an account on which the employee will draw once the employee retires. These accounts are often known as 401(k) or 403(b) accounts.

A. Employer-Sponsored Defined Contribution Plans

Employer-sponsored defined contribution plans are governed by the federal Employee Retirement Income Security Act (ERISA). ERISA preempts state law on a number of issues, and that preemption has significant implications for estate planning purposes.

First, when a married employee establishes an account pursuant to an employer-sponsored defined contribution plan, the employee's spouse automatically becomes the beneficiary of that plan

---

[5] Restatement (Third) of Property (Wills and Other Donative Transfers), § 7.2, cmt. e.

upon the employee's death. The employee has no discretion to choose another beneficiary, unless the spouse waives his or her statutory rights by filing appropriate documents with the plan administrator. Moreover, even upon divorce, the ex-spouse remains the beneficiary of the plan unless either the ex-spouse waives those rights or the employee obtains a Qualified Domestic Relations Order (QDRO). A settlement agreement by the terms of which the spouse relinquishes all interest in the retirement account is not sufficient, under federal law, to remove the spouse as the beneficiary of the plan.

Second, even when the employee is not married, the employee may not change the designated beneficiary except in accordance with the plan documents. The Supreme Court has held that the rights to plan assets at the employee's death are governed by the terms of the plan; ERISA preempts state law. As a result, a state may not, by statute or case law, permit a will to override the employee's beneficiary designation.

These rules present a challenge for estate planners because many employees are not aware who they designated as a plan beneficiary, and may not even be aware that they designated any beneficiary at all. In most cases, the employee does not initiate the beneficiary designation; the opportunity to designate a beneficiary appears on one of the many forms the beneficiary must sign in order to set up the retirement account. Often, decades will have passed since the employee designated a beneficiary. The employee thinks of the account as "his" account, and assumes that it will pass in accordance with the will or revocable trust instrument he signs when he consults his lawyer for estate planning advice.

As a result, the lawyer must be careful to review retirement plan documents, and must adjust the client's estate plan accordingly. If the client and the client's spouse want someone other than the spouse to be the beneficiary of the plan, the client and the spouse must execute the appropriate plan documents. In any event, the lawyer will have to make sure that the client understands that the client's will or revocable trust will *not* be effective to distribute plan assets, no matter how explicit the language of the will or trust instrument.

B.   IRA Accounts

Congress has authorized many individuals not covered by employee-sponsored plans to establish Individual Retirement Accounts (IRAs), which enjoy some of the same tax advantages as employer-sponsored plans. IRAs, however, are not ERISA plans, and therefore not governed by the broad preemption rules applicable to employer-sponsored plans. As a result, state law rules of construction and state law rules dealing with revocation upon divorce, apply to IRAs while they do not apply to ERISA plans.

To complicate matters further, when an employee covered by an employer-sponsored defined contribution plan retires, the employee is generally entitled to "roll over" the plan assets into an IRA. Once the assets are rolled over into an IRA, they are not subject to the same ERISA rules; a married employee has power to designate a beneficiary other than a spouse, and state law determines what documents suffice to change the designated beneficiary.

Nevertheless, most states hold that to change the beneficiary of an IRA account, the account holder must execute the documents required by the financial institution at which the account is established; a will provision explicitly leaving the IRA account to someone other than the designated beneficiary is insufficient to change the account beneficiary. Again, the primary objective appears to be to protect financial institutions who make payments in reliance on documents executed by the beneficiary. Some states, however, take the opposite approach and enforce will provisions that explicitly devise an IRA account to a person other than the designated beneficiary.

IV. Life Insurance

Many people buy life insurance to assure financial security for their dependents. Because the primary purpose of life insurance is to protect beneficiaries—not to accumulate wealth for the policy-holder, life insurance purchasers tend to be more aware of the beneficiaries designated on their policies than is typically the case with retirement accounts. Nevertheless, conflicts can arise, especially when the insured does not change the policy beneficiaries after significant life events, such as divorce.

Because a life insurance policy is a contract between the insured and the insurance company, most courts assume that the company's obligation is to pay in accordance with the insured's beneficiary designation, even if the insured's subsequent will purports to change that beneficiary designation. Even in New York, which permits a will to override a Totten Trust designation, the insurance beneficiary of record prevails over the beneficiary named in the insured's will. For instance, the New York Court of Appeals has held that a former spouse who divorced the insured when he contracted multiple sclerosis was nevertheless entitled to collect as the designated beneficiary of his life insurance policy, even though the insured's will named his father—who had cared for him during his illness—as the beneficiary of the policy.[6]

---

[6]   McCarthy v. Aetna Life Ins. Co., 92 N.Y.2d 436, 681 N.Y.S.2d 790, 704 N.E.2d 557 (1998).

The Restatement (Third) of Property (Wills and Other Donative Transfers) has suggested that the insurance company can be adequately protected in this situation by a rule that shields it from liability for good-faith payout of the insurance proceeds, while otherwise giving effect to the wishes expressed in the insured's will.[7] As yet, however, scant case authority supports the Restatement's position.

In any event, the competent estate planner must ask the client about the existence of any life insurance policies, and must ascertain the beneficiaries of those policies, in order to co-ordinate the client's estate plan. Sometimes, that will require changing the beneficiary in accordance with the policy's provisions. In other circumstances—as where the insured has transferred ownership of the policy to someone else during the insured's lifetime—no change in designation will be possible. Tax considerations may make it advantageous for the insured to make a lifetime gift of all or part of the premiums, and in that event, the estate planner's job is to make sure the client directs the remainder of her estate in a way that best effectuates the client's overall estate planning objectives.

Problems

1.   Teresa's Will, properly executed in 2000, reads in relevant part as follows:

> The residuary of my estate I devise to the Trustee of the Teresa Testator Revocable Living Trust, executed simultaneously herewith.

Immediately after executing her will, Teresa also executed a document titled "The Teresa Testator Revocable Living Trust," by signing the document in front of a notary. She transferred no assets to that trust, but she made both her 401K plan and her life insurance policy payable, at her death, to the trustee. Clause One of the Trust, not at issue here, named Teresa as trustee, provided that the trust was revocable at Teresa's option, and gave Teresa full rights to income and principal as Teresa, in her discretion, deemed necessary or appropriate. Clause Two of the trust document provided that at Teresa's death, the trust should continue for the benefit of her children for their lives, with a remainder in two of her grandchildren. She made no provision for her third grandchild, Norman.

Teresa has died, and Norman has challenged the trust itself and the pour over provision in Teresa's will, arguing that the trust is invalid for the following reasons: the trust had no property, the trustee had no duties during Teresa's life, Teresa failed to appoint a

---

7   Restatement (Third) of Property (Wills and Other Donative Transfers) § 7.2, Reporter's Note 6.

trustee to succeed her after her death, and the trust is a testamentary document that fails to comply with testamentary formalities. Will Norman succeed in invalidating the trust? If so, on what grounds?

2. Sara Settlor executes a revocable trust instrument naming herself as trustee during her lifetime and naming her two children as beneficiaries at her death. She attaches a schedule of property to the trust instrument, and the schedule includes $200,000 in bearer bonds kept in her safe deposit box. The trust instrument provides that "during settlor's lifetime, trustee shall distribute to or for the benefit of the settlor such sums, at such times, and for such purposes, as the settlor shall direct."

Six months after creating the revocable trust, Sara sells the $200,000 in bearer bonds and transfers her funds to her brokerage account. The following week she directs her broker to buy $200,000 in Microsoft stock. The following year, Sara dies. Her will leaves all of her property to her husband, Harry. How should the Microsoft stock be distributed?

3. Decedent established the following accounts during her lifetime:

a. an IRA account, established 30 years ago, naming her husband as primary beneficiary, and providing that if her husband shall not be alive at the account-holder's death, the account should be distributed to Decedent's (then five-year old) daughter, Ann.

b. an employer-sponsored retirement account, established 20 years ago, naming her husband as primary beneficiary, and providing that if her husband shall not be alive at the account-holder's death, the account should be distributed, in equal shares, to Decedent's two children, Ann and Bill (then aged 15 and 8).

c. a POD account, established 5 years ago, directing the bank to pay over the account proceeds to Decedent's husband upon Decedent's death.

Suppose Decedent dies with a will, executed one year before her death, leaving "my entire estate to the American Red Cross." Decedent's Husband, Harry, survived her.

If Decedent's only significant assets are in the three accounts described, how should those accounts be distributed?

4. Assume Decedent had established the same accounts as in Problem 3, but her will provided "I revoke any designations I have previously made in any documents establishing bank accounts or

retirement accounts, and I direct that all of my assets, including those accounts, should be distributed to the American Red Cross."

Again, if the Decedent's only significant assets are in the three accounts described, how should those accounts be distributed?

5.   Assume again that Decedent has established the same accounts as in Problem 3, but her will provided "I leave my entire estate to my husband, Harry."

If Decedent died in an automobile accident, and Harry died the next day after suffering injuries in the same accident, how should the accounts be distributed?

6.   Assume that Decedent has established the same accounts as in Problem 3, and left a will executed 20 years ago, leaving her entire estate "to my husband, Harry, if he survives me, otherwise to my daughter, Ann."

If Decedent obtained a divorce from Harry six months after executing the will, and Harry survived Decedent, how should the accounts be distributed at Decedent's death?

Chapter Nine

POWERS OF APPOINTMENT

The power of appointment is a mechanism for introducing flexibility into the estate plan. In particular, powers of appointment permit a property owner to designate a person she trusts to decide how that property should be distributed at some time in the future—often long after the property owner's death.

Consider a property owner who would like to provide for her only daughter during the child's lifetime, but to assure that the property will ultimately be distributed to the daughter's children. The property owner could, of course, create a trust with directions that income be distributed to the daughter for life, and principal be divided equally among the daughter's issue at the daughter's death. But property owner would not, at the time she creates the trust, know what needs her current and future grandchildren will have at the daughter's death. Perhaps one will be a multimillionaire while another is a starving artist. Perhaps one will be in debt, or another will be enmeshed in a bad marriage to a spouse who threatens to make claims against the grandchild's assets. The property owner may not be able to anticipate these eventualities, but there is a much better chance that by her daughter's death—which may come decades later—the daughter will be in a position to evaluate the relative needs and deserts of the grandchildren. To take advantage of the daughter's more complete information about the family's evolution, the property owner might forego equal division of the trust principal, and instead give the daughter a power to appoint the property among the property owner's grandchildren.

In addition to the flexibility powers of appointment bring to estate planning, they also have the potential to generate significant estate tax advantages. Suppose, for instance, the property owner would like to give property to her daughter outright, but would also like to assure that the property does not pass through her daughter's own estate. Giving the daughter a lifetime income interest, combined with a power to appoint the property among the daughter's relatives (or some other broad group), would give the daughter a great degree of control over the property without subjecting the property to estate taxation in the daughter's estate.

I.   Terminology

A.   The Parties to a Power of Appointment

The person who creates the power of appointment—the person whose money or property will be distributed when the power is exercised—is called the **donor** of the power of appointment. The person who exercises the power—the person who decides how the donor's property should be distributed—is called the **donee** of the power. Note, however, that the donee does not necessarily share in the appointive property; instead, the donee effectively acts as the donor's agent in selecting the ultimate beneficiaries of the power.

The people to whom the donee appoints the property—the ultimate beneficiaries of the appointed property—are the **appointees**. Often, the donor restricts the people to whom the donee may appoint. The class of people eligible to receive the appointive property are called the **objects of the power**, or sometimes the **class of permissible appointees**.

Finally, consider what happens if the donee never exercises the power of appointment. The people who would take in the absence of exercise, whether or not they are explicitly named in the instrument creating the power, are called the **takers in default** (or takers in default of appointment).

B.   The Scope of the Power

The donor of a power of appointment can give the donee complete freedom to choose appointees, or the donor can choose to limit appointment to a more narrowly defined class of objects of the power. Under state property law, powers are classified as either **general** or **special**. When the donor imposes no limits on a power's objects, authorizing the donee to appoint even to herself or her estate, the power is a **general power**. The Restatement (Third) of Property defines a general power as one which is "exercisable in favor of the donee, the donee's creditors, the donee's estate, or the creditors of the donee's estate."

Frequently, however, the donor wants to limit the donee's freedom to choose appointees. If the donor prohibits the donee from appointing to herself, her estate, her creditors or the creditors of her estate, the power is **special**. Of course, the donor can create even greater restrictions on the exercise of a special power. Thus, the donor might give the donee power to appoint property "among donee's children" or "among donee's blood relatives."

When the donor creates a special power, the donee is not generally obligated to appoint to every object of the power. Instead, the donee may exclude some or many members of the class. As a result, we label the power as an **exclusive** power. By contrast, if the donor explicitly requires the donee to appoint some assets to every member of the class, we say that the power is **non-exclusive**. The problem with construing a power as **non-exclusive** is that the donor generally has provided no guidance about how much the donee must appoint to each object of the power. As a result, courts construe powers as exclusive in the absence of express language to the contrary.

Sometimes, the donor of a power gives the donee the power to appoint immediately; at other times, the donor postpones the donee's exercise of a power of appointment. Typically, although not always, when a donor postpones the donee's exercise, the donor permits the donee to exercise the power only by will, which does not become effective (or irrevocable) until donee's death. When the donee has a power that the donee is free to exercise immediately, the donee's power is **presently exercisable**. When the donee's power is not presently exercisable, the donee holds a **postponed** power. And when the postponed power can only be exercised by will, the donor has created a **testamentary** power of appointment.

Because the IRS must identify taxable interests in trusts, the Internal Revenue Code (the "Code") also defines powers of appointments. The Code largely tracks the state property law approach to defining powers, with a few differences. First, the Code rejects the term "special power" in favor of the term **"non-general power."** Second, the Code includes within its definition of powers trustees' fiduciary powers to invade and distribute principal. Third, a donee who has the power to invade principal for her own benefit has a general power *unless* her power to invade is limited by an **"ascertainable standard,"** in which case the power is "non-general."[1] The Code suggests that the power to distribute principal for a beneficiary's "health, education, support, or maintenance"—or some combination of those terms—would be an ascertainable standard. The definition matters because property subject to a general power is part of donee's taxable estate, whereas property subject to a non-general power is not. For example, if Barbara is the trustee of a trust and has the power to invade principal as necessary to provide for her own "support, health, education and maintenance," her power would be non-general and the trust property would not be taxed in her estate. If Barbara had the power to invade principal "as necessary for her comfort, happiness and enjoyment," the power would be general, and the trust assets would be taxed in Barbara's estate at her death.

---

[1]   I.R.C. §§ 2041(b)(1)(A), 2514(c)(1).

II. Creation and Exercise

Almost invariably, the donor of a power of appointment creates the power as an incident to donor's will or inter vivos trust instrument. Typically, the will or trust instrument names the trustee. The instrument also indicates whether the power is general or special, and whether it is testamentary or presently exercisable. Thus, the instrument might provide "I give to my daughter Daphne a power to appoint the trust principal, by will, among those of my descendants who survive her." With that language, donor has created a special testamentary power of appointment in Daphne. If donor wanted to make the power general, donor could eliminate the words after the last comma. If donor wanted to make the power presently exercisable, donor could do so by eliminating the words "by will." Whatever the nature and scope of the power, the donor should then specify what will happen to the property if the donee fails to appoint; that is, the donor should name takers-in-default. For example, the donor could provide: "if my daughter fails to exercise this power, I direct that the trust principal be divided among my descendants, *per stirpes.*"

Once the donor creates the power, the focus shifts to the donee. What acts of the donee constitute exercise of the power? If the donee is sufficiently precise, donee's exercise will be clear. Frequently, the residuary clause in donee's will includes a blanket exercise of all powers the donee might have: "I leave the remainder of my estate, including any property over which I hold a power of appointment, to . . . " Blanket provisions like this one are sufficient to exercise any powers the donee has, unless the donor has required donee to use more precise language. Authorities diverge, however, on whether the residuary clause of donee's will exercises powers of appointment held by the donee when the residuary clause makes no mention of powers of appointment. A majority of states, supported by the Restatement of Property, have taken the position that a will disposing of all of the donee's property does not manifest an intention to exercise any powers possessed by the donee. In New York and a number of other states, however, an effective exercise of a power of appointment does not require an express reference to the power; a will disposing of all of donee's property exercises the power unless the will provides to the contrary, either expressly or by necessary implication. Uniform Probate Code section 2–608, takes an intermediate position. Under the UPC, a general residuary clause exercises a power of appointment if the power is general and if the donor did not make provision for takers in default. If the power is special, or if the donor did make provisions for takers in default, the will exercises the power only if it manifests an intention to include the property subject to the power.

Why do courts disagree about whether a naked residuary clause exercises a power of appointment? Perhaps because dramatically different circumstances can lead to a residuary clause in which donee does not explicitly exercise a power of appointment. First, the donee might have written the will without knowing of or thinking about the power of appointment. In that case, the intent of the donor and the donee would most likely be advanced by treating the residuary clause as effectively exercising the power of appointment. After all, the donor has indicated that she wants the donee to use her judgment in exercising the power. The donee, in turn, would most likely have exercised the power in favor of the beneficiaries of her own estate. For this situation, then, the New York rule makes good sense.

In other cases, however, the donee writes her will knowing of the power, and does not mention the power because she does not want to exercise the power (perhaps because she is happy to have the appointive property pass to the takers-in-default named by the donor). In that situation, the Restatement rule would better effectuate the intention of the donor and the donee. Which of these situations is more likely to explain donee's failure to mention the power is difficult to determine. Different states have made different judgments on the issue, leading to the disparate doctrinal rules.

Of course, the donor can anticipate and resolve these difficulties with appropriate language in the instrument creating the power. For instance, the donor can give the donee a power of appointment, and provide explicitly that donee's execution of a will shall constitute exercise of the power even if the will makes no mention of the power. Conversely, the donor can provide explicitly that donee's will shall be deemed to exercise the power only if the will makes explicit reference to the power. Indeed, donor can be still more explicit, providing that donee's will shall be deemed to exercise the power only if it refers to the power by the date of the instrument creating the power.

When the instrument creating the power of appointment requires that the power be exercised by a reference to the power or its source, it is generally presumed that the donor's intention was to prevent inadvertent exercise of the power (UPC section 2–704). On the other hand, if donee's will purports to transfer the appointive property, but never makes reference to the power itself, some courts have held that the donee has not satisfied the specific reference requirement, and that the donee's exercise is therefore ineffective.[2]

III. Consequences of the Donee's Failure to Appoint

The donee of a power of appointment has no obligation to exercise the power; the donee is effectively the donor's agent, with

---

[2] *See, e.g.*, Cessac v. Stevens, 127 So.3d 675 (Fla. App. 2013).

authority to act on the donor's behalf, but no duty to act. What happens, then, when the donee fails to exercise the power? Where the power is general and the donor has specified takers-in-default, the answer is simple: the appointive property passes to those takers-in-default. When the instrument creating the power does not specify takers-in-default, the general rule is that the appointive property passes through the donor's estate. The rationale for the rule rests on the theory that the appointive property is the donor's property, not the donee's property; if the donee has not exercised the power the donor has given to her, the property passes as it would have passed if the donor had never created the power at all. So, for instance, if donor executes a trust instrument requiring the trustee to pay trust income to donor's wife for her life, and also gives the wife a "power to appoint, by will, the trust principal," if the wife fails to exercise the power, the principal passes to the beneficiaries of the estate of the donor/husband at the death of the wife/donee.

The consequences of failure to appoint, however, are different when the power is a special power. As with general powers, the donor's express provision for takers-in-default would control. But when the donor has not explicitly named takers-in-default, courts often conclude that the appointive property should be distributed among the objects of the power. This doctrine is often called the **powers in trust** doctrine. Consider, for instance, a donor who creates a trust, with trust income to be paid to donor's sister for life, and principal to be distributed "among my sister's issue as my sister shall appoint by will." The donor intended to give the sister discretion to choose the proportions in which the sister's issue would benefit, but the terms of the grant make it clear that donor had earmarked that property for the sister's issue. If the sister fails to appoint, the powers in trust doctrine would require distribution among the sister's issue rather than having the property pass back to donor's estate (which would permit other family members, or non-family members, to share in the appointive property).

The powers in trust doctrine applies when the objects of a special powers constitute a well-defined class, making distribution to class members feasible. If the donor had granted donee a power to appoint "to anyone except herself or her estate", the powers in trust doctrine could not apply because there would be no mechanism for deciding what share should be distributed to which objects of the power.

IV. Consequences of Ineffective Appointments: The Capture Doctrine and Allocation of Assets

Consider now the problem of the donee who has exercised the power of appointment, but has done so ineffectively. When the power is general, an exercise may be ineffective because it violates the Rule

Against Perpetuities, or perhaps because the donee has exercised in favor of a person who is now dead, or an institution that no longer exists. One might expect the consequences of an ineffective appointment to be the same as the consequences of a failure to appoint.

Often, however, statutes and case law treat ineffective exercise differently from non-exercise. First consider general powers. When a donee attempts to exercise the power, it is often fair to assume that the donee would have preferred to have the appointive property pass to the beneficiaries of his own estate rather than having the property pass back to the donor's estate. This assumption is especially fair when donee's will blended the appointive property with his own—for instance, if the donee disposed of "all my property, including the property over which my father's will gave me a power of appointment, to my cousin Nancy." Suppose Nancy died before both the donor and the donee, leaving no issue. The donee's exercise would be ineffective, because the provision for Nancy would have lapsed. (An exercise might also be ineffective because it violated the Rule Against Perpetuities). By statute or case law, many states have concluded that the donee's ineffective attempt to exercise the power of appointment "captures" the appointive property for the donee's estate. As a result, the appointive property would be distributed to the beneficiaries of the donee's estate rather than to the beneficiaries of the donor's estate. This doctrine, known as the **capture doctrine**, rests on the presumed intent of the donor, who gave the donee unlimited power to dispose of the appointive assets.

Neither the capture doctrine nor its rationale applies to special powers. With a special power, the donor has restricted the donee's discretion, and has not authorized donee to appoint the property to the donee's estate. Hence, the donor's intent would be frustrated if donee could channel the appointive property to donee's estate simply by exercising the power ineffectively. Thus, the consequence of an ineffective exercise is generally the same as the consequence of non-exercise: the property passes to the takers-in-default; if takers-in-default are not specified, the appointive property passes to the objects of the power if the class of objects is well-defined, and otherwise to the beneficiaries of the donor's estate.

Suppose, however, the donee's will has blended the appointive property with donee's own property, and has disposed of both in part to objects of the power, and in part to non-objects of the power. The **allocation of assets doctrine** provides that the assets should be "allocated" or "marshaled" to give maximum effect to the donee's wishes. That is, the appointive assets should be allocated, as far as possible, to those beneficiaries of the donee's estate who are objects of the power, and adjustments should be made to allocate more of donee's personal estate to those beneficiaries who are non-objects of the power.

For example, if donee has a special testamentary power to appoint among her children, and her will disposes of "the remainder of my estate, together with any powers of appointment I may have, one-half to my husband and one-half to my son", consider how a court would distribute donee's $800,000 estate and the $400,000 over which donee has a power of appointment. Donee had no power to appoint to her husband. Rather than invalidate half of donee's appointment (which might channel some of the appointive assets to a child whom the donee has determined is not needy, or not deserving), a court would be likely to allocate all of the appointive property to the son (an object of the power). Then, to give maximum effect to donee's wishes, the court would allocate $600,000 of donee's personal estate to the husband, and the other $200,000 to the son— leaving the husband and the son with $600,000 each, while still giving effect to donor's limitation on exercise of the power.

The allocation of assets doctrine is also applicable, to both special and general powers, when the donee has made a disposition which would be invalid under the Rule Against Perpetuities with respect to the appointive property, but valid with respect to donee's own estate. In that case, too, courts will allocate assets to maximize the effectiveness of donee's intended dispositions.

V. Contracts to Appoint

In many respects, the donee of a power of appointment acts as the agent of the donor; the donor has entrusted the donee to make decisions that advance the donor's agenda. As a result, legal doctrine limits the donee's power to make enforceable contracts about the appointive property in ways that would be inconsistent with the donor's reasons for giving the donee the power of appointment. The donee is not free to contract about the appointive property as if it was her own.

First, the donee may not contract to appoint to an object of a special power in return for the object's agreement to share the appointive property with a non-object of the power. That non-object might be the donee herself, or a third party. Such a contract is sometimes called a "fraud on the power", because the donee and the object have colluded to subvert the donor's intention. As a result, the contract is unenforceable, and any appointment made to the object who has contracted with the donee is ineffective. The entire appointment is ineffective because a court has no way to know how much the donee would have appointed to that object in the absence of the contract.

Even when the contract does not benefit non-objects, contracts to appoint can frustrate donor's intention. When the donor creates a testamentary power of appointment—whether the appointment is special or general—the donor seeks to postpone the donee's decision about how to appoint until the latest possible moment, to enable the donee to take into account as many facts as she can before deciding how donor's property should be distributed. If the donee, by contract, binds herself to a particular appointment, the donee no longer has the same freedom to change her mind to take into account facts learned after the contract is made. Moreover, if the power is a special power, the contract may well benefit the donee personally, in violation of the donor's limitations, which prevent the donee from appointing in favor of herself or her estate.

As a result, a contract to appoint is generally unenforceable whenever the power is a testamentary power. That is, even if the promisee has paid consideration to the donee of the power in return for the donee's promise to appoint, the promisee has no recourse against the appointive property if the donee appoints to someone other than the promisee. In New York, a statute gives the donee a claim for restitution against the donee's personal estate, but not against the appointive property. Even this rule, however, may frustrate the donor's wishes by increasing the likelihood that the donee will perform on the contract in order to avoid subjecting her personal estate to claims by the donee.

Although a contract to appoint is unenforceable with respect to a testamentary power, authority suggests that an appointment made pursuant to an unenforceable contract is nevertheless a valid appointment. This authority suggests that the donee's judgment will remain unclouded by the contract so long as the contract is not enforceable; hence, the mere existence of the contract should not operate to invalidate an otherwise permissible appointment. These authorities, however, are less than persuasive, especially if a disappointed promisee has a restitution claim against the donee's personal estate.

These limitations on contracts to appoint do not apply to general, presently exercisable powers of appointment. Because the donee of a general, presently exercisable power can appoint to herself, she is entirely free to contract with respect to the appointive property. Even with respect to a special, presently exercisable power, the donee may contract to appoint to one or more objects of the power, so long as the contracts do not benefit any non-object (including the donee herself). Because the donee could appoint to any object immediately, the donee is also free to promise the object that she will appoint to the object at a later time or on specified conditions.

VI. Releases

Although the donee of a testamentary power is not generally free to contract with respect to the power, the donee is free to release the power, in whole or in part, unless the donor has manifested an intent to prevent the donee from releasing the power. Suppose, for instance, donee has a general power to appoint property, and donee's daughter is the taker-in-default. Donee might then release her power, guaranteeing that her daughter will receive the appointive property. The effect of a release is often similar to the effect of a contract: donee binds herself to a particular disposition of the appointive property, even though the donor wanted donee to keep her options open for as long as possible. Nevertheless, courts and legislatures have explicitly authorized releases of powers of appointment. Initially, tax advantages were the impetus for making powers releasable. Today, those advantages have disappeared, but the doctrine permitting release has remained.

The effect of a total release of a power of appointment is to benefit the takers-in-default, who need no longer fear that an appointment will divest them of the appointive property. A donee can also execute a partial release, which narrows the freedom of choice otherwise available to the donee, but does not eliminate that freedom. For instance, if the donor gives the donee a general testamentary power to appoint, the donee might execute an instrument releasing her power to appoint the property to anyone but her issue. The release converts the general power into a special power, but nevertheless leaves the donee with considerable discretion. Similarly, if the donor gives the donee a special testamentary power to appoint among the donee's blood relatives, the donee might release her power to appoint to anyone but her issue, again narrowing the scope of donee's alternatives.

Sometimes, promisees of contracts to appoint have sought to enforce the contracts as enforceable releases rather than unenforceable contracts. Thus, if a donee has a general power to appoint, and then contracts to appoint in favor of a particular group of children, those children might assert a claim against the appointive property if the donee were subsequently to exercise the power of appointment in favor of his wife. Their claim would be that the donee has converted the general power into a special power. Hence, applying the powers in trust doctrine, the donee's exercise in favor of a non-object of the special power would lead to an equal distribution among the objects of the power: the beneficiaries of the purported release of the power.

Although there is authority to support the position of the promisees, there is also authority on the other side. In particular, the

New York legislature, after experience with the problem, enacted a statute providing that where the donor of a power designated takers-in-default, a release must serve to benefit all the takers-in-default. The statute limits the power of a donee to use a release to convert a general power into a special power, or to narrow the scope of a special power.

VII. Rights of Donee's Creditors in the Appointive Property

Suppose the donor has given the donee a power to appoint the principal of a $1,000,000 trust. What rights do creditors have to the appointive property? First consider creditors of the *donor*. If the donor has creditors at the time the donor creates a power in an *inter vivos* instrument, the donor's creditors would be free to attack the transfer that created the power as a fraudulent transfer (assuming the creditors could establish the requisites of fraudulent transfer law). But subsequent creditors of the donor would not have any rights against the appointive property.

Next, consider the rights of creditors of an appointee. If the donee appoints to an appointee who is in debt, the appointee's creditors may reach the appointive property. Of course, if the donee knows about those creditors, the donee may choose not to appoint to that appointee, and the creditor has no right to the appointive property until after the donee makes the appointment. These issues do not generate much controversy.

More significant issues arise when creditors of the donee seek to reach the appointive property. If we conceptualized the donee as merely an agent of the donor, distributing the donor's property as the donor wishes, then the donee's creditors should have no rights against the appointive property. But in reality, the donee frequently is in a position to derive personal benefit from the appointive property, especially when the power is general, and that potential for benefit suggests that creditors should be entitled to reach the appointive property. Doctrine in the area is settled with respect to some issues, but not with respect to others.

First, consider a principle that is beyond dispute: when the donee holds a special power of appointment, the donee's creditors cannot reach the appointive property. When the power is special, the donee cannot appoint in favor of herself. Instead, the donor has made the donee a mere agent, with power to choose among beneficiaries designated by the donor. In that circumstance, there is little reason to enable the donee's creditors to reach the appointive property at the expense of the donor's chosen beneficiaries. If the donor had chosen instead to give the property directly to the objects of the power, the donee's creditors would have had no claim to the property; donee's creditors should be no better off merely because donor has empowered the donee to choose among those objects.

Second, consider a principle that should be beyond dispute: when the donee holds a general, presently exercisable power of appointment, the donee's creditors should be entitled to reach the appointive property. When the donee holds a general, presently exercisable power, the donee can immediately appoint to herself and make the property her own. When the donor has given her such complete dominion over the appointive property, there appears to be little reason to treat the appointive property differently from the donee's personal assets—which would generally be available to the donee's creditors. That is the position taken by the Third Restatement of Trusts, and by statutes in New York and California. The principal holdout is a preliminary draft of the Third Restatement of Property, which would apply the equitable assets doctrine to all general powers, whether they are testamentary or presently exercisable.

That brings us to the issue that generates the most controversy: what rights do creditors of the donee have when the donee holds a general testamentary power? The common law rule—retained by the Third Restatement of Property—is that the donee's creditors can reach the appointive property *only if (and when) the donee actually exercises the power.* This rule, known as the **equitable assets doctrine**, effectively permits the insolvent donee to choose between having the appointive assets pass to his creditors, or to the takers-in-default. If, as is often the case, the takers-in-default are the donee's close family members, the donee is likely to choose not to exercise the power, leaving the creditors without redress. The rationale for the equitable assets doctrine lies in the common law's treatment of the appointive property as the property of the donor, despite the broad powers the donor has conferred on the donee. Only when the donee exercises the power does the donee make it her own, and thereby subject it to the claims of her own creditors.

A number of authorities reject the equitable assets doctrine, from a variety of different perspectives. At one extreme lies New York, which holds that the creditors of a donee have no rights against property subject to a general testamentary power—whether or not the donee exercises the power. By contrast, California would permit the donee's creditors to reach the appointive property at the death of the donee—but only if the donee's personal assets are insufficient to satisfy creditor claims. The Third Restatement of Trusts would go further, treating appointive property as the equivalent of the donee's personal property, except that creditors may not reach the appointive property until the donee's death.

Finally, if the donee becomes bankrupt during his lifetime, only general presently exercisable powers become a part of the bankruptcy estate. Because the donee could not exercise a special power, or a general testamentary power, in favor of his own current creditors, those creditors cannot reach the appointive property in a bankruptcy proceeding.

Problems

1.   Mother M died, leaving a will that created a trust, and directed that at the death of her son, S, the trust principal should be distributed "among S's descendants as S shall appoint by will." The residuary clause of M's will left the "remainder of my property to the Trustees of Bates College." When S died ten years later, S left a will providing "I leave all of my property to my daughter, X." S was survived by his only two children, X and Y.

At S's death, how should the trust principal be distributed?

How, if at all, would your answer be different if M's will had provided "if my son fails to appoint, I direct that the trust property be distributed, at my son's death, to my grandson, Y."?

2.   Mother M died, leaving the same will as in Problem 1. S died ten years later, leaving a will providing "I leave $100,000 to my daughter X, and the remainder of my property to the Roman Catholic Church." (Assume the value of S's net probate estate, at the time of S's death, was zero).

At S's death, how should the trust principal (now worth $500,000) be distributed?

3.   Mother M died, leaving the same will as in Problem 1. S died ten years later, leaving a will providing "I leave all of my property, including the property subject to the power of appointment created in my mother's will, to be divided in equal shares between my daughter X and the Roman Catholic Church."

At S's death, the trust principal is worth $300,000, and S's net probate estate is worth $500,000. How should the trust principal and S's net probate estate be distributed?

4.   Wife W created a trust providing income for husband H during H's lifetime, and giving H a power to appoint the trust principal, by will, in favor of the couple's children. The couple had two children, S and D. After W's death, H contracts to appoint in favor of D in return for D's promise of lifetime care. D cares for H for the rest of his life. H's last will, executed after the promise, exercises the power of appointment in favor of S, and leaves his entire estate to S.

To what is D entitled if the appointive property is valued at $300,000 and H had a personal estate of $100,000?

How, if at all, would your answer be different if the power was a power to appoint by will, and H released the power after contracting with D and before executing his last will?

5.   T's mother created a trust, giving T a right to income during T's lifetime, and giving T a general power to appoint the trust principal, by will. The trust instrument provided that in default of appointment, the trust principal should be distributed to T's issue, *per stirpes*. At T's death, T was survived by his son S and his daughter D. The appointive property was then worth $300,000, T had no personal assets of his own, and debts of $200,000.

How should the appointive property be distributed if

a.   T's will exercises the power of appointment in favor of his daughter;

b.   T's will provides "I do not exercise the power of appointment created in my mother's trust"; or

c.   T, during his lifetime, executed an instrument releasing his power of appointment?

6.   How, if at all, would your answers to Problem 5 change if

a.   T's mother had given T a power to appoint "by will or by deed"?

b.   T's mother had given T a power to appoint "by will, among his descendants"?

Chapter Ten

FUTURE INTERESTS

Wills and trust instruments frequently create interests designed to become possessory in the future. Decades may pass between the time the will or trust instrument takes effect and the time a holder of a future interest becomes entitled to possession. Unanticipated events are likely to occur in that period. In particular, some named beneficiaries may die, and other relatives may be born to the testator or the settlor of the trust. Especially when instruments are inartfully drafted, it may be difficult to determine how settlor would have wanted the trust property distributed had she known what events would actually occur. These uncertainties require principles of construction—principles that guide courts in effectuating the intention of the drafter of the instrument, and that guide drafters in crafting wills and trust instruments. An understanding of those construction principles, however, requires some familiarity with our system for classifying future interests.

I. Classification

A. What Is a Future Interest?

A future interest is one that does not become possessory immediately upon its creation. A future interest may follow an interest in trust or a legal life estate. Suppose, for instance, a settlor transfers property to T as trustee, with directions to pay income to B for life, and to distribute the principal to C at B's death. C's interest is a future interest because her right to possession is postponed until a time in the future—the time of B's death. (By contrast, B's interest is a present interest because B is entitled to the immediate beneficial enjoyment of the trust property).

Even if a future interest will not become possessory until some time in the future, the future interest is an enforceable legal right from the moment it is created. The word "present" or "future" preceding the word "interest" refers to the time of beneficial enjoyment, not to the existence of the legal right. That is, if settlor creates a trust with directions that at B's death, the trustee should distribute the trust principal to C, C has a future interest at the moment settlor creates the trust.

That future interest creates a variety of rights in C. First, C may bring an action against T for any acts by T that would impair C's interest. In particular, T might be liable to C for breach of fiduciary duty if T mismanages or misappropriates the trust property. In addition, C, as the holder of a future interest, may sell that interest even before the interest becomes possessory. Moreover, if the future interest follows a legal life estate in land, the holder of the future interest may bring an action for "waste" if the holder of the life estate takes actions that impair the value of the future interest. As a result of these rights, the future interest has an immediate present value to its holder.

B. Categories of Future Interests

In classifying a future interest, the first step is to determine who holds the future interest at the moment the future interest is created. At that moment, the future interest will be held either by the grantor of the property, or by someone else. If the future interest is held by the grantor, the future interest falls into one of three categories: a possibility of reverter, a right of entry (sometimes called a power of termination), or a reversion. By contrast, if the future interest is held by a transferee—someone other than the grantor—then the future interest must either be a remainder or an executory interest. So, in identifying a particular future interest, it is easiest to proceed by process of elimination: if the grantor created a future interest in herself, the grantor did not create a remainder or an executory interest; if the grantor created a future interest in a third party, the grantor did not create a reversion, a possibility of reverter, or a right of entry.

1. Future Interests in the Grantor

Future interests held by the grantor are less important for estate planning purposes than are future interests held by third parties. Few people seeking to transmit wealth intentionally create future interests in themselves. As a result, the differences among the three future interests a grantor may create in herself are of limited practical importance.

A possibility of reverter is the future interest remaining in a grantor who has created a determinable interest in someone else. A determinable interest is generally conceptualized as an interest that will end automatically upon the happening of a particular event. Thus, if O conveys land "to B and her heirs so long as the premises are used for residential purposes," B's interest will terminate automatically if and when the land ceases to be used for residential purposes. As a result, O holds a possibility of reverter.

By contrast, a right of entry is the future interest remaining in a grantor who has created, in someone else, a possessory interest subject to a condition subsequent. An interest subject to a condition subsequent is conceptualized as an interest that does not terminate automatically upon the happening of a particular event, but which the grantor may elect to terminate upon the happening of that event. Thus, if O conveys land "to B and her heirs, but if the property is used for nonresidential purposes, O may enter and terminate B's estate," O has a right of entry, not a possibility of reverter.

The differences between these two interests are not as well defined in practice as they are in theory, although an occasional case turns on the distinction between the two. By far the most common future interest retained by the grantor is the reversion—which can most easily be defined as any future interest in the grantor that is not a possibility of reverter or a right of entry. Thus, a reversion arises if a grantor who owns property in fee simple absolute conveys a life estate without specifying what happens at the expiration of the life estate. And when a grantor creates a future interest that is invalid under the Rule Against Perpetuities, the result is often a reversion in the grantor.

2. Future Interests in Persons Other than the Grantor: Remainders

Remainders are by far the most important of the future interests. In most circumstances, when a grantor creates either a life estate or a trust, the grantor will also create a remainder to take possession after the expiration of the life estate or the termination of the trust. Thus, if grantor creates a trust, with directions that the trust income be paid to her husband for his life, with the trust principal to be distributed to her children at the husband's death, the grantor has created a remainder in her children.

A grantor can create one of four different types of remainders. The four types are:

Indefeasibly Vested Remainders

Vested Remainders Subject to Partial Divestment (or Subject to Open)

Vested Remainders Subject to Complete Divestment

Contingent Remainders

An **indefeasibly vested remainder** is the easiest remainder to identify and understand. Subject to unimportant qualifications, a remainder is indefeasibly vested if the remainder is certain to become possessory whenever and however the preceding estates end, and if there can be no event which might act to divest or diminish the remainderman's interest, either before or after the remainder becomes possessory.

Thus, if T's will creates a trust, and provides that the trust income should be paid to T's husband H during his lifetime, with the trust principal to be distributed to T's daughter D at the husband's death, D has an indefeasibly vested remainder. D's remainder is certain to become possessory immediately upon H's death; it is not subject to any conditions. If D happens to die before H does, D's death does not divest D of the remainder; instead, the remainder passes through D's estate, either to the beneficiaries of D's will or, if D has left no will, to D's intestate heirs.

A **vested remainder subject to partial divestment**, like an indefeasibly vested remainder, is certain to become possessory. But unlike an indefeasibly vested remainder, a vested remainder subject to partial divestment may be diminished in size if events occur that increase the number of persons entitled to share in the remainder. Typically, a vested remainder subject to partial divestment arises when a grantor makes a gift to a class of persons, and the class is an "open" class: more members might be added to the class, principally by birth. For that reason, this remainder is often known as a *vested remainder subject to open.*

Suppose, for instance, T's will creates a trust, with income to be distributed to T's son, S, for life, remainder at S's death "to be distributed among S's children." At the time of T's death, S has two children, Y and Z. If S is still alive at T's death, S could have more children. As a result, the remainder in Y and Z, although vested, is subject to open or subject to partial divestment. That is, at T's death, Y and Z are certain to share in the remainder, but their current share—half of the remainder apiece—could easily shrink to a smaller percentage if S were to have more children after T's death.

Indefeasibly vested remainders and vested remainders subject to partial divestment are certain to become possessory estates. Some remainders, however, will never become possessory. Suppose, for instance, T's will creates a trust for the benefit of T's wife for life, with a remainder "to my son S if S survives my wife, and otherwise to my daughter D." If S dies before the wife, S's interest will not become possessory at all. We call S's interest a **contingent remainder**. We can generally tell whether a remainder is contingent by asking two questions.

First, is the remainder held by some ascertained person? If the answer is no, the remainder is contingent. Suppose, for instance, T creates a trust with the income to be paid to the daughter for life, with a "remainder to my daughter's children." At the time of T's death, his daughter has no children. No ascertainable person holds a remainder. Because a vested remainder must be vested in some person or persons, the remainder cannot be vested. As a result, the remainder in the daughter's children must be a contingent remainder.

Second, if the remainder is held by some ascertained person, one must ask whether the remainder is subject to a condition precedent. If the remainder is subject to a condition precedent, it is classified as a contingent remainder—even if the remainder is held by an ascertained person.

Some remainders are subject to conditions, and therefore are not certain to become possessory, but are nevertheless classified as vested remainders. When a remainder is subject to a condition subsequent rather than a condition precedent, the remainder is classified as a **vested remainder subject to complete divestment**.

These two remainders—the contingent remainder and the vested remainder subject to complete divestment—are the hardest to distinguish. The distinction between the two turns largely on the difference between a condition subsequent and a condition precedent. And that distinction is largely a matter of language rather than substance. The standard formulation provides that if the condition appears in the same clause as the grant to the remainderman, or in a clause before the grant to the remainderman, then the condition is a condition precedent, and the remainder is a contingent remainder. By contrast, if the only condition appears in a clause after the language of the grant, the condition is a condition subsequent, and the remainder is a vested remainder subject to complete divestment.

Consider some examples. First, suppose T devises property in trust "to A for life, remainder to B if B survives A, otherwise to C." The condition on B's grant appears in the same clause as the grant to B. As a result, the condition is a condition precedent, and the remainder is contingent. The same result would apply if the grant were "to A for life, then, if B survives A, remainder to B, otherwise to C." Here, the condition appears in a clause before the grant, and, once again, the condition is precedent. Consider, by contrast, a devise in trust "to A for life, remainder to B, but if B fails to survive A, then to C." Classic theory teaches that in this case, the condition on B's remainder is a condition subsequent: it appears in a clause after the clause making the grant to B. As a result, B's remainder is vested subject to complete divestment.

This distinction between contingent remainders and vested remainders subject to complete divestment may appear unduly fine. After all, in substance, the condition in these examples is identical: B's remainder becomes possessory if and only if B outlives A. In facts, courts do not often confront cases in which a lot turns on the placement of the comma. When they do confront such cases, they are likely to give the classic formulation some weight, but it is not invariably determinative. Courts are at least as likely to examine the identity of the beneficiaries and the effect of the alternative constructions on the grantor's dispositive scheme before deciding whether the remainder is contingent or vested.

3. *Future Interests in Persons Other than the Grantor: Executory Interests*

Although most future interests in persons other than the grantor are remainders, executory interests arise in two situations. First, by definition, a remainder cannot cut short or "divest" a vested remainder in fee simple. If a future interest in someone other than the grantor would operate to cut short a vested remainder in fee, that future interest must be an executory interest. Thus, executory interests typically follow vested remainders subject to complete divestment.

For instance, if T devises property in trust "to A for life, remainder to B, but if B fails to survive A, then to C", C holds an executory interest. Because B's interest is a vested remainder (albeit a vested remainder subject to complete divestment), the interest that follows B's interest cannot be a remainder. Hence, by process of elimination, C's interest is an executory interest. That is, any future interest in a person other than a grantor that is not a remainder is defined to be an executory interest.

The second category of executory interests arises when there is certain to be a time gap between the end of the prior estate and the time the future interest will become possessory. By definition, for a future interest to be a remainder, the interest must be one that is capable of becoming possessory upon the natural expiration of a prior estate created in the same instrument. If the interest cannot become possessory until after a "gap" in time, the interest cannot be a remainder, and must, again by process of elimination, be an executory interest.

For instance, if T's will creates a trust and directs that income be paid "to A for life, and one year after her death, I direct that the principal be distributed to B", B has an executory interest. B's future interest cannot become possessory immediately upon the expiration of A's life estate, and cannot, therefore, be a remainder.

Today, there is little practical difference between a remainder and an executory interest. Indeed, in some states, the distinction has been abolished altogether, by statute.

4. *Restatement Simplification*

In an effort to simplify the law of future interests, the Restatement (Third) of Property (Wills and Other Donative Transfers) abolishes the distinctions among contingent remainder, vested remainders subject to open, vested remainders subject to partial divestment, and executory interests. The Restatement distinguishes only between contingent and vested interests, and labels an interest as contingent if "it might not take effect in possession or enjoyment." The Restatement recognizes that for most purposes, the real issue facing both estate planners and estate litigators is not classification of future interests, but construction of those interests—a subject to which we now turn.

II. Construction of Future Interests

Classification of future interests has little intrinsic importance. Classification is important for two principal reasons: first, classification is essential to determine an interest's validity under the Rule Against Perpetuities, an issue reserved for Chapter Nine; second, classification is helpful in assisting courts in the construction of language that appears in wills or trust instruments. The language of the common law classification system has become a shorthand for discussing the grantor's intent. This section focuses on those construction issues.

A. The (Increasingly Modest) Preference for Early Vesting

Common law courts developed, as a principle of construction, a preference for the early vesting of estates. That is, in cases of ambiguity, common law courts historically preferred to construe estates as vested rather than contingent. This preference rested on several foundations other than the intent of the grantor. First, at common law, vested interests were alienable while contingent interests were not, so that the preference for early vesting increased alienability of land, and therefore efficiency of land use. Second, construing interests as vested often avoided invalidity under the Rule Against Perpetuities. Third, vested remainders accelerated into possession upon premature termination of preceding estates, while contingent remainders did not. For instance, suppose T's will devised property in trust to his brother B for life, remainder at B's death to B's nephew Y, but if Y fails to graduate from college, then to A. If Y's remainder were construed as contingent, and B disclaimed his interest, Y would not be entitled to possession, because contingent remainders could not accelerate into possession. By contrast, if Y's remainder were construed as vested, Y could take possession upon B's disclaimer.

The reasons for the preference for early vesting are not as strong today as they were a century ago. First, today, most property subject to future interests is held in trust, with a trustee who enjoys power to sell the trust property. As a result, concerns about alienability are less significant. Second, in most states, the Rule Against Perpetuities has been modified to reduce the number of instances in which the Rule would invalidate a future interest. Third, disclaimer statutes generally deal with the problem of premature termination by treating the disclaiming beneficiary as if she predeceased testator. Finally, when the future interest follows an interest held in trust, termination of the present interest before the remainder becomes possessory does not present overwhelming practical problems: the trustee can manage the trust property.

Moreover, the preference for early vesting can generate two significant costs. First, the preference will sometimes require reopening of a beneficiary's estate to permit distribution of the vested remainder when the remainder becomes possessory. Second, in some cases, the preference for early vesting can generate adverse estate tax consequences: if Y dies with a vested remainder, the remainder passes through, and is taxed in, Y's estate. By contrast, if courts construe Y's remainder as contingent, Y's death does not trigger any tax liability, because Y had no remainder to transmit.

As a result, courts today are less likely to rely on the preference for early vesting as a basic principle in construction of a future interest. Instead, courts are likely to focus more heavily on the intent of the grantor.

B.   Gifts to Individuals

Trust instruments do not always anticipate the wide variety of events which might occur between the time the settlor creates the trust and the time designated for distribution of the trust principal. In particular, trust instruments often fail to specify what should happen if some or all of the designated beneficiaries die before the time for distribution. For instance, suppose T's will creates a trust, with instructions to pay the income from the trust to T's brother B for life, "remainder at B's death to be divided between my nephew Y and my niece Z." What happens if, at the time of B's death, Y, or Z, or both, have died?

In some ways, the problem is analogous to the "lapse" problem that arises with respect to will construction. In each case, the problem is that a named beneficiary has died before the beneficiary has become entitled to possession of the property. But the problems are not identical. A will typically has no effect until testator's death. By contrast, when settlor has created a trust, the remainder beneficiaries of the trust have a property interest—a future interest—from the moment the trust becomes effective. (For this purpose, it doesn't matter whether the trust was created by will or by *inter vivos* trust instrument).

It is incorrect, therefore, to state that a gift of a future interest lapses if the beneficiary dies before her interest becomes possessory. It is also incorrect to apply anti-lapse statutes to such gifts. Drafters must be careful to anticipate, and to provide explicitly for, as many contingencies as possible. Rules of construction, however, have developed to deal with the unexpected death of beneficiaries.

1.   No Implied Condition of Survivorship

Consider a will or trust instrument in which T provides a life interest to his brother B for life, "remainder at B's death to my nephew Y." Suppose Y has died before B, leaving a surviving daughter, D, and a will disposing of all of his property to his wife, W. How should the trust remainder be distributed at B's death?

Note that the question is ultimately one of ascertaining T's intent: what meaning did T intend to convey with the words he used in the trust instrument? The problem, of course, is that T did not anticipate that Y would die before B (and his lawyer did not suggest the possibility—or any solutions—to him!). More precise drafting could have eliminated any ambiguity in the trust instrument.

In the absence of that precise drafting, three distributions of the remainder are plausible:

1.   A court could determine that Y's remainder was indefeasibly vested at the time the trust was created, and that Y was therefore free to dispose of the remainder as he wished. On this theory, W, as the beneficiary of Y's will, would take the remainder.

2.   A court could imply a condition of survivorship into Y's remainder, concluding that Y's remainder was contingent, and that upon Y's failure to survive, the remainder should be distributed to the residuary legatees or intestate heirs of T.

3.   A court could apply principles analogous to those embodied in the anti-lapse statute, concluding that Y's remainder was contingent upon survivorship, and that Y's issue had an alternative contingent remainder in the event that Y did not survive. On this theory, because Y did not survive B, Y's daughter would take the remainder.

Common law courts have generally embraced the first of these three alternatives: no conditions of survivorship will be implied. They have done so for a variety of reasons. First, common law courts did not consider alternative (3), largely because in the absence of language in the trust instrument suggesting an alternative contingent remainder in Y's issue, there appeared to be little basis for finding such a remainder. Second, alternative (2) would typically frustrate T's intentions. T does not typically expect that the trust assets will revert to his own estate after that estate has been fully distributed. Moreover, in most instances where T devises the remainder of a trust to Y, T would prefer that Y's chosen beneficiaries (who will often be Y's issue or other close family) should take that trust remainder rather than having the property pass to other relatives of T. Often, having the property pass to other relatives of T would distort T's estate plan. For instance, suppose T divided his estate among three separate trusts, one for the family of each of his three siblings, A, B, and C. If the trust for B provided for the remainder to be paid to Y and B's death, and if courts were to imply a condition of survivorship, the share allocated to B's family would instead be distributed to A's trust and C's trust, while B's grandchild would take nothing. The common law rule—no implied conditions of survivorship—recognizes that in most circumstances, T would want to avoid such a result.

2. *Express Conditions of Survivorship*

Grantors are free to impose express survivorship conditions on future interests. Too often, however, the language used by grantor is unclear, raising construction issues. Two problems recur: how express must the survivorship condition be, and how long must the holder of the future interest survive?

a. *Ambiguous Survivorship Language*

Consider first the grantor who imposes ambiguous survivorship conditions. The classic problem involves a grantor whose trust instrument imposes express survivorship conditions in the event the holder of the future interest dies with surviving issue, but says nothing about survivorship if the holder of the future interest dies without surviving issue. Should the grant be construed to require survivorship in all circumstances, or only in the limited circumstances specified in the grant?

Thus, suppose the trust instrument provides that the trust income should be distributed to settlor's wife for her life, and at the wife's death, the principal should be distributed

> "to my children A and B. If, however, either A or B should die before the death of my wife, leaving issue, I direct that the issue should take the share their parent would have taken if then living, share and share alike."

In this instance, grantor has provided expressly (1) that A takes A's share if A survives the wife; and (2) that A's issue take A's share if A does not survive the wife, but dies leaving issue. The grantor has, not however, provided at all for (3) A does not survive the wife, but dies without issue (perhaps leaving a will calling for distribution to A's spouse, or a charity, or other friends or relatives).

The most common response to this problem is to hold that if A predeceases the wife without issue, A's estate takes the future interest. The rationale typically offered is that grantor has created a vested remainder subject to complete divestment. The only divesting condition expressed in the grant, however, is death before the wife leaving issue. If the divesting condition is not met, because A had no issue, then, upon A's death, the remainder vested indefeasibly in A's estate.

This solution, however, undoubtedly frustrates the intent of some grantors, because it diverts property away from grantor's blood relatives. Nevertheless, courts have invoked the preference in favor of early vesting, together with the omission of words of survivorship, to support the conclusion that A's estate takes the remainder.

b.   *Survivorship of Whom?*

Sometimes, a trust instrument expressly imposes a survivorship requirement, without expressly identifying the person the holder of the future interest must survive. Consider, for instance, a grant "*to my wife for life, remainder to my surviving children.*" The grantor certainly intended to exclude the estates of children who do not survive, but the grantor has not expressly indicated whether the children must survive the grantor himself or the wife. The difference can be significant. Suppose, for instance, one child survives the decedent, but not the decedent's wife. If the grant were construed to require survivorship of the wife, the other children would share the remainder, to the exclusion of the deceased child. If, on the other hand, the grant were construed to require survivorship only of the decedent, the deceased child's estate would take the deceased child's share.

Courts generally resolve this problem by holding that when the grant includes a survivorship requirement, but includes no language specifying the date to which the beneficiary must survive, the beneficiary is entitled to take only if the beneficiary survives until the date at which the beneficiary's interest becomes possessory. Thus, if the grant provides "to my wife for life, remainder to my surviving children," children must survive the wife to be eligible to share in the remainder. That is, in this situation, courts do not apply the preference for early vesting.

3.   Uniform Probate Code Section 2–707

In 1990, the drafters of the Uniform Probate Code promulgated section 2–707, a controversial provision which, if widely accepted, would revolutionize the construction provisions applicable to future interests. Section 2–707(b) provides: "A future interest under the terms of a trust is contingent on the beneficiary's surviving the distribution date." In other words, the statute would reverse the common law principle that survivorship conditions should not be implied. The statute would not, however, permit future interests to fail if the holder of the interest dies before the distribution date. Instead, the statute provides that "a substitute gift is created in the beneficiary's surviving descendants." Suppose, for instance, T, by will, creates a trust, income payable to T's husband H for his life, remainder at H's death "to H's niece, N." The statute provides that N's interest is contingent; if N fails to survive H, N doesn't take. However, if N leaves surviving descendants, those descendants take the trust property at H's death.

The UPC also changes the effect of trust language expressly creating a survivorship condition. Suppose a trust instrument provides "to my wife, W, for life, remainder to my cousin C if she survives W." As we have seen, at common law, C would be entitled to take only if C survived W. Otherwise, the trust property would, at W's death, pass back to settlor's estate, and ultimately through the residuary clause of settlor's will, or through intestate succession. UPC § 2–707, however, would instead create a substitute gift in favor of C's descendants—even though the language of settlor's trust instrument expressly requires C to survive W!

The UPC provision has some advantages. In particular, the statute reduces the number of transmissible remainders testators might inadvertently create, and thus has the potential to reduce the tax bills of estates served by poorly-trained lawyers. On the other hand, many fear that the statute has the potential to frustrate the intention of many grantors whose lawyers fail to adjust to the statute's radical changes.

C.   Class Gifts

1.   Introduction

A class gift is a gift to members of a class rather than to particular designated individuals. Thus, if a trust settlor gives his wife an income interest in trust, and provides that at the wife's death, the trust principal should be divided among "my children" or "my nieces and nephews" or "my issue by representation," settlor has made a class gift.

Why would a trust settlor make a class gift rather than a gift to individuals? First, the settlor knows that his family will change over time. If settlor created a future interest only in children or grandchildren identified by name, afterborn children or grandchildren would not be entitled to share in the future interest. By making a class gift, settlor can provide for relatives he did not know at the time he created the trust.

Class gifts, however, raise a number of significant construction questions. Most of these questions can be avoided by careful drafting. Unfortunately, not all drafters are careful. Courts have developed principles of construction to deal with wills and trust instruments that are less-than-explicit about the drafter's intent. This section explores those principles.

2.   *Increases in the Class: The Class Closing Rule of Convenience*

Suppose a trust settlor creates a trust during her lifetime, and directs that the trust income be paid to her sister for life, with the principal to be distributed at her death "to my grandchildren in equal shares." Which grandchildren share the trust principal?

Consider first the easiest question: should grandchildren born after creation of the trust, but before sister's death, be entitled to share? The answer is yes. By making a class gift to "grandchildren" rather than gifts to individual grandchildren by name, settlor signaled that the principal should not be limited to those grandchildren alive when the trust was created. If settlor had wanted to limit the remainder to those grandchildren alive at creation of the interest, settlor could have identified them by name. Moreover, no good practical reason exists for excluding grandchildren born after creation of the trust, but before the sister's death.

Move to a more difficult question: should grandchildren born after the sister's death be entitled to share in the trust remainder? The common law's answer is no. The common law has developed a **"class closing rule"**, also called the **"rule of convenience"**, which *closes membership in a class when at least one member of the class has become entitled to possession of the property that is the subject of the class gift.*

Consider the reasons for the class closing rule. Suppose we adopted a rule permitting all grandchildren, whenever born, to share in the trust principal. How much could we distribute to those grandchildren alive at the sister's death? If each grandchild would be entitled to an equal share, we have to know how many shares there will be before we can make a distribution. But we will not know definitively how many shares there will be until the death of settlor's last surviving child—which may occur long after the sister's death. Therefore, if we permitted all grandchildren to share, we could make no distribution to grandchildren living at the sister's death. Would that result reflect settlor's intent? Almost invariably, the answer is no. When settlor provides for distribution of principal to her grandchildren at the sister's death, she intends that her grandchildren will receive money at that time—not years later when it is no longer physiologically possible for additional grandchildren to be born.

To summarize, then, when a grantor makes a class gift, membership in the class may continue to increase until at least one member of the class becomes entitled to possession. When one member becomes entitled to possession, the class "closes" and subsequently-born members of the class are excluded from participating in the class gift.

Consider an example of the rule's application. Suppose O creates an inter vivos trust, and directs that trust income be paid to his son S until his son's marriage. O directs that at S's marriage, the trust principal should be distributed "to my nieces and nephews." O had one niece, X, at the time she created the trust. Another niece, Y, was born before S's marriage, and at the time of S's marriage, it appears likely that O's brother will have more children. Who is entitled to share in the trust principal? X and Y may both share, but subsequently born children of O's brother may not share. The class "closed" at the time of S's marriage, because at that time, X and Y became eligible to participate. If we allowed subsequently born nieces and nephews to share, we would not be able to distribute anything to X or Y until the class of nieces and nephews closed "naturally" upon the death of O's last surviving sibling. (Once O's last surviving sibling dies, no additional nieces and nephews can be born, so we say that the class of nieces and nephews closes naturally at that time).

The common law recognizes one significant exception to the class closing rule: if, at the time an interest is intended to become possessory, no member of the class has yet been born, then the class closing rule will not apply, and we will wait for the class to close naturally. Thus, in the previous example, if, at the time of S's wedding, none of O's siblings yet had children, the class would not close upon the birth of O's first niece or nephew; the remainder would not be distributed until the death of all of O's siblings, when the class of nieces or nephews would close "naturally" or "physiologically."

Recently, there has been a move to create another narrow exception, applicable only to children conceived after the death of a genetic parent through the use of frozen sperm or frozen embryos. In limited circumstances, UPC § 2–705(g) would keep the class open for up to 45 months after the scheduled date for distribution in order to accommodate children of assisted reproduction.

3.   *Single-Generation and Multiple-Generation Class Gifts: Survivorship Issues*

If a grantor makes a gift of a future interest "to my children" or "to my grandchildren" or "to my brothers and sisters", the members of the class of beneficiaries are all of the same generation—either the grantor's own generation (as in the case of "to my brothers and sisters") or the generation of grantor's children or the generation of grantor's grandchildren.

By contrast, if the grantor makes a gift of a future interest "to my issue" or "to my descendants" or to "my brothers and sisters and their issue", the members of the class of beneficiaries may be of different generations. Grantor's issue or descendants include his children, grandchildren, and great grandchildren. The issue of grantor's brothers and sisters include nieces and nephews, but also grandnieces and grandnephews.

a.   *Multiple Generation Class Gifts*

Multiple-generation class gifts typically raise fewer construction questions than single-generation class gifts. When a grantor creates a future interest in "issue" or "descendants", the issue or descendants are determined at the time the interest becomes possessory. A remainder to "issue" or "descendants" is by definition a contingent remainder; a grantor would only use these terms if the grantor intended (a) to include persons born after creation of the remainder and (b) to include only persons who are alive at the time the interest becomes possessory. The distribution of shares among issue will generally be determined in accordance with the jurisdiction's intestate succession statutes, unless the will or trust instrument specifies another method of distribution.

Thus, if a trust settlor creates a trust for the benefit of his daughter, X, for life, with the remainder to be distributed at X's death "to my descendants," the principal of the trust will be distributed as if the decedent had died intestate at the moment of X's death. For instance, suppose, at X's death, decedent's surviving issue included decedent's son, A, X's daughter, B, and two children, C and D, of a deceased son. If the jurisdiction's intestate succession statute provides generally for a "modern per stirpes" distribution, A and B would each take one-third of the principal, while C and D would each take one-sixth; if the jurisdiction's statute were based on the Uniform Probate Code's representation scheme, A would take one-third, and B, C, and D would each take two-ninths.

b.   Single Generation Class Gifts: No Implied Conditions of Survivorship

Construction issues are more complicated when a grantor creates a single-generation class gift. The most basic question is similar to the question that arises with gifts to individuals: should we imply a condition of survivorship? And the most common answer—although not an invariable one—is the same as with gifts to individuals: conditions of survivorship should not be implied.

Consider for instance a will in which testator creates a trust for the benefit of her husband for life, and directs that, after her husband's death, trust principal should be divided among "my children." Suppose testator had three children, two of whom were alive at the husband's death. Suppose further that the third child had died survived by a wife and daughter, and a will leaving all of his property to his wife. At common law, the remainder in the children was indefeasibly vested at settlor's death. As a result, upon the husband's death, the property would generally be divided into equal shares, one to each of the two living children, and the third to the estate of the deceased son—which would be distributed to the son's wife in accordance with the son's will.

The no-implied-condition-of-survivorship rule has been applied most frequently when the deceased member of the class died intestate, or died leaving a will devising his estate to some or all of his descendants. In that situation, the rule almost certainly reflects the intent of the grantor.

When, by contrast, the deceased class member's will left his estate to a spouse, or to a person outside the family, the rule may frustrate the intent of the grantor. In that situation, if the deceased class member died without issue, some courts might imply a survivorship condition, thus preserving the trust property for blood relatives of the grantor. But if the deceased class member died with issue, that result, too, threatens to frustrate grantor's intent, because it leaves one branch of decedent's family—the descendants of the deceased class member, with no share of the remainder. A third approach would be to treat the single-generation class gift to children as a multiple-generation class gift to issue—thus permitting descendants of the deceased class member, rather than devisees of that class member, to take the class member's share of the trust principal.

Many courts, however, have refused to treat a gift to children as a gift to issue, noting that if the grantor had wanted the issue of the deceased class member to take rather than the class member's devisees, the grantor could have made a multiple-generation class gift—to issue, or to descendants. Because the grantor (or the grantor's lawyer) instead created a single-generation class gift to children, these courts conclude that we should presume the grantor intended something different—a vested remainder in the children, which includes a right to devise the remainder. These courts, therefore, adhere to the no-implied-condition-of survivorship rule.

c.   Single-Generation   Class   Gifts: Express   Survivorship Conditions

A grantor might try to avoid the no-implied-conditions-of-survivorship rule by imposing an express condition of survivorship. For instance, grantor could create a trust for the lifetime of her husband, and then provide that at the husband's death, the principal should be distributed "to my surviving children, in equal shares." Unfortunately, this language, too, invites litigation about construction of the trust instrument. The problem is this: did the grantor intend to exclude issue of deceased children from sharing in the trust principal?

The traditional answer is yes: if the grantor had wanted to provide for issue of deceased children, grantor would have made a multiple-generation class gift to issue or descendants, not a single-generation class gift to children. If grantor made a single-generation class gift, and included a survivorship condition, only surviving members of the single generation are entitled to take.

Again, the traditional answer has been subject to considerable criticism. The critics contend that the gift to "surviving children" does not, in most cases, reflect a deliberate decision to exclude issue of deceased children, but reflects instead inadequate lawyering by the drafter of the trust instrument. As we shall see, the critics have prevailed in the drafting of section 2–707 of the Uniform Probate Code.

Another construction problem arises when the grantor includes ambiguous survivorship language in a class gift. The most common example is the grant that directs distribution of principal "in equal portions among my children, the children of any deceased child taking their deceased parents' share." As with gifts to individuals, this sort of grant makes it clear that (1) surviving children share in the remainder and (2) the interests of deceased children who leave children are divested in favor of those children. The grant does not make it clear what happens to the interests of children who die without leaving children. The traditional approach is to conclude that the quoted language creates a vested remainder that is subject to divestment only in one circumstance: when a child has died before the distribution date leaving children. If the child has died without leaving children, then the divesting condition has not occurred, and the property is distributed through the deceased child's estate.

Each of these construction problems can be avoided by the drafter who takes care to avoid single-generation class gifts. In most cases, when a grantor wants to make a class gift, the grantor's intention is to make a multiple-generation class gift. In cases where that is not the grantor's intention, the grantor's lawyer should, in any event, use careful language to indicate expressly what should happen to the future interest of a class member who does not survive until the date of distribution.

4.　*UPC § 2–707*

Section 2–707 of the Uniform Probate Code would significantly alter the common law's traditional construction principles surrounding class gifts. First, section 2–707(b)(2) abandons the no-implied-conditions-of-survivorship rule. The statute adopts instead a construction that treats a single-generation class gift as if it were a multiple-generation class gift. That is, if a trust settlor were to provide that trust income be paid to her husband for life, remainder at the husband's death to her children, the remainder would be distributed to (1) those children who survived the husband and (2) the surviving descendants of any deceased children. The estates of deceased children would not share in the trust principal. Put in other terms, the Uniform Probate Code does not treat a class gift to a single generation class as a vested remainder; instead the Code treats the gift as remainder contingent upon survivorship until the date of distribution.

Section 2–707 also rejects the common law's treatment of express survivorship conditions. The statute provides that words of survivorship are not, in the absence of additional evidence, sufficient to preclude descendants of a deceased beneficiary from sharing in the future interest. That is, the statute creates a substitute gift in descendants of a deceased class member, even if the trust instrument, by its terms, requires survivorship. Suppose, for instance, a settlor creates a trust for the life of her daughter, and provides that at the daughter's death, the principal should be distributed "among my surviving grandchildren." The UPC would entitle all surviving grandchildren to share in the trust remainder, but would also entitle issue of deceased grandchildren to share in the remainder. The assumption behind the statute is that use of the term "surviving grandchildren" reflects careless drafting by the settlor's lawyer, not an intent in the settlor to exclude issue of deceased grandchildren.

The statute does, however, provide that if the trust instrument includes an alternative devise for situations in which the class member does not survive to the date of distribution, the alternative devise prevails over the statute's "substitute gift" to issue. Thus, if the trust instrument provides that upon the death of settlor's child, the trust property should be distributed "among my surviving grandchildren, but if any grandchild fails to survive my last surviving child, that grandchild's share shall be divided among my surviving grandchild", issue of deceased grandchildren would not be entitled to share in the trust principal; the language of the trust instrument is sufficiently clear to overcome the statutory presumption that settlor intended the equivalent of a multiple-generation class gift. Similarly, if a trust instrument were to provide that upon the death of settlor's child, the trust property should be distributed "among my grandchildren, but if any grandchild fails to survive my last surviving child, that grandchild's share should be distributed to the grandchild's estate," a deceased grandchild's share would pass through the estate, and not to the grandchild's descendants. In other words, UPC § 2–707 develops rules of construction, but clear language in the trust instrument prevails over the statutory construction rules.

5.   *Gifts to Heirs*

In some circumstances, the grantor of an interest in trust creates a future interest in "my heirs" or in the heirs of some other person. The gift to the class of heirs is a gift to the persons who would take under the intestate succession statute of the jurisdiction. The principal construction difficulty is determining at what moment the heirs should be determined. A hypothetical illustrates the problem. Suppose testator's will creates a trust for the benefit of his wife for life, with the remainder at the wife's death to be distributed "to my heirs." At testator's death, his heirs, under the applicable intestate succession statute, are his wife, a brother, a sister, and a niece (the child of a deceased brother). The wife outlives the testator by twenty years, and at the wife's death, testator's sister has died childless with a will leaving all of her property to the American Red Cross, and the niece has died, survived by a son and a husband, and a will leaving all of her property to her husband. How should the trust principal be distributed?

One approach, influenced by the common law's preference for early vesting, is that the grantor's heirs are to be determined at the moment of the grantor's death. That is, the brother and sister who survived testator, together with the niece, each have indefeasibly vested remainders from the moment of testator's death. When the wife dies, the brother takes his share, the sister's share passes by her will to the American Red Cross, and the niece's share passes by her will to her husband. (Even though testator's wife would have been a taker under the intestate succession statute, she would not have been treated as an heir, and her estate would not have shared in the trust principal).

An alternative approach, endorsed by Uniform Probate Code Section 2–711, is that heirs should be determined at the moment of distribution. That is, we would determine who would be entitled to take testator's estate if testator had died at the moment of his wife's death, survived by relatives then alive. On this approach, the trust principal would be equally divided between testator's brother and his grandnephew (the only child of testator's only niece). Those were testator's only living relatives at the time of his wife's death, and equal division would be required by virtually any intestate succession scheme.

Both approaches find support in the case law. Moreover, the problem arises not only with an express gift of a future interest to heirs, but also when grantor has failed to dispose of a future interest, or has done so invalidly (perhaps because of a violation of the Rule Against Perpetuities). The advantage of the common law approach is that it avoids long-term contingency—the very policy that underlies the Rule Against Perpetuities. The advantage of the Uniform Probate Code approach is that there is less need to reopen the estate of people long dead to distribute the principal of the trust, and a reduced possibility of adverse estate tax consequences.

6.   Class Gifts of Income

A final construction issue involves class gifts of income. Suppose, for instance, settlor creates a trust, and directs that income from the trust be divided "among my children until the death of my last surviving child, at which time the trust principal should be distributed to the American Red Cross." What happens to the trust income as various of settlor's children dies? The standard approach is to treat the children as the equivalent of joint tenants with a right of survivorship: as each child dies, the remaining children share in the trust income until the income interest terminates with the death of the last surviving child.

There are circumstances, however, in which courts might hold that the trust's language demonstrates sufficient contrary intent to overcome the standard construction. Suppose the trust instrument includes the same language creating an income interest, but a different remainder: the trust income is to be divided "among my children until the death of my last surviving child, at which time the trust principal should be distributed among my descendants, by representation." On these facts, a court might conclude that if settlor wants descendants of deceased children to share in the trust principal, settlor would also want descendants of deceased children to share in the trust income.

Problems

1.   T's testamentary trust provides that income shall be distributed to T's wife, W, during W's lifetime, with the remainder at W's death to be distributed among W's sisters, A, B, and C.

At T's death, A has already died, survived by her husband D and a will leaving all of her property to her son, E. B dies after T's death, but before W's death, survived by her daughter, F. B's will left all of her property to the American Red Cross. C survived W.

How and when should the principal of T's trust be distributed?

How, if at all, would your answer change if UPC 2–707 is in effect?

2.   T's testamentary trust provides that income shall be distributed to T's wife, W, during W's lifetime, and the principal should be distributed at W's death "to my sister S, if she survives W." T's will includes a residuary clause leaving the remainder of T's estate "to my brother, B."

S died after T's death, but before W's death. S's will left all of her property to her husband, H, and nothing to her daughter, D.

How should the trust principal be distributed at W's death?

How, if at all, would your answer change if UPC 2–707 is in effect?

3.   T's testamentary trust provides that income shall be distributed to T's husband, H, during H's lifetime, with the remainder at H's death to be distributed "in equal shares to my grandchildren."

At T's death, T has two grandchildren, A (age 15) and B (age 10). H survives T by 10 years. By the time of H's death, T has three more grandchildren, C, D, and E. In addition, A has died, leaving a daughter, F, and a will leaving her property to her husband, G. After H's death, T's daughter gives birth to two more children, J and K.

How and when should the principal of T's trust be distributed?

How, if at all, would your answer change if UPC 2–707 is in effect?

4.   T's testamentary trust provides that income shall be distributed to T's sister S, during S's lifetime, with the remainder at S's death to be distributed "in equal shares to my grandchildren."

S dies a year after T. At the time of S's death, T has no grandchildren. T's only daughter, D, ultimately has three children, X (born two years after S's death), Y (born five years after S's death), and Z (born seven years after S's death).

How and when should the principal of T's trust be distributed?

5.   T's testamentary trust provides that income should be distributed to his children for life until the death of his last surviving child. At the death of that child, trust principal should be distributed "to my grandchildren in equal shares, the children of any deceased grandchild taking their deceased parent's share."

T had three children, A, B, and C. C was the survivor of the three. At C's death, A's only child, D, was still alive. Two of B's children, E and F, predeceased C, leaving no issue, and leaving B's third child, G, as their only heir. C left one surviving child, H. C's other child, J, predeceased C, with a will leaving all of her property to her husband, K. J and K have an only child, L.

At C's death, how should the principal of T's trust be distributed?

Chapter Eleven

THE RULE AGAINST PERPETUITIES

I. Introduction

The Rule Against Perpetuities limits the power of trust settlors to create contingent future interests. The Rule's legendary intricacy has frustrated many an estate plan, spawned countless litigations, and tortured many law students. Dissatisfaction with the Rule has, in recent decades, generated significant reform and, in a number of states, outright abolition of the Rule. Nevertheless, the common law Rule remains in effect in a number of states, and remains the foundation for perpetuities reform statutes in other states. An understanding of the Rule remains important to avoid drafting errors and to navigate through the reform legislation.

This chapter focuses primarily on the common law Rule Against Perpetuities. After we explore the common law Rule, we will turn to the various types of reform legislation—some, but not all, of which build on the common law Rule. First, consider the classic statement of the Rule:

> *No interest is good unless it must vest, if at all, not later than twenty-one years after some life in being at the creation of the interest.*

The Rule Against Perpetuities originally arose as a judicially-developed compromise between wealthy landowners who wanted to tie up their land for generations and those who wanted to escape from restrictions imposed by their ancestors. If a landowner were able to tie up land with an endless succession of contingent life interests, the landowner would effectively make the land inalienable into the future: no group of people would be able to sell the land, even if all living current owners agree that the land would be used more efficiently by a prospective purchaser. Thus, by limiting the duration of future contingent interests in land, the Rule Against Perpetuities promoted efficient use of land.

These concerns about inalienability are less significant with respect to interests held in trust: the trustee holds legal title to trust property, and is free to sell it to persons when sale would benefit the trust beneficiaries. But claims of intergenerational equity remain. Many people believe it is simply unfair to permit members of the current generation, by tying up property with future interests and trusts, to prevent members of future generations from giving effect to their own preferences about use and disposition of property.

211

The premise behind the Rule is that people with property should be permitted to tie up their property for a reasonable period of time—but no longer. The Rule defines reasonableness indirectly, in terms of life events rather than a period of years. For instance, the Rule permits a person to tie up property for the lifetime of any person known to decedent—for the lifetime of any person alive at the time decedent creates that person's interest. In this way, the Rule permits a wealthy person to provide for a child or other relative with a known propensity to squander money. Indeed, the Rule allows a wealthy person to extend his control even further. Suppose, for instance, that at the death of the profligate beneficiary, decedent's ultimate beneficiaries, perhaps his grandchildren, are minor children. The Rule permits decedent to keep the property in trust, and thus to avoid distribution to ultimate beneficiaries, until 21 years past the death of people alive when decedent created the interest. In effect, then, the Rule Against Perpetuities permits the wealthy decedent to control the disposition of her property for the lifetime of persons whose propensities she knows or fears, and for 21 years thereafter.

By contrast, a wealthy decedent has no reason to know which of his more remote descendants might need protection from their own imprudence. Under these circumstances, the Rule deems it unreasonable for decedent to impose contingencies on the power of these remote descendants to use the property. Put in other terms, the general idea behind the Rule is that it is unreasonable for a decedent to attempt to control property beyond the period during which decedent might plausibly assert some special knowledge of the propensities of one of her beneficiaries. This basic understanding of the Rule's policies might make it easier to understand and apply the existing Rule.

II. The Rule's Operation

A. What Interests Are Subject to the Rule?

The Rule Against Perpetuities is a rule against contingency. The Rule requires that every interest "vest" or "fail" within the Rule's period: lives in being plus 21 years. A corollary to this principle is that a rule that is vested upon its creation can never violate the Rule Against Perpetuities.

First, present possessory interests are, by definition, vested interests, and therefore not subject to the Rule Against Perpetuities. Thus, if a grantor creates a life estate, or a life interest in trust that entitles a beneficiary to an immediate right to possession, or an immediate right to income from the trust, the interest cannot violate the Rule because the interest is already vested.

Second, future interests held by the grantor of an interest in property are by definition vested, and hence not subject to the Rule Against Perpetuities. This rule is not of significant importance in estates practice, because few grantors execute wills or trust instruments that create future interests in themselves; their objective is to transmit their wealth, not to arrange for its return to their estate.

The primary application of the Rule Against Perpetuities is to future interests in parties other than the grantor. And with respect to those interests, the Rule's focus is on contingency. Contingent interests increase the opportunity for a dead property owner to control ownership or use of property from the grave. Once an interest has vested in a particular beneficiary, the dead property owner has lost the opportunity to control the property (or his family). By limiting the duration of contingency, the Rule Against Perpetuities limits the settlor's ability to control his family from the grave.

As a result, interests vested when created are always valid. Only interests that are not vested when created are subject to the Rule, and require more careful evaluation. For purposes of the Rule, two kinds of interests—indefeasibly vested remainders and vested remainder subject to complete divestment—are vested interests. *Vested remainders subject to partial divestment (or subject to open) are not vested remainders for purposes of the Rule.* We will explore that counterintuitive statement when we discuss class gifts. Our principal concern, then, is identifying vested remainders subject to open, contingent remainders, and executory interests. Those are the interests to which the Rule applies.

B.   Applying the Rule

1.   *"Vesting" of Interests*

The Rule Against Perpetuities requires that an interest must vest, if at all, within lives in being plus 21 years measured from the moment of the interest's creation. That is, the Rule Against Perpetuities is a rule designed to limit the duration of contingent interests. A contingent interest stops being contingent in one of two ways: it becomes a vested interest, or it fails altogether—that is, facts evolve to ensure that the condition that made the interest contingent will never be satisfied.

To understand the Rule, then, it is essential to understand what it means for an interest to vest, and what it means for an interest to fail to vest. Future interests change over time. As we have seen, if an interest is vested at the time of creation, the interest is valid under the Rule Against Perpetuities. But interests that are initially contingent may become vested over time. For instance, suppose settlor creates a trust directing that income should be distributed to his wife, A, for her life, with the principal to be distributed "to my daughter D if she has then graduated from college, otherwise to my niece, N." At the time the trust is created, D's remainder is contingent, because she has not yet satisfied the condition attached to her remainder—she has not graduated from college. If, however, D graduates from college five years after settlor creates the trust, the contingency has been removed and D's interest has vested indefeasibly; even if she is not yet entitled to distribution of the trust principal (because her mother is still alive), her interest is certain to become possessory at her mother's death. This example illustrates an important principle: *a future interest may vest before it becomes possessory.* This principle is important because the Rule Against Perpetuities does not require that an interest become possessory within the period of the Rule; it requires only that the interest *vest* within the period of the Rule. In evaluating a contingent future interest for compliance with the Rule, then, one must determine the last moment at which the interest could be transformed into a vested interest.

Not all contingent future interests will vest. Indeed, when we label an interest "contingent," we are conceding that the interest will vest only if a particular contingency actually occurs. If the contingency does not occur, the interest fails; that is, the interest will never vest and never become possessory.

Reconsider the trust to settlor's wife, A, for life, with principal to be distributed "to my daughter D if she has then graduated from college, otherwise to my niece, N." If D graduates from college five years after the grant, while her mother is still alive, we have seen that D's interest vests indefeasibly. But D's graduation from college also has an effect on N's contingent remainder: as a result of D's graduation, N's interest fails. The condition necessary for N's interest to vest—D's failure to graduate from college during her mother's lifetime—can never occur.

Note that whether a contingent remainder fails has nothing to do with the Rule Against Perpetuities. Contingent interests fail because the required contingencies do not occur. In order to avoid a common confusion about application of the Rule Against Perpetuities, the following proposition is critical to understand: *to say that a contingent interest fails is not equivalent to saying that the interest is invalid under the Rule Against Perpetuities!* The grant in the preceding paragraph illustrates the principle. At the time settlor created the trust, it was certain that either the interest in D or the interest in N would eventually fail. But both interests are perfectly valid under the Rule Against Perpetuities. Why? Because we will know whether the interests will vest or fail at the death of A, settlor's wife—and that is a time within the period of the Rule. Neither D's interest nor N's interest can remain contingent past the date of A's death, and the Rule, as we have seen, is a rule against contingency.

2.   *Measuring Lives*

To be valid, an interest must vest, in Gray's words, "not later than twenty-one years after some life in being at the creation of the interest." The Rule Against Perpetuities is a rule of proof: if you can *prove* that an interest will vest within the period of "twenty-one years after some life in being," you have proven that the interest does not violate the Rule. In evaluating an interest under the Rule, one must seek to identify a life in being—a so-called "measuring life" or "validating life"—where it is possible to guarantee that the interest in question will vest within twenty-one years after the measuring life dies. That is, a future interest is valid under the Rule if it is possible to point to a living person (or to a group of living people) and to guarantee that within 21 years after the death of that person (or the death of the last member of that group), the interest in question will have vested or failed.

a.   *Using a Group of Individuals as Measuring Lives*

The Rule does not require identification of a single person during whose lifetime (plus 21 years) the interest in question will vest; an interest is valid under the Rule if it is possible to identify a group of living people and to guarantee that the interest in question will vest within 21 years of the death of the last survivor of the members of the group. In other words, *even if the interest is not certain to vest within the lifetime of a single person, the interest is valid if it is certain to vest within the lifetime of a group of people, all of whom are alive at the time of the conveyance.*

Consider a common example. T's will leaves property in trust, and provides that the income from the trust should be distributed to T's children for their lives, and, "at the death of my last surviving child, the trust principal should be distributed to those of my grandchildren who are alive at the time of the death of my last surviving child." Suppose at the time of T's death, T is survived by three children, A, B, and C. Who can be used as a measuring life to validate the interest in surviving grandchildren? Note that neither A, nor B, nor C individually can be used as measuring lives because at the time of T's death, it is impossible to know which of the three will survive the others. For instance, A cannot be used as a measuring life, because B and C might survive A by more than 21 years, and we will not know in which grandchild the remainder vests until the death of the last of the children. But A, B, and C collectively can be used as measuring lives. It is possible to point to A, B, and C collectively and guarantee that by the death of the survivor, the contingent interest in grandchildren will have vested or failed.

b.   *Strategies for Choosing Measuring Lives*

In evaluating interests for compliance with the Rule Against Perpetuities, the goal is to identify a measuring life (or a group of measuring lives) who satisfy two criteria:

1.   the interest in question must vest within 21 years after the death of that measuring life; and

2.   the measuring life must be a person alive at the time the interest was created.

If there exists even one measuring life (or group of measuring lives) who satisfy these two criteria, the interest in question is valid under the Rule Against Perpetuities.

The first step in identifying measuring lives is to determine what event or events will trigger vesting of the interest in question. Most contingent interests will vest (1) at a time defined in the instrument creating the interest (2) if a specified contingency occurred. Both the time of vesting and the contingency generally have some relationship to lifetime events. That is, the interest is likely to vest at the death of a particular person, or at the time a particular person reaches a specified age. The most common contingency is survivorship: the grantor may provide, for instance, that the interest vests in those children of A who survive A.

Once one identifies the event that will trigger vesting, the next step in selecting measuring lives is to make a list of all those people during whose lifetime, or at whose death, or within 21 years of whose death, the interest in question will vest or fail. Some scholars find it useful to speak of assembling the lives causally related to vesting. *Basically, this step involves listing all persons who satisfy the first criterion for measuring lives.*

Consider, for instance, a grant "to A for life, remainder to A's children for so long as a child of A is still alive, remainder to B if B is then alive, and if not, remainder to A's surviving grandchildren." If one wants to determine whether B's future interest is valid under the Rule, one would first note that B's interest will vest at the death of A's last surviving child, but only if B herself is then alive. So we know that the interest will vest or fail during the lifetime of (1) A's children; and (2) B. So, both A's children as a group, and B, satisfy the first criterion for measuring lives.

Once the list of persons who satisfy the first criterion has been assembled—the list of persons during whose lifetime (or within 21 years of whose death) the interest must vest or fail—it is time to turn to the second criterion: are the persons on the list certain to be alive at the creation of the interest? *If any persons or group of persons on the list are certain to be alive at the creation of the interest, then they satisfy the second criterion for measuring lives, and the interest is valid under the Rule Against Perpetuities.*

Consider the same hypothetical grant. Ask whether A's children were lives in being at the creation of the interest. If A was alive at the time of the grant, the answer is no: A was capable of having another child (the Rule presumes that people—men and women—can have children at any age). Therefore, we do not know at the time of the grant that all of A's children have been born, and we cannot be certain that A's children were lives in being at the creation of the interest. As a result, we cannot use A's children as measuring lives. That does not, however, mean that the interest in B is invalid under the Rule, because we still have to check the other person on our list of persons who satisfy the first criterion: B herself. Was B alive at T's death? Yes. (If B was named in the instrument, we can assume that B was alive at the time the instrument was drafted). Therefore B satisfied both criteria for measuring lives, and the interest in B is valid.

Consider now another interest created in the same hypothetical grant: the interest in A's surviving grandchildren. Is that interest valid under the Rule? Using the same approach, recognize first that the interest in grandchildren will vest (1) at the death of A's last surviving child (2) if the grandchildren are then alive. So two groups satisfy the first criterion for measuring lives: A's children, and A's grandchildren. Move next to the second criterion: can we be certain that these persons are lives in being at the creation of the interest. As before, the answer is no with respect to A's children; so long as A is alive, A could have additional children after creation of A's interest. With respect to A's grandchildren, the answer is also no; A could certainly have more grandchildren after creation of the interest. Since neither set of lives satisfy the second criterion for measuring lives, the interest in A's surviving grandchildren is invalid under the Rule Against Perpetuities. Does that invalidity affect the validity of the interest in B? No. Each interest is evaluated separately under the Rule Against Perpetuities.

To summarize, then, evaluation of a future interest under the Rule Against Perpetuities involves three steps:

1. *Determine when the interest will vest or fail, and upon what contingencies;*

2. *List all persons during whose lifetime, or at whose death (or within 21 years of whose death) the contingencies will occur, causing the interest to vest or*

fail. This list is a list of persons who satisfy the first criterion for measuring lives;

3. *Check to see whether any of the persons on the list were certain to be alive at the creation of the interest. That is, check to see which of the persons on the list satisfy the second criterion for measuring lives. If any of the people on the list satisfy the second criterion, the interest is valid under the Rule Against Perpetuities. If none of the persons on the list satisfy the second criterion, the interest is invalid under the Rule.*

What impact do frozen embryos, sperm banks, and other modern technologies have on the measuring life calculus? To date, no court has held an interest invalid under the Rule because of the possibility that a child might be born years after the death of its genetic parents. The reason is obvious: if contingent interests were to be invalid because of the possibility that children might be born to their parents long after the death of those parents, even the most innocuous future interests would be invalid. A devise "to my husband for life, remainder to my husband's youngest child" would create an invalid interest because of the possibility that a child might be born to the husband 30 to 40 years after the husband's death.

Two other points bear mention. First, in testing the validity of the interests created by a single instrument, *it is not necessary to use the same measuring life to validate each interest*. Different measuring lives may be used to establish the validity of different interests created in the same instrument. Second, *the measuring life need not be a person named in the instrument*. For instance, consider a will that leaves property "to my sister and her heirs until the birth of my first grandchild, and upon the birth of my first grandchild, the property should be distributed to that grandchild." Suppose further that at testator's death, no grandchildren have yet been born, but testator has two surviving children. The interest in the grandchild is valid because we can use the testator's children as measuring lives— even though the children are nowhere named in the grant. By contrast, the sister does not satisfy the first criterion for measuring lives, and the grandchild does not satisfy the second criterion, so neither can be used as measuring lives.

3. Twenty-One Years

So far, the focus has been on the "lives in being" aspect of the Rule Against Perpetuities. But the Rule requires that an interest be certain to vest, if at all, within "lives in being plus 21 years." What impact does the 21-year period have on analysis of future interests?

In most circumstances, the 21-year period has no impact at all, unless the creator of the interest has expressly postponed vesting by 21 years, or has included a condition requiring survivorship to a specified age. The reason is apparent. If we cannot guarantee that an interest will vest within a person's lifetime, we will not generally be able to guarantee that the same interest will vest within 21 years of her death—unless the instrument expressly postpones vesting until 21 years after the person's death, or the instrument provides for vesting in those children who reach age 21.

The 21-year period may also be used without any measuring life. Thus, if T devises property "to those of my descendants alive 21 years after my death," the devise is valid because the interest will vest within 21 years of the creation of the interest.

Although the 21-year period can be tacked on to the end of a life in being, it cannot precede a life in being. Thus, T may not direct that trust principal be distributed "to those of my descendants alive at the death of the last survivor of all of my issue born within 21 years after my death."

III. Recurring Problems

A. When Does the Perpetuities Period Start to Run?: Revocable and Irrevocable Inter Vivos Trusts

The Rule Against Perpetuities requires a future interest to vest within "lives in being plus 21 years" from the creation of the interest. But when is the creation of the interest? First, consider a will. Because the will does not become effective until decedent's death, the period for future interests created in a will runs from the moment of decedent's death, not from the moment the will is executed.

Next, turn to inter vivos trusts. Generally, if the decedent creates a future interest in an instrument designed to take effect immediately, the period starts to run from the date of the instrument. This fact creates a trap for the drafter. When the decedent makes an inter vivos transfer, the transferor might have children born after the transfer. As a result, the transferor's children will not meet the second criterion for measuring lives—they might not all be lives in being at the creation of the interest. By contrast, when testator makes a disposition by will, testator's children, as a class, are available as measuring lives because testator can't have additional children after his death.

Suppose, however, decedent creates an inter vivos trust, but one that is freely revocable until decedent's death. Because the decedent is the practical owner of the trust property until his death, courts have held that the perpetuities period should be measured from the moment the trust becomes irrevocable—decedent's death—rather than the moment the trust becomes effective. When the trust instrument gives the settlor only a limited power to revoke, or a limited power to withdraw principal, courts measure the perpetuities period from the time the trust was executed, not from the moment of decedent's death.

B.   Remote Possibilities

Many perpetuities problems arise from a drafter's failure to consider realistically implausible, but theoretically possible, events which might cause future interests to vest beyond the period of the Rule. The Rule is a rule of logic, not of probabilities. If an extraordinarily unlikely event could cause an interest to vest beyond the period of the Rule, the common law invalidated the interest from its inception rather than waiting to see whether the unlikely event actually occurred. Many of these unlikely events have generated their own names. This section considers the drafting pitfalls associated with these remote possibilities.

1.   The Fertile Octogenarian

The common law Rule presumes that men and women can have children at any age. This presumption has created invalidity under the Rule, because the Rule refuses to treat as closed classes groups of persons that are practically certain never to add new members. For instance, suppose a 90-year-old testator devises property in trust, "income payable to my sister's children until the death of my sister's last surviving child, and at that time, the principal should be distributed among my then-living issue, per stirpes." Assume T's sister is alive, and 86, at the time of the grant. The interest in testator's issue is invalid under the Rule. The interest will vest at the death of the last surviving child of T's sister. Consider measuring lives who satisfy the first criterion: (1) T's sister's children; and (2) the issue of testator who are alive at the time of T's sister's death. The issue do not satisfy the second criterion, because issue can be born at any time after testator's death (as long as T had surviving issue). And T's sister's children do not satisfy the second criterion because the sister could have more children after testator's death. Because neither set of measuring lives satisfy the second criterion, the interest in issue is invalid under the Rule.

2.   The Unborn Widow

A widow of a decedent is the person married to the decedent at the time of the decedent's death. But when a future interest is created in a "widow" of the decedent at a time when the decedent is still alive, there is no guarantee that the widow is a person alive at the time of the grant. For instance, a father might create a trust for the benefit of his son for life, remainder to the son's widow for life, remainder to the son's then-living issue. When the father creates the trust, the father does not know that the son's eventual widow is a person who is yet alive. The son might, in the future, marry a much younger woman—a woman so much younger that the woman was not alive when the father created the trust.

This fact does not invalidate the future interest in the widow. If the widow's interest vests at the son's death, the son can be used as a measuring life to validate the widow's interest. But what of the interest that follows the widow's interest—the interest in the son's then-living issue? Note that their interest vests at the widow's death, but the widow cannot be used as a measuring life, because the widow might be born after the creation of the trust. Hence, the interest in the son's issue is invalid—because of the possibility of an unborn widow!

3.   *The Slothful Executor*

Suppose a will or trust instrument directs distribution of trust assets upon completion of an administrative task, in the reasonable expectation that the task will be performed expeditiously. If the distribution is contingent on meeting specified conditions at the time the task is performed, the interest in the beneficiaries violates the Rule Against Perpetuities, because there is no assurance that the task will be performed within lives in being plus 21 years.

Consider, for instance, a will that leaves property to "the officers of the Moose Lodge in office at the time my estate is distributed." Some courts have held that the interest in the officers is invalid under the Rule because there is no guarantee that the executors will distribute the estate within lives in being plus 21 years.

C.   **Application to Charitable Gifts and Trusts**

Although the Rule Against Perpetuities applies to charitable interests as well as non-charitable interests, application to charitable interests is different in some respects.

First, consider the similarities. If a will or trust instrument creates non-charitable present interests, followed by a charitable future interest, the future interest is subject to the Rule. That is, so long as there is a possibility that the charitable future interest will not vest within the Rule's period, the interest is invalid. The classic example involves a bank president whose will devised land to his bank for so long as the bank continued to exist, and then to the managers of a charitable entity. The interest in the charity was invalid because it was not vested at its creation, nor was there any guarantee that the interest would vest within twenty-one years of the death of any person alive at the bank president's death.

Conversely, if a will or trust instrument creates a charitable present interest, followed by a non-charitable future interest, the future interest is subject to the Rule. The classic case involves a devise of land to a church, with a provision that if the church should be dissolved, the land should pass to designated individual beneficiaries. Because the interests in the individual beneficiaries might not vest within twenty-one years of the death of any individual alive at the time of the devise, those interests were invalid under the Rule. (Remember that we cannot use the designated individual beneficiaries as measuring lives, because the interest might vest in the beneficiaries of their estates long after their deaths).

Now consider the differences between the Rule's treatment of charitable interests and the Rule's treatment of non-charitable interests. First, charitable trusts and foundations can endure in perpetuity, while non-charitable trusts cannot (at least in those jurisdictions that retain the common law Rule). Private trusts must have identifiable beneficiaries, and the interests of each of those beneficiaries must vest within the Rule's period. As a result, a private trust cannot last forever. Once all of the beneficiaries whose interests vested within the Rule's period have died, the trust must end because there is no beneficiary to whom the trustee can distribute trust funds. By contrast, because a charitable trust need not have identifiable beneficiaries, the Rule imposes no limits on trust duration. As a result, a charitable trust can endure forever.

A second unique feature of the Rule's treatment of charitable interests is that a trust settlor can create a succession of charitable interests without violating the Rule. Thus, if the settlor creates one charitable interest, and directs that upon some contingency, the trust shall pass to another charitable beneficiary, the interest in the second charitable beneficiary is valid under the Rule. Thus, if the settlor were to devise property "to the American Red Cross, but if the Red Cross is ever dissolved, to the United Way", the interest in the United Way is valid. The theory behind this rule is that the perpetual use of the property by charities is a benefit that exceeds any harm resulting from the long-term contingency.

D. Consequences of Invalidity

When the Rule Against Perpetuities invalidates a provision in a dispositive instrument, what happens to the property subject to the invalid provision? As the New York Court of Appeals has put it, the answer to that question "is not strictly law; it is a matter of good judgment."[1] That is, generalization is dangerous, because the various provisions of a will or trust instrument generally reflect a scheme on the part of the testator or trust settlor, making it difficult to treat individual provisions in isolation. Nevertheless, a few general principles have emerged.

In general, if an interest is invalid under the rule, the invalid interest is excised from the trust instrument, leaving the rest of the instrument to take effect. So, if the instrument includes a succession of interests, each designed to vest upon the expiration of the preceding interest, if a particular interest is invalid, all of the preceding interests remain valid. At the moment the instrument provides for the invalid interest to take effect, the property would pass back to the grantor or to the grantor's estate. Suppose, for instance, testator's will leaves her estate, in trust, "income to be paid to my children for life, then to my grandchildren for life, principal to be distributed, at the death of my last surviving grandchild, to my great grandchildren in equal shares." The interest in great-grandchildren is invalid under the Rule. But the invalidity does not affect the interests in children and grandchildren; they remain valid. What happens to the trust property at the death of the last surviving grandchild? If the trust was not created in the will's residuary clause, the trust property would fall into the residue, and pass to the testator's residuary beneficiaries. If testator devised the entire residue of his estate to the trust, then the property would pass by intestate succession to the testator's heirs.

The principle that the invalid interest is excised from the dispositive instrument operates differently when the invalid interest would operate to divest a prior vested interest. In that case, the effect of invalidity will generally be to make the prior interest absolute. Suppose, for instance, testator devises her home "to my daughter for life, remainder to my daughter's children, but if any of my daughter's children should become a lawyer, that child's share of the house shall be divided among his or her siblings." The final interest is invalid under the Rule. When we excise that interest from the will, we are left with an instrument that reads "to my daughter for life, remainder to my daughter's children." There is no need in this case for the invalid interest to pass through the testator's estate; instead, the prior interest becomes absolute as a result of the invalidity of the divesting condition.

These general principles do not apply if a court could give effect to more of testator's dispositive scheme by invalidating a broader range of interests. When it would appear that invalidation of multiple interests, or even the entire will, would better effectuate

---

[1]   In re Durand's Will, 250 N.Y. 45, 164 N.E. 737, 740 (1928).

testator's intent than would invalidation of a single interest, the doctrine of *infectious invalidity* permits a court to invalidate valid interests as well as invalid ones. For instance, imagine a will in which testator leaves half of his estate to his son outright, and the other half in trust, income to his daughter for life, "remainder to those of my daughter's children who reach age 40." The remainder interest in the daughter's children is invalid. If a court were simply to have that interest pass through testator's estate, testator's son could end up with more than half of testator's estate—a result testator did not intend. A court might instead conclude that testator would prefer to have her entire estate pass by intestacy. The doctrine of infectious invalidity would permit the court to invalidate the entire will.

IV. Class Gifts

A. The All-or-Nothing Rule

The Rule Against Perpetuities creates special problems in its application to class gifts—gifts to classes such as children, grandchildren, or nieces and nephews. In particular, the Rule *invalidates gifts to every member of the class if it would be possible for the gift to vest in any member of the class at a time beyond the Rule's period*—lives in being plus twenty one years.

Consider an example. Suppose testator's will leaves the residue of her estate in trust, with income to be paid "to my grandchildren for so long as one of my grandchildren remains alive", and "upon the death of my last surviving grandchild, principal is to be distributed to my great-grandchildren." Let us assume that at testator's death, testator's children are still alive, and two great-grandchildren have been born to testator. Note that at testator's death, those great-grandchildren have vested remainders subject to open. Are their interests valid under the Rule Against Perpetuities? The answer is no. They are beneficiaries of a class gift—a gift to a class of great-grandchildren. But the interest in other members of the class might vest long past the death of all persons alive at testator's death. (For instance, one of testator's children could have a child immediately after testator's death; testator's other children, grandchildren, and great-grandchildren could then die; subsequently, forty-years later, great-grandchildren could be born to the afterborn grandchild). So long as the interest in some member of the class of great-grandchildren is invalid under the Rule, the interest in the existing great-grandchildren is also invalid. This rule, sometimes called the *"all or nothing rule,"* can be expressed another way: *a vested remainder subject to open is not a vested interest for purposes of the Rule Against Perpetuities.*

As counterintuitive as it might seem, the "all or nothing rule" sometimes effectuates the grantor's intent better than a rule that would permit some members of the class to take when the interests of other members are invalid. When a grantor makes a class gift, he generally expects members of the class to be treated equally. The all-or-nothing rule generates equal treatment; a rule that recognizes partial invalidity would not. Reconsider the example of the future interest in great-grandchildren. The all-or-nothing rule treats all great-grandchildren alike—by invalidating their interest. The effect of invalidation is to pass the invalid interest by intestate succession—which in all likelihood will benefit the great-grandchildren as a class. So the great-grandchildren will still benefit, and will do so more equally than if the Rule saved the grant for the great-grandchildren alive at testator's death!

Of course, there are instances in which the all-or-nothing rule would frustrate the intent of the grantor. The point is that the all-or-nothing rule sometimes generates sensible results.

B. The Effect of the Class Closing Rule of Convenience

Chapter Eight discusses the Class Closing Rule of Convenience, which holds that when a grantor makes a class gift, the class "closes" when one member of the class becomes entitled to distribution of a share of the gift. Subsequently born members of the class will not share in the gift. The class closing rule of convenience is a rule of construction applicable even to gifts that are entirely valid under the Rule Against Perpetuities.

Consider, for example, a will in which testator creates a trust, and directs that income be paid to her unmarried 50-year-old daughter for life, and that principal be paid, at the daughter's death, "to those of my son's children who reach age 21." The grant to the son's children is entirely valid under the Rule Against Perpetuities, because the interests in every member of the class of the son's children will vest within 21 years of the son's death (so that the son satisfies the first criterion for measuring lives). Because the interest became valid at testator's death, the son was necessarily a life in being at the creation of the interest (so that the son satisfies the second criterion for measuring lives).

As a construction question, however, which of the son's children take, if at the time of the daughter's death, the son has three children, ages 25, 20 and 15? The class closing rule tells us that the 25-year-old is entitled to one-third of the principal at the daughter's death, and the two younger children will each be entitled to one-third of the principal if they survive to age 21. If the son has any children born after the daughter's death, those children will not be entitled to share in her grandmother's trust. We say that the class of eligible takers "closed" when the 25-year-old became entitled to possession. This rule makes it possible for the trustee to distribute a share of trust principal to the 25-year-old; if it were not for the Rule of Convenience, trustee would not be safe in distributing any principal to the 25-year-old because, in theory, testator's son could have an infinite number of additional children, each of whom might become entitled to an infinitely small share of the trust principal.

Because the Class Closing Rule of Convenience operates to close a class artificially before the class would close "naturally" by the death of the parent of the class members, the Rule of Convenience sometimes operates to save class gifts that would otherwise be invalid under the Rule Against Perpetuities. If we can be sure that the interest in members of the class will vest (or fail) by the time the Rule of Convenience closes the class, the class gift will be valid under the Rule Against Perpetuities even if the class might not close "naturally" until beyond the Rule's period.

For example, suppose T's will creates a trust, directs that the trustee distribute income "to my sister for life," and directs that the trustee then distribute principal "to my sister's grandchildren." Suppose further that at T's death, T's sister has a son, N, who in turn has a three-year-old daughter, G. T's devise of trust principal is valid under the Rule Against Perpetuities. T's grandniece, G, has a vested remainder subject to open—an interest not treated as vested for purposes of the Rule Against Perpetuities. But note that the Class Closing Rule of Convenience entitles G to take a share of the principal at the death of T's sister, and also provides that any grandnieces and grandnephews not yet born by the death of T's sister *will never become entitled to share in the trust principal.* We need not, therefore, worry about their interests. The only interests that could ever vest are interests in grandnieces and grandnephews alive at the death of T's sister—a person alive at the creation of the interest. Those interests will vest or fail within 21 years of the death of T's sister, and are therefore valid under the Rule Against Perpetuities. So, because of the Rule of Convenience, no interest may vest in a member of the class more than 21 years after the death of T's sister. As a result, the all-or-nothing rule does not invalidate the devise to G.

V. The Rule Against Perpetuities and Powers of Appointment

The Rule Against Perpetuities applies to powers of appointment, and in that context creates particularly serious traps for the careless drafter. When applying the Rule to powers of appointment, two questions require analysis: first, is the power itself valid, and second, when the power is exercised, is the exercise valid under the Rule.

A. Validity of the Power of Appointment

Recall the different types of powers of appointment: powers may be general or special, and they may be testamentary or exercisable by an *inter vivos* instrument. Different types of powers are treated differently for Rule Against Perpetuities purposes.

Consider first a general power exercisable by will or by *inter vivos* instrument. Once a donee acquires the right to exercise such a power, the donee has the equivalent of fee simple ownership; the donee can exercise the power in favor of herself, and eliminate all contingencies in the instrument creating the power. Since the Rule Against Perpetuities is designed to prevent interests from remaining contingent for too long, the Rule's purposes are not frustrated if we can be certain that a donee will be able to exercise the power in favor of herself within the Rule's period. Hence, *when a power is general and exercisable by an inter vivos instrument, the power is valid under the Rule Against Perpetuities if the power is certain to become exercisable during the period of the Rule.*

Other powers—special powers, and general testamentary powers—present different considerations, and are subject to a different rule. When a donee holds a special power, or a general testamentary power, the donee does not have the equivalent of absolute ownership; the donee will never be able to exercise in favor of herself. For so long as it remains possible for the donee to exercise the power, interests in the appointive property might remain contingent. Hence, the Rule Against Perpetuities invalidates these powers *if there is any possibility that the power might be exercised beyond the Rule's period*—lives in being plus 21 years.

Most donors who create powers of appointment confer those powers on people they know and trust. The Rule Against Perpetuities will never invalidate those powers. If the donor gives a power—even a special testamentary power—to her spouse, or to one of her children, or to a trusted sibling—the power will be exercised within the donee's lifetime. So long as the donee was identified (and therefore alive) at the time the donor created the power, the power cannot possibly be exercised beyond the period of the Rule.

The risk that a power of appointment will violate the Rule Against Perpetuities is greatest when a careless donor creates a discretionary trust, and gives the trustee a power to pay (or not to pay) income to designated beneficiaries. Suppose, for instance, T's will creates a trust, designates a corporate trustee, and directs the trustee to distribute among T's daughter D and D's children as much or as little trust income as the trustee believes appropriate. The will directs that at the death of D's last surviving child, the trust principal is to be distributed to the American Red Cross. The future interest in the Red Cross is valid (because it is vested at creation of the interest), but the power of appointment in the corporate trustee is invalid. Because D's children might not all be born at the time of T's death, D's children cannot be used as measuring lives. As a result, the trustee might still be exercising the power well beyond the period of lives in being plus 21 years.

Nevertheless, it bears repeating that invalidity of a power itself is rare; so long as the instrument creates the power in an identified, living person, the power is valid. The more difficult problems involve validity of the exercise of the power—the subject of the next section.

B.   Validity of the Power's Exercise

If a power itself is invalid, then any exercise made pursuant to the power will, of course, be ineffective. But suppose, as will usually be the case, that the power is valid. What constraints does the Rule Against Perpetuities impose on exercise of the power?

First, when the donee of a power makes outright appointments to identified beneficiaries, exercise of the power raises no perpetuities problems. The donee has not, by making outright appointment, prolonged the contingency of any interests. Hence, the donee's appointments do not violate the Rule.

Perpetuities issues arise, however, when the donee exercises the power by creating a trust with contingent future interests. The principal question that arises is whether the perpetuities period starts to run from the moment the donor created the power, or from the moment the donee exercised the power.

1.   *The Scope of the Relation-Back Doctrine*

Recall that the donee of a power of appointment is often treated as the donor's agent. That is, the donee acts on the donor's behalf to "fill in the blanks" in a disposition made by the donor when the donor created the power. The donor could not foresee future events—births, deaths, changes in wealth, etc.—that might affect the donor's preferred disposition of the appointive property, so the donor gave the donee power to adjust dispositions to take into account those future events. Application of this "agency" theory of powers of appointment would suggest that the perpetuities period should be measured from the time the donor created the power of appointment, not from the time the donee exercised the power. Courts, however, have applied the agency theory to some, but not all, powers of appointment.

If the donor creates a special power of appointment, courts typically embrace the agency theory, and apply the *relation-back doctrine*. That doctrine holds that we should read the donee's appointment back into the instrument in which the donor created the power. The relation-back doctrine requires that we measure the perpetuities period from the time the donor created the power.

Suppose, for instance, T's will creates a trust, giving his wife W, an income interest for life and a special power to appoint the principal in favor of "our descendants." At T's death, the couple's only son, S, is alive and childless. W dies 30 years later, outliving S. W's will exercises T's power by creating a trust to pay income to S's only daughter G, for life, and to distribute principal among G's children at G's death. W's exercise of the power of appointment violates the Rule Against Perpetuities. Because T created a special power, we measure the perpetuities period from the time T created the power—T's death. At T's death, G was not yet born, and would not qualify as a measuring life. Hence, the remainder interest in G's children is invalid under the Rule.

By contrast, courts do not apply the relation-back doctrine when the donor gives the donee a general power exercisable by an *inter vivos* instrument. In that event, courts uniformly hold that the perpetuities period should be measured from the time of exercise. The rationale is a familiar one: the donee's interest is the functional equivalent of an absolute interest, because the donee could appoint in favor of herself. As a result, we treat any appointment just as we would treat any other property disposition made by the donee. The agency theory of powers of appointment simply doesn't fit when the donor has given the donee power to exercise in favor of herself during her own lifetime.

Thus, in the preceding example, suppose T's will had created a trust, giving his wife W a general power to appoint the principal in favor of herself by *inter vivos* instrument. If W were to exercise the power by creating a further trust, with income to her granddaughter G for life, and distribution of principal among G's children at G's death, W's exercise of the power of appointment would be entirely valid. The perpetuities period would be measured from the time of W's exercise, and G could therefore be used as a measuring life, assuring that all interests vest within the period of G's lifetime.

Finally, when a donor has created a general testamentary power of appointment, courts divide on the application of the relation-back doctrine. A majority of courts have held the doctrine applicable, and have therefore held that the Rule's period runs from the time of the power's creation, not from the moment of exercise. Some courts, however, have rejected application of the relation-back doctrine to general testamentary powers.

2. The Second-Look Doctrine

The relation-back doctrine provides that for special powers and, in many jurisdictions, for general testamentary powers, the Rule's period is measured from the time the power is created, not from the time of exercise. The *second-look doctrine* ameliorates the impact of the relation-back doctrine by providing that in evaluating the validity of an interest, we can take into account all facts known at the time the donee exercises the power.

The common law Rule Against Perpetuities focuses on possibilities. If a remote series of events could cause a future interest to remain contingent beyond the Rule's period, the future interest is invalid, however unlikely that series of events might be. Consider, for instance, a testator whose will leaves her property in trust for the benefit of her 60-year-old daughter for life, then to her daughter's children for life, with the principal to be distributed to the daughter's grandchildren at the death of the daughter's last surviving child. The remainder in the daughter's grandchildren would be invalid under the Rule, because the daughter's children might not all have been lives in being at the time of testator's death.

Suppose, now, that testator's will creates a trust for the benefit of her daughter for life, and gives the daughter a special testamentary power to appoint among the daughter's descendants. The daughter appoints by creating a testamentary trust for the benefit of her children for life, with the principal to be distributed to the daughters' grandchildren at the death of the daughter's last surviving child. Assume further that the daughter has had no additional children after the original testator's death.

In this situation, the second-look doctrine prevents the daughter's appointment from violating the Rule Against Perpetuities. Recall that the relation-back doctrine instructs us to measure the Rule's period from the time the mother created the power. At that time, the daughter was still alive and, at least theoretically, could have more children. If we read the daughter's appointment back into the mother's will, and ask whether the appointment is valid, taking into account only those facts known at the mother's death, then the daughter's appointment would be invalid.

The second-look doctrine rejects this approach, and permits us to take into account all facts known at the time of the daughter's death—in particular, the fact that all of the daughter's children were actually born by the time of the death of the original testator— daughter's mother. Hence, even though the relation-back doctrine requires us to measure the Rule's period from the time of the mother's death, we can use the daughter's children as measuring lives, and the daughter's appointment is valid. Of course, if at the time of the daughter's death, she had given birth to another child born after her mother's death, the appointment would be invalid, because even if we take into account facts known at the time of the daughter's exercise, we still could not be sure that the interest in the daughter's grandchild would vest within the period of the Rule. (The daughter's afterborn child could not be used as a measuring life, and the interest in the daughter's grandchildren would not vest until the afterborn's death).

The second-look doctrine applies only to interests created under powers of appointment. The doctrine is not equivalent to the "wait and see" doctrine adopted in a number of jurisdictions to salvage interests invalid under the Rule Against Perpetuities.

C.   Validity of Gifts in Default of Appointment

Suppose a trust settlor creates a power of appointment in a donee, and also provides for takers-in-default—the persons to whom the appointive property should pass if the donee fails to exercise the power. The disposition to takers-in-default is subject to the Rule Against Perpetuities, and the Rule's period is measured from the time the power is created. Some courts have held, however, that the second-look doctrine should apply to gifts in default of appointment.

Thus, in one leading case, settlor created an inter vivos trust which disposed of trust principal in a way that would have violated the Rule. But settlor also reserved to himself a general testamentary power of appointment. The court held the second-look doctrine applicable, enabling the court to examine facts in existence at the time of settlor's death—facts which would have eliminated the remote possibilities that could have invalidated the original trust.

This approach makes considerable sense. If settlor had exercised the power of appointment to create a new trust, different in insignificant respects from the original trust, the second-look doctrine would have applied to the appointment. No reason appears why the settlor's disposition should be invalid simply because settlor did not exercise that power.

VI. Perpetuities Reform

The common law Rule Against Perpetuities is on the wane. Most jurisdictions have modified it in some way; some have abolished the Rule altogether. The section examines the most common reforms.

A.   Construction and Reformation

A number of states have enacted statutes requiring construction and reformation of wills and trust instruments to avoid violation of the Rule Against Perpetuities. That is, if an interest violates the common law Rule, these statutes require a court to alter its dispositive provisions to comply with the rule while effectuating the settlor's purpose to the greatest extent possible.

New York takes a similar, but more limited approach. New York creates a number of statutory presumptions targeting the remote possibilities most likely to invalidate future interests. For instance, the New York statute mandates reduction of age contingencies to 21 years, and creates a presumption that a woman over 55 cannot have children.

B.   Wait-and-See

For many years, the most common form of perpetuities reform was adoption of the wait-and-see doctrine, either by courts or by legislatures. The common law Rule Against Perpetuities upsets a future interest if it is possible, at the time of the interest's creation, that the interest might not vest within the period of the Rule. The wait-and-see doctrine, by contrast, instructs courts to wait and see whether those future interests would actually remain contingent for longer than the Rule's period.

Wait-and-see was subject to two criticisms. First, unlike the common law Rule, which enables courts to determine the validity of all interests immediately upon their creation, the wait-and-see doctrine would itself increase contingency by making it impossible to determine—often for years after an interest's creation—whether the interest would be valid under the Rule. If the purpose of the Rule is to reduce contingency, wait-and-see to some extent undermines that purpose.

Second, wait-and-see creates controversies about how long courts should wait before determining whether an interest is valid under the Rule. Different jurisdictions took diverse approaches to this question.

C.   USRAP

Scholars unhappy both with the common law Rule and with wait-and-see developed another approach, now embodied in the Uniform Statutory Rule Against Perpetuities (USRAP). Under USRAP, a contingent future interest is valid if (1) it satisfies the common law Rule Against Perpetuities, or (2) the interest actually vests within 90 years from the time of its creation.

That is, for an interest not valid under the common law Rule, we wait until 90 years after the interest's creation, and if the interest is still contingent, the interest is invalid.

D.   Abolition of the Rule

In recent years, a number of states have abolished the Rule Against Perpetuities altogether. The movement has largely been tax driven. Trust settlors who want to take maximum advantage of the exemption from the Generation-Skipping Transfer Tax can permanently insulate the trust corpus from taxation if the trust never terminates. The Rule Against Perpetuities, however, requires termination at some point, and eventually requires the trust proceeds to pass through the estate of some trust beneficiary.

Some states have discovered that if they abolish the Rule Against Perpetuities, they can attract trust business from settlors seeking to avail themselves of the tax benefits offered by perpetual trusts. The move toward abolition has accelerated in recent years. Whether that trend will continue may depend in part on the future of federal estate tax policy. So far, Congress has retained the federal estate tax, albeit only for very wealthy testators, and at somewhat reduced rates. If Congress abolishes the estate tax altogether, the pressure for abolition of the Rule might abate. Otherwise, competition among states may make the Rule largely irrelevant in the near future.

Problems

1.   T creates a testamentary trust, with trust income to be distributed to T's wife W for her life, then to T's surviving children for so long as one of T's children remains alive, then to T's grandchildren until the last of T's grandchildren graduates from college, at which time the trust is to terminate, and the principal is to be distributed "in equal shares to T's grandchildren."

Does any provision in T's trust violate the Rule Against Perpetuities? If so, which one?

2.   T creates a testamentary trust, with income to be distributed to T's daughter for life, then to T's grandchildren until the death of T's last surviving grandchild, at which time the trust is to terminate, and the principal is to be distributed "to those of my great-grandchildren alive at the death of my last surviving child."

Is the disposition of trust principal valid under the Rule Against Perpetuities?

How, if at all, would your answer change if the trust had been an irrevocable inter vivos trust?

3.   T creates an irrevocable inter vivos trust, with income to be distributed to T's husband for life, and then to T's surviving children until the death of T's last surviving child, at which time the trust

principal is to be distributed "among my grandchildren in equal shares."

Is the disposition of trust principal valid under the Rule Against Perpetuities?

How, if at all, would your answer change if the trust had been a testamentary trust?

4.   T creates a testamentary trust, with income to be distributed to T's wife for life, remainder at the wife's death to T's grandchildren until the death of T's last surviving grandchild, at which time the trust principal is to be distributed:

   a.   "to my cousin, Charlie."

   b.   "to my cousin, Charlie, if he is then alive."

   c.   "to my nieces and nephews, in equal shares."

   d.   "to my surviving nieces and nephews, in equal shares."

At the time of T's death, T's parents and siblings are dead. Which of these potential dispositions of trust principal would be valid under the Rule Against Perpetuities?

Would any of your answers be different if, at the time of T's death, T's parents or siblings were alive?

5.   T creates a testamentary trust, with income to be distributed to T's wife for life, and then to T's surviving children until the death of T's last surviving child, at which time the trust principal is to be distributed "to my brother's grandchildren." At T's death, T's only brother is still alive and has one 30-year-old child.

Is the disposition of trust principal valid under the Rule Against Perpetuities?

How, if at all, would your answer change if T's brother also has a grandchild alive at the time of T's death?

Chapter Twelve

ADMINISTRATION: THE PROBATE PROCESS

I. The Need for Administration

A decedent's death does not automatically trigger administration of the decedent's estate. Some living person must start the administration process. In many circumstances, no one will start the process because there will be no need for estate administration.

Suppose, for instance, the decedent died without a will, survived by her only daughter. Suppose further that decedent's assets at her death consisted of household furniture and a bank account held by decedent "in trust for" decedent's daughter. And finally suppose decedent had been punctilious about paying her debts, and the daughter is confident that no creditors have outstanding claims against decedent. In these circumstances, there would be little reason for decedent's daughter to seek estate administration. There is no dispute about who will receive decedent's assets, and a simple death certificate will enable the daughter to collect the bank account proceeds. Administration would generate costs with no commensurate gain.

Only when a decedent's family situation is more complicated, or when a decedent's financial assets are more sophisticated, does estate administration become necessary. Estate administration accomplishes several objectives. First, administration finally determines who is entitled to estate assets. A decedent may leave one or more wills of disputed validity, or, even in the absence of a will, disputes might arise about the identity of decedent's closest surviving relatives. Administration of decedent's estate provides a mechanism for final resolution of these disputes.

Second, administration makes it possible for estate beneficiaries to collect the decedent's assets from banks and financial institutions. Decedent's children may know that there is no dispute over disposition of decedent's assets, but the local bank does not know that. The bank, then, may be reluctant to turn over decedent's bank accounts to one or all of decedent's children unless a court has authorized some person to act on the estate's behalf to collect the estate's assets. Without such formal authorization, the bank might worry about paying the wrong person, and ultimately subjecting itself to double liability. Therefore, administration will typically be necessary where decedent's assets are held by financial institutions, and where decedent has made no arrangements for the assets to pass outside the probate system. By contrast, when decedent's assets are already in a form which permits them to pass to a beneficiary outside of the probate system—for instance where the assets are held in P.O.D accounts—administration will typically not be necessary to collect those assets.

Third, administration facilitates orderly disposition of creditor claims against the estate. Suppose a decedent owed money at his death—perhaps to business suppliers, or to credit card companies. Those creditors would not normally have to bring action to collect those debts until expiration of the ordinary statute of limitations on their claims. As a result, distribution of the decedent's assets to beneficiaries would leave the beneficiaries subject to the fear that at some time in the future, the beneficiaries might have to return those assets to the decedent's creditors. Administration ameliorates that problem because, typically, once an estate administrator provides notice to creditors of the decedent's death, creditor claims become subject to a short statute of limitations, permitting timely distribution of estate assets.

Finally, estate administration enables the estate administrator to sell clear title to the decedent's real property (and to any other "titled" assets the decedent might own). Suppose, for instance, the decedent owned the house in which she lived. At her death, if her only daughter were to put the house up for sale, purchasers would be reluctant to purchase from the daughter; purchasers could not, for instance, be sure that decedent had no other children, or had not died with a will leaving the house to some other person or institution. Administration of decedent's estate provides prospective purchasers with assurance that the seller—the estate's personal representative—has authority to convey good title to the house.

Most significant estates need administration for one or more of these reasons. Some, however, do not, and most small estates need no administration at all. When there are few assets to administer, there is little reason to incur the costs of administration.

II. Jurisdiction

Suppose the beneficiaries of decedent's will or decedent's intestate heirs decide to seek administration of decedent's estate. Where would they go to seek administration? Typically, they would seek administration in the probate court (or its equivalent) in the state of decedent's domicile. In some states, a separate court is devoted to probate matters; in others, a court of general jurisdiction handles probate issues. All states share the principle that the state of decedent's domicile has jurisdiction to administer decedent's estate.

The jurisdictional issue, however, is not without its complications. Although all states agree that a person has only one domicile, and states agree, in general terms, on the definition of domicile, a decedent's domicile is ultimately a legal conclusion, not a provable fact. Moreover, a decedent's survivors sometimes have reason to disagree about decedent's domicile. A surviving spouse, for instance, might have reason to seek administration in a state which provides a generous elective share, while the beneficiaries of decedent's will might have reason to resist such a choice. Multiple states may have an interest in collecting taxes on decedent's estate.

Unfortunately, a determination by one state's courts that decedent was domiciled within that state is not binding on persons (and states) not parties to the administration proceeding. As a result, it is possible for two or more states to conduct parallel—and potentially inconsistent—administrations of decedent's estate. On a few occasions, that possibility has been realized, sometimes resulting in multiple taxation of decedent's estate.

The more common problems, however, arise not out of inconsistent determinations of domicile, but out of narrow conceptions of the power of a court-appointed estate representative to act beyond the borders of the state in which the representative was appointed. Suppose, for instance, a New York court appoints a personal representative of decedent's estate. If decedent had several bank accounts in Florida, must a Florida bank turn those accounts over to the New York representative? The traditional answer has been no. The Florida bank should not have to evaluate the authority conferred by the "foreign" piece of paper appointing the personal representative. As a result, the personal representative would have to bring a separate **ancillary administration** proceeding in the Florida courts.

Ancillary administration is typically co-operative. When personal property is involved, states typically respect the primacy of the administration conducted in the state of decedent's domicile. Indeed, sometimes, ancillary administration is unnecessary, because financial institutions in the state where the assets are located will turn over decedent's assets to an out-of-state personal representative without any local judicial intervention.

When decedent owned out-of-state real property, ancillary administration will almost always be necessary. Typically, the law of the state in which the land is located—not the law of decedent's domicile—governs disposition of the land by will or intestate succession. Moreover, a deed executed by an out-of-state representative would present serious title issues, making the land less marketable than it would be if a local personal representative were appointed to administer local property. Nevertheless, modern law encourages co-ordination of the domiciliary administration proceeding and the ancillary administration proceeding, whenever possible.

III. Appointment of the Personal Representative and Issuance of Letters

In order to begin the process of collecting and distributing an estate, some person or institution (or group of persons and institutions) must seek appointment as the estate's personal representative. The function of the personal representative is the same whether the decedent left a will or died intestate, but the commonly-used labels are different. When the decedent has left a will, the personal representative is typically called an **"executor"** because the representative will "execute" the decedent's instructions. By contrast, when the decedent has died intestate, the personal representative is typically called an **"administrator."**

The process for administering an estate differs significantly from state to state. Moreover, many states offer more than one process for administering an estate. A common pattern, reflected in the Uniform Probate Code, creates two separate mechanisms, one for **"informal"** probate or appointment proceedings, and another for **"formal"** probate or appointment proceedings. (In some jurisdictions, informal probate is known as probate "in common form," while formal probate is known as probate "in solemn form.") Informal proceedings are best suited to estates in which there is no significant dispute about ultimate distribution of the estate assets; administration is necessary primarily to enable the estate to resolve creditor claims, to collect estate assets from financial institutions, or to convey good title to estate property. Informal proceedings typically permit appointment of a personal representative without prior notice to all heirs and will beneficiaries; after appointment, the representative must provide notice of the appointment to heirs or beneficiaries, who may then institute formal proceedings if they object to the appointment.

Formal proceedings, by contrast, are more litigation-like. A person seeking appointment as personal representative, or seeking probate of a will, must provide notice to heirs and will beneficiaries, who have the opportunity to object before the court makes any appointment.

Whether the person seeking appointment as personal representative chooses formal or informal proceedings, the person typically seeks "letters" from the relevant court or agency. These letters—called **"letters testamentary"** when there is a will and **"letters of administration"** when there is no will—authorize the personal representative to act on behalf of the estate. When the personal representative gives copies of these letters to banks and other financial institutions, those institutions can turn the decedent's funds over to the representative without fear of liability to future claimants; the letters serve as proof that the institution turned the funds over to an authorized person.

When the decedent has left a will, the will typically names an executor or co-executors. The named executors typically are entitled to issuance of letters testamentary, so long as they are otherwise eligible to serve as fiduciaries. (Some states impose residency or other requirements on service as a fiduciary).

When the decedent has died intestate, statutes typically establish an order of priority for issuance of letters of administration. For instance, a surviving spouse typically enjoys the highest priority, followed by children, and then grandchildren. When multiple persons within one category seek letters, courts might have discretion to grant letters to one, or more, persons within that category. As with executors, the statutes might impose eligibility criteria.

IV. Marshaling and Managing Estate Assets

The personal representative's primary objective is to wrap up estate administration as quickly and inexpensively as possible, distributing as much as possible to the estate beneficiaries. The administration process, however, inevitably takes time. To take a prime example, the personal representative must make sure all taxes owed by the estate are paid before closing the estate and making distribution to the beneficiaries. Those taxes include not merely estate taxes, but income taxes on income earned by the decedent in the year of decedent's death (and, perhaps, in prior years as well), together with income taxes due as a result of the personal representative's sale of estate assets during the process of administration.

Moreover, the personal representative must collect estate assets before the representative can begin to distribute them. Sometimes, collection of assets is straightforward; when a bank or financial institution is presented with letters testamentary or letters of administration, the institution will generally turn decedent's assets over to the personal representative without significant difficulty. But suppose that at the time of her death, decedent had outstanding (and perhaps disputed) claims against contract debtors or tortfeasors. Those claims are assets of the estate, and it is the personal representative's duty to marshal those assets along with decedent's jewelry and bank accounts.

In order to marshal estate assets effectively, the personal representative must have powers that enable the representative to act as the owner of estate property. Typically, when decedent's will names an executor, the will also enumerates powers granted to that executor. But powers are equally important when the will is silent, or when the personal representative is an administrator of an intestate estate. State statutes typically confer on personal representatives a wide array of powers that permit the representative to conduct business on behalf of the estate. Uniform Probate Code section 3–715 is illustrative, enumerating 27 powers held by a personal representative "except as restricted or otherwise provided by the will. . . ." These powers include, for instance, the power to effect compromises with debtors and the power to acquire or dispose of estate assets.

The powers held by the personal representative are powers held in a fiduciary capacity. The scope of fiduciary duties is explored later in this chapter.

V.   Creditor Claims

The claims of a decedent's creditors generally enjoy priority over the claims of the beneficiaries of decedent's estate. If decedent died with assets of $1 million, but debts amounting to $1 million, decedent's beneficiaries are in the same position as if decedent had no assets and no liabilities: they are entitled to nothing from the estate, because there is no estate. The decedent's debts constituted a personal obligation, and after the decedent's death, that obligation became an obligation of the personal representative. Hence, disposition of creditor claims is a matter of critical importance to estate beneficiaries, and to the personal representative. In broad terms, creditor claims are of two types: claims that arose out of actions taken by the decedent before the decedent's death, and claims that arose out of actions taken by the personal representative after the decedent's death. The two types of claims raise distinct legal issues.

A.   Pre-Death Claims

The personal representative faces several challenges in disposing of creditor claims against the decedent. First, the personal representative must discover the existence of such claims. Second, the personal representative must evaluate their merit. And third, the personal representative must resolve those claims quickly, because outstanding claims make it unsafe for the personal representative to distribute the estate to estate beneficiaries. Because the personal representative owes a duty to creditors, if the personal representative distributes to the beneficiaries without paying creditor claims, the representative risks personal liability to the creditors for amounts wrongfully distributed to estate beneficiaries.

Consider the problem facing the personal representative. In the absence of a special statute, the decedent's creditors would not be required to assert their claims against the estate until the expiration of the statute of limitations on the particular claim involved—which in some circumstances could be several years after the decedent's death. To deal with this situation (which would make distribution of any of decedent's assets very risky), most states have enacted "nonclaim statutes." These statutes require creditors to assert claims against a decedent's estate far earlier than required by the general statute of limitations that would apply if decedent were still alive.

Nonclaim statutes are of two types. Some statutes bar creditor claims unless they are asserted within a specified period measured from decedent's death. Others bar claims unless they are asserted within an even shorter period, but measure from the time the creditor receives notice from the personal representative that the creditor is obligated to present his claim. Some statutes, including the Uniform Probate Code, incorporate both sorts on nonclaim provisions.

Nonclaim statutes, however, are subject to federal constitutional constraints. In *Tulsa Professional Collection Services, Inc. v. Pope*,[1] the United States Supreme Court held that when a nonclaim statute purports to cut off creditor claims within a specified period after the personal representative gives notice to creditors, the Due Process clause requires that the notice to known or reasonably ascertainable creditors be actual notice, not notice by publication.

In *Pope*, decedent had incurred expenses associated with a hospital stay before his death. After decedent's wife initiated probate proceedings, the court issued letters testamentary to her. The applicable Oklahoma statute required the executor to give notice to creditors that they must present claims to the executor within two months of the date of first publication of the notice. Failure to file within the two month period would bar the claim forever, subject to a few statutory exceptions. The statute provided only for notice by publication. Decedent's wife published the notice, as required by the statute, but the hospital did not file a claim within the two-month period. When the wife, as executor, rejected the hospital's claim based on the Oklahoma nonclaim statute, the hospital challenged the statute on due process grounds.

---

[1]   485 U.S. 478 (1988).

The United States Supreme Court started its analysis by distinguishing Oklahoma's nonclaim statute from an ordinary statute of limitations. Because ordinary statutes of limitation are self-executing, the state's limited involvement does not constitute the type of state action required to implicate the protections of the due process clause. Oklahoma's nonclaim statute, by contrast, involved more extensive action by the state, and the Court held that the statute was not self-executing. The Court emphasized that the statute did not become applicable until someone instituted probate proceedings, a state official appointed an executor, and that court-appointed executor provided notice to creditors. The Court held that in these circumstances, "state involvement is so pervasive and substantial that it must be considered state action subject to the restrictions of the Fourteenth Amendment."

Once the Court concluded that the government action implicated the Due Process clause, the court turned to the sufficiency of notice by publication. The court conceded that the state had a legitimate interest in expeditious resolution of probate proceedings, but concluded that the executor was nevertheless required first to make reasonably diligent efforts to uncover the identities of creditors, and second to provide actual notice to those creditors. Only with respect to creditors who are not "reasonably ascertainable" will publication notice suffice.

The Court's opinion in *Pope* left open two significant questions. First, the Court expressly declined to consider whether the Due Process clause applies to nonclaim statutes running from the date of the debtor's death, rather than from the date notice is provided by a court-appointed executor. Those statutes might be characterized as self-executing, and therefore treated like ordinary statutes of limitations. Second, the Court indicated that even the actual notice requirement does not apply to creditors with "mere 'conjectural' claims." Some courts have read this language to dispense with the need for notice to contingent creditors. On this analysis, if the decedent was a contractor who guaranteed his work, decedent's executor would not be obligated to provide actual notice to the various beneficiaries of decedent's guarantees.

B.   Post-Death Claims

In many cases, decedent's estate consists not merely of passive investments—bank accounts or stocks and bonds—but of a going concern: the family farm, or decedent's shoe store. In these cases, the personal representative will often want to preserve the going concern value of the operation, perhaps with an eye to selling the business. If, however, the personal representative wants to preserve that going concern value, the personal representative may have to operate the business (with the help of employees) until a prospective purchaser emerges. And if the personal representative operates the business, the personal representative will have to make contracts (potentially to suppliers and purchasers), and will engage in activity that generates some risk of tort liability (inadequately shoveling the snow in front of decedent's shoe store). Even if the personal representative wants to sell the asset as quickly as possible (as might be the case with real property), the personal representative might have an obligation to maintain the property in the interim, and could engender contract litigation based on any sale contract he makes with a prospective purchaser.

Who bears the loss when actions taken by the representative on behalf of the estate generates tort or contract liability? There are three basic alternatives: (1) the representative is personally liable for his actions, with no recourse against estate assets; (2) the estate, and not the executor personally, is liable; and (3) the representative is personally liable, but has a claim against the estate for reimbursement.

In the absence of a statute, the common law has generally endorsed alternative (3). Courts have held the personal representative personally liable for breach of contracts made on behalf of the estate, and for torts committed while the personal representative holds legal title to the estate. The personal representative is entitled to recover from the estate, to the extent that the personal representative's actions were reasonably taken for the benefit of the estate. But recourse against the estate would not help a personal representative whose liability exceeded the value of the estate.

With respect to contract claims, the personal representative can insulate himself from personal liability by including contract terms expressly excluding personal liability by the personal representative. That option, however, is not available with respect to tort liability; to protect himself, the personal representative must purchase adequate liability insurance.

These common law rules are not typically in the interest of estate beneficiaries. A personal representative concerned about personal liability might choose not to preserve a firm's going concern value, because continued operation of the business could subject the personal representative to liability that the representative could avoid by selling the business more quickly, or by abandoning it altogether. As a result, many states have enacted statutes that endorse alternative (2). These statutes limit the personal liability of the representative. Uniform Probate Code § 3–808 is illustrative. Subsection (a) of the statute reverses the default rule for contracts entered into by the personal representative, providing that the personal representative is not personally liable unless the contract provides otherwise. Subsection (b) then provides that the personal representative is personally liable for torts committed in the course of administration "only if he is personally at fault." As the comment to section 3–808 explains, the statute is designed to "make the estate a quasi-corporation for purposes of such liabilities." That is, the personal representative is liable for his actions only if an agent for a corporation would be liable under the same circumstances. At the same time, tort claimants and contract claimants have a direct remedy against estate assets, even if they do not have a remedy against the personal representative's personal assets.

VI. Distributing Assets and Closing the Estate

After marshaling assets and paying taxes and creditor claims, the personal representative's objectives are (1) to distribute estate assets to the estate beneficiaries in accordance with the provisions of the will or the intestate succession statute, and (2) to close out the estate.

Although the personal representative may have to sell large assets in order to make appropriate distribution to the various beneficiaries, the personal representative may make distributions in kind rather than in cash, and should try to make distributions in kind where possible. First, when a testator has made a specific bequest, there is a strong presumption that testator intended that the beneficiary receive specific property—not the cash value of the property. For instance, if testator's will leaves her diamond engagement ring to her only daughter, testator does not expect the personal representative to sell the ring and distribute the proceeds of the sale to the daughter.

Second, even when a decedent has not made a specific devise, income tax considerations may lead the estate beneficiaries to prefer distributions in kind—especially of assets that have appreciated in value since decedent's acquisition of those assets. Consider, for instance, a decedent who, twenty years before his death, purchased 1,000 shares of Acme stock at $10 per share (or a total of $10,000). Suppose further that at decedent's death, the Acme stock is worth $100,000. If the personal representative sells the shares and distributes the proceeds, decedent's estate will have realized $90,000 worth of capital gain, which is subject to income taxation. By contrast, if the personal representative distributes the shares of stock, there has been no realization of gain, and the beneficiaries take a "stepped-up basis", which assures that when they sell the shares they will be taxed only on the difference between their sale price and the $90,000 value of the stock at the time of decedent's death. In these circumstances, there is every reason for the personal representative to make distributions in kind rather than in cash. If, on the other hand, a particular beneficiary (other than a specific devisee) requests payment in cash rather than in kind, the personal representative may be obligated to sell assets as necessary to facilitate cash payment.

When the estate's assets consist of publicly-traded securities, valuation poses no obstacle to distribution in kind. When the assets are less liquid, the personal representative is well advised to have the assets appraised before they are distributed in kind. Appraisal reduces the risk of challenge by disappointed beneficiaries.

Once the personal representative has arranged final distribution of estate assets, the personal representative has discharged his or her duties. Suppose, however, that an estate beneficiary or a creditor concludes that the personal representative has retained estate assets, or has made an improper distribution. Must the personal representative remain in limbo until such claims are advanced? The standard answer is no. The personal representative may petition a court to approve an accounting and distribution of estate assets. Although procedures vary significantly from state to state, the accounting is generally designed to foreclose further litigation by beneficiaries with respect to matters fully disclosed by the personal representative in the accounting proceeding. Once the final accounting is complete, the personal representative is relieved of responsibility for estate assets.

VII. Compensating the Personal Representative and the Estate's Lawyer

Administration of an estate takes work and skill, both by the personal representative and, in most cases, by the estate's lawyer. Both the personal representative and the lawyer are entitled to compensation for their work; without compensation, they might have inadequate incentive to act in the estate's interest.

The fees paid to the personal representative cannot generally be set by contract: who but the personal representative would contract to set the representative's fees? Statutory law generally governs the compensation paid to personal representatives, but the statutes vary considerably from state to state. A common statutory approach entitles the personal representative to commissions based on the size of the estate; the percentage declines with the size of the estate. For instance, in California, the personal representative receives four percent of the first one hundred thousand dollars of the estate's value, three percent of the next one hundred thousand dollars, with progressively smaller percentages for each additional increment of estate value. Statutes like California's assume that administration of a $200,000 estate does not require twice as much effort as administration of a $100,000, so that a personal representative should not receive twice as much compensation. Nevertheless, compensation on a large estate can be sizable. Under the California statute, the personal representative of a $5,000,000 estate would be entitled to $67,000 in commissions.

In other states, statutes entitle the personal representative to "reasonable" compensation. (*See, e.g.* UPC § 3–719). How is reasonableness to be determined? Under the UPC, the personal representative may, in the first instance, set her own compensation, but must give all interested persons an opportunity to establish that the compensation is unreasonable. (UPC § 3–721). Ultimately, a court will determine whether the compensation is reasonable.

Statutes also regulate the compensation payable to the estate's lawyer. Theoretically, the personal representative could negotiate a fee with the estate's lawyer, but there are reasons to doubt that the personal representative will negotiate the best deal possible for the estate. First, in many cases, a personal representative who is a family member of the decedent will not "shop around," but will simply go to the lawyer who drafted decedent's will, and assume that the lawyer's fees will be reasonable. Second, if the personal representative is a "professional" rather than a family member, the personal representative may have an interest in currying favor with the lawyer, who might be a source of repeat business. As a result, in many states (again, California is an example), the fees payable to the estate's lawyer are fixed by a statute that mirrors the compensation payable to the personal representative. In other states, the personal representative and the lawyer may contract for a fee, but the fee will be subject to reasonableness review by a court.

If commissions and lawyer fees were based solely on the value of decedent's estate, neither the personal representative nor any lawyer would have a reason to administer an estate whose debts approach or exceed its assets; because the overall value of the estate is low (or even negative), statutory compensation would be small or non-existent. Yet both the estate's creditors and sometimes its beneficiaries would benefit from administration of that estate, because a diligent personal representative might look for other assets, or seek to reduce the estate's liabilities. As a result, statutes sometimes include escape valves that permit courts to award additional compensation in exceptional circumstances.

Finally, a personal representative (or a lawyer) may waive compensation, and serve for free. Compensation waivers are most common when the personal representative is a close relative of the decedent (and often an estate beneficiary).

Problems

1. Decedent, who owned and managed a toy store, never incorporated the enterprise. During her lifetime, she sold all merchandise with a "lifetime, money-back guaranty." At decedent's death, her niece is appointed personal representative. The personal representative conducts a review of decedent's records, and emerges with the reasonable belief that all of decedent's suppliers have been fully paid. The PR closes the store and distributes all of decedent's assets to decedent's husband and children.

   Does the PR bear personal liability for subsequent claims by decedent's suppliers or customers?

2. Decedent, who owned and managed a toy store, never incorporated the enterprise. After decedent's death, personal representative continued to operate the store. A patron tripped and injured herself when she slipped on a wet floor and hit her head on a large, metal, toy truck.

   Assuming the fall was the result of negligence by an employee hired by the personal representative, from whom may the injury victim recover?

   How, if at all, would your answer change if the personal representative were the only person working in the store?

3. Decedent's will provides for equal division of his estate among his three children. Decedent's assets include a $100,000 commercial store (originally purchased for $10,000), a $40,000 stamp collection (purchased by decedent over the years with a total purchase price of $5,000), and $160,000 in cash.

   The personal representative proposes to sell the store and the stamp collection at auction and distribute the proceeds equally among the children. Would the PR's actions subject him to liability to the children?

Chapter Thirteen

SOLUTIONS TO PROBLEMS

Chapter Two: Intestate Succession

1. $225,000 to H, $25,000 each to A, B, and C.

UPC 2–102(4) applies because one of decedent's surviving descendants—C—is not a descendant of H. As a result, H is entitled to $150,000 plus one-half of any balance of the intestate estate ($75,000), for a total of $225,000. The remaining $75,000 is divided equally among I's three children, A, B, and C (*see* UPC 2–103(1); 2–106).

If C had never been born, H would take $225,000 + $37,500, for a total of $262,500, and A and B would take $18,750 each.

UPC 2–102(3) would apply because all of I's descendants would also be H's descendants, but H has a descendant who is not a descendant of I. Therefore, H is entitled to $225,000 plus one-half of the balance, for a total of $262,500. The remaining $37,500 is divided equally between I's two children, A and B.

2. $150,000 to Z; $50,000 to A; $25,000 each to Y and T; $16,667 each to Q, R, and P.

I is not survived by descendants, parents, or descendants of parents. As a result, UPC 2–103(4) is applicable. That statute directs that half of the estate passes to descendants of paternal grandparents. Z is the only such descendant, so Z takes one-half of the estate, which is $150,000. The remaining half passes to descendants of maternal grandparents by representation. UPC 2–106(b) describes the representation scheme. The closest generation in which there are surviving descendants is the generation of I's uncles and aunts. We divide into as many shares as there are living uncles or aunts (1: A) and deceased uncles and aunts who left surviving descendants (2: B and C), for a total of three shares of $50,000 each. A takes one of those shares, and the remaining two shares ($100,000) are recombined for distribution to the descendants of deceased uncles and aunts. The statute then directs that the $100,000 be divided among Y, T, Q, R, and P as if A and A's descendants had predeceased I. As a result, we would divide the $100,000 into four shares, two for living first cousins (Y and T), and two for descendants of deceased first cousins who left descendants (X and V). Y and T would each take one of the $25,000 shares, and the remaining two shares ($50,000) would be recombined and distributed equally among Q, R, and P.

If Z had predeceased I and the jurisdiction provided for strict per stirpes distribution, distribution would be $100,000 to A, $50,000 each to Y, P, and T; $25,000 each to Q and R.

First, all distribution would be to descendants of maternal grandparents, because there are no paternal grandparents. We would divide into three equal shares, one for each uncle and aunt. A would take her own share, B's share would be divided between V and T, with P taking V's share; C's share would be divided between Y and X, with Q and R splitting X's share.

3.   P would take I's entire estate. If, however, P died leaving I as her only surviving relative, P's estate would escheat to the state. Section 2–103(4) permits P to inherit from I because P is a descendant of I's grandparents. I, however, is not a descendant of P's grandparents, but is instead a descendant of P's great-grandparents. As a result, I's estate passes to the state under UPC 2–105.

4.   A, Y and Z would each take $212,500.

Because H survived W by more than 120 hours, at W's death, H would be entitled, under UPC 2–102(4), to $150,000 plus $175,000 (one half of the remaining $350,000 in W's estate), for a total of $325,000. The remaining $175,000 would pass to A. Then, at H's death, H's estate would total $425,000—his own $100,000 plus the $325,000 he inherited from W. That $425,000 would be divided equally between his sisters, Y and Z.

If H had only survived W by two days, A would take $500,000, and Y and Z would each take $50,000.

In that event, UPC 2–104 provides that H should be treated as if H predeceased W for purposes of distribution of W's estate. As a result, A would inherit W's entire $500,000 estate. Y and Z would share H's $100,000 estate.

5.   B takes one-third of the estate; D, E, and F each take two-ninths.

The estate would first be divided at the level of I's children, into three shares. Under UPC 2–106, B would take one share, and the remaining two shares (2/3 of the estate) would be recombined, and distributed equally among D, E, and F. (1/3 of 2/3 is 2/9).

If B disclaimed, G, H and J would take B's share; each would take 1/9 of I's estate; D, E, and F would each take two-ninths.

UPC 2–1106(b)(3)(B) provides generally that if a person disclaims an interest in an estate, the disclaimed interest passes as if the disclaimant died immediately before the time for distribution (in the case of an intestacy proceeding, this means the time of the decedent's death). In this case, that would mean that the estate would be distributed as if I were survived by six grandchildren, and each of the grandchildren would each take one-sixth of the estate. Such a result, however, would create an incentive for B to disclaim to obtain for himself and his children a larger share of the estate (one-half) than they would receive if he did not disclaim. The UPC was drafted, however, to prevent B from disadvantaging the families of his siblings in this way. UPC 2–1106(b)(3)(C) provides that if the descendants of the disclaimant (G, H, and J) would share in the disclaimed interest by representation if the disclaimant (B) were to predecease the decedent, the disclaimed interest passes only to the descendants of the disclaimant who survive the time of distribution. The disclaimed interest passes by representation to G, H, and J. That is, G, H, and J would share B's interest rather than taking in their own right.

6.　　A, B, and C would take equal shares of I's estate.

　　I in this case is survived by descendants of parents. Under UPC 2–103(3), descendants of decedent's parents, or either of them, would take I's estate. UPC 2–107 makes it clear that half-siblings share equally with full siblings. As a result, A and B (half siblings) share equally with C (a full sibling) so that each takes one-third of I's estate.

If X had adopted I, X would take I's entire estate.

　　In this case, I is survived by a parent. UPC 2–118(a) provides that an adopted individual is the child of her adopting parent. As a result, UPC 2–103(2) would leave I's entire estate to her surviving parent, X.

If X had adopted I and then died before I, I's estate would be divided equally between B and C.

　　In this case, as in the first case, I is survived by descendants of parents. UPC 2–119(b) provides that a parent-child relationship exists between an individual who is adopted by the spouse of either genetic parent and:

(1)　　the genetic parent whose spouse adopted the individual; and

(2)　　the other genetic parent, *but only for the purpose of the right of the adoptee or a descendant of the adoptee to inherit from or through the other genetic parent* (emphasis added).

In other words, I would have the right to inherit from A, but A has no right to inherit from I.

Chapter Three: Family Protection

1.   H has a right to elect $200,000 more than W provided for him; he would be entitled to 20% of the irrevocable trust and 20% of W's interest in the beach house to satisfy that $200,000.

Start by computing the augmented estate, which includes the following items:

$500,000	net probate estate (included under § 2–204)
$500,000	2006 trust, with released power to revoke (included under § 2–205(3)(A)
$800,000	2008 irrevocable trust (included under § 2–205(2)(A)
$200,000	W's share of beach house (included under § 2–205(1)(B))
$600,000	H's own assets (included under § 2–207)
$2,600,000	TOTAL Augmented Estate

(Note that the 2006 trust is included within the estate because the release of the power to revoke occurred within two years before W's death. As a result, the release is treated like a gift made within two years before W's death).

Next, we determine that because the marriage was longer than 15 years, the marital property portion of the augmented estate is 100%. H's elective share is **$1,300,000**—50% of the marital property portion of the augmented estate.

Then we must determine what is charged against H's elective share under UPC § 2–209(a). The following are included:

$500,000	The entire net probate estate, all of which was left to H
$600,000	The marital property portion (100%) of H's own assets
$1,100,000	TOTAL amount charged against H

Therefore, there is an unsatisfied balance of $200,000, the difference between $1,300,000 and $1,100,000. That balance is to be satisfied, under § 2–209(b), from amounts included under the augmented estate—other than amounts included pursuant to § 2–205(3)(A) and (C). Hence, the balance must come from the $800,000 2008 trust and the $200,000 of beach house. Because the total of those two amounts is $1,000,000, and the unsatisfied balance is

$200,000, H takes 20% of each amount—$160,000 from the trust, and $40,000 (or a 20% share) from the beach house.

If H and W had been married for 10 years, the augmented estate would have been the same, but the marital property portion would have been 60%, or $1,560,000. The elective share would have been half of that, or $780,000. The $500,000 net probate estate would have been charged against the husband under § 2–209(a), together with 60% of the husband's own assets. Sixty percent of $600,000 is $360,000. Therefore, H is charged with a total of $860,000, which is larger than his elective share. As a result, he has no right to take amounts beyond what W has provided.

If W's 2006 trust had been irrevocable when created, it would not have been included in the augmented estate at all. W's trust would have left W with no general power of appointment under § 2–205(1), and would have left W with no right to possession under § 2–205(2), and the transfer would not have been included under § 2–205(3) because it was not made within two years before W's death.

As a result, the augmented estate would have been $2,100,000. Assuming a 30-year marriage, H's elective share would have been $1,050,000. But H is charged with $1,100,000—the $500,000 he received from the net probate estate, and the $600,000 in his owns assets. As a result, H would have no right to take amounts beyond what W has provided.

2.   W has a right to elect $50,000 beyond what H has provided for her, but electing would not be in W's interest, because she would have to give up an income interest in a $1,900,000 trust—an interest worth far more than $50,000.

H's augmented estate includes the following amounts:

$2,000,000	net probate estate (§ 2–204)
$300,000	W's life insurance policy (§ 2–206(3))
$500,000	S's life insurance policy (§ 2–205(1)(D))
$200,000	POD Account (§ 2–205(1)(C))
$3,000,000	TOTAL augmented estate

Because the parties have been married for five years, the marital property portion of the augmented estate is $900,000 (30%). The elective share is half of that, or $450,000. The wife is charged, under § 2–209(1), with the $100,000 she received outright from the net probate estate, and with the $300,000 life insurance policy, for a total of $400,000. That leaves her with a right to take an additional $50,000. But in order to elect, she would have to disclaim the income interest in H's residuary trust. Give the wife's relatively young age and life expectancy, that life interest is worth far more than $50,000; indeed, in the first year after H's death, it is likely to generate more than $50,000 in income for the wife.

3.   The wife has a right to elect an additional $120,000, but she would be better off claiming under the UPC's premarital will provision, which would leave the wife with $500,000.

For elective share purposes, H's augmented estate equals $1,200,000—the total value of H's estate added to W's own assets. The marital property portion is 30% of that, $360,000. W's elective share is 50% of that, for a total of $180,000. 30% of W's own assets would be charged against her elective share. Thirty percent of $200,000 equals $60,000. As a result, the wife can elect an additional $120,000: $180,000–$60,000.

If, however, W claims under UPC § 2–301, she can claim her intestate share of the portion of H's estate not left to H's children. In other words, W can take her intestate share of the $900,000 designated for the Red Cross. Under UPC § 2–102(4)—the intestate share statute—W would be entitled to $150,000 plus half of the balance of $750,000, for a total of $375,000.

4.   A would be entitled to nothing. UPC § 2–302(1) would entitle A to his intestate share. But in this case, if T had died intestate, T's entire estate would pass to T's husband, H. (UPC § 2–102(1)(ii)). Because A would take nothing in intestacy, A also takes nothing under the pretermitted child statute.

The answer would not change if B had been born before execution of T's last will. UPC § 2–302(2) makes no provision for an afterborn child in the situation in which testator's before-born children take nothing under testator's will.

If T had made a general bequest to B of $10,000, UPC § 2–302(2) provides that the $10,000 would be divided into two shares, and A would take one of those two shares, with B taking the rest. Each child, therefore, would take $5,000.

Chapter Four: Wills

1.   Will 2 does not comply with the formalities required by the UPC, because the will was witnessed by only one witness. Nevertheless, UPC § 2–503's dispensing power would permit probate of Will 2 because there is clear and convincing evidence that Testator intended the document to be her will. She invited a notary and executed the will in front of the notary and other witnesses, even if only one of the witnesses signed the will. (If the notary had actually acknowledged Tomasina's signature on the will, rather than just Martha's signature on the self-proving affidavit, that by itself would

have been sufficient under UPC § 2–502(a)(3)(B)). Testator's failure to obtain the signature of a second witness was undoubtedly the product of neglect, not second thoughts about the will's provisions.

Lance might try to argue that the will was executed based on a mistake of fact: Testator executed the will believing he was dead. This argument is problematic, however, because the mistake is not clear from the face of the will, nor is the disposition Testator would have made had she been aware of the truth; there is every reason to believe that she would have wanted Sue Ellen to take something even if she had known that Lance was alive. In these circumstances, a court would not be likely to invalidate the will for mistake of fact.

If Will 2 is admitted to probate, Will 1 is not entitled to probate because Will 2 revoked Will 1 by inconsistency.

If, however, the court concludes that UPC § 2–503 is not applicable, Will 1 should still not be admitted to probate. First, Will 1 was revoked by physical act: crumbling of the will constitutes destruction, and the destruction was accomplished in front of witnesses with a clear intent to revoke.

Lance might try to invoke the doctrine of dependent relative revocation (DRR) and argue either that the revocation of Will 1 was conditioned on the validity of Will 2, or that it was dependent on testator's belief that Lance was dead. These arguments, however, are unlikely to succeed. DRR is designed to effectuate a testator's intent. Here, probate of Will 1 is less likely to effectuate Testator's intent than intestacy. In light of Testator's reconciliation with Sue Ellen, it appears more likely that she would prefer an even split between the two children to a disposition that leaves her entire estate to Lance.

2.a. Objections to Probate of Will 1: The will was revoked by inconsistency (execution of Will 2 if Will 2 is valid under section 2–503). Destruction of Will 2 did not revive Will 1, because the UPC includes a presumption against revival. Lance's only argument is that the presumption has been overcome by Testator's statement. The statement, however, is equivocal, because Lance would be "taken care of" even in intestacy.

b.   Attempt to Probate Will 2: Sue Ellen has no arguments for probate of Will 2, which was revoked by physical act. DRR is inapplicable here. If Sue Ellen tried to argue that the revocation of Will 2 was dependent on restoration of Will 1, the natural response would be that intestacy more closely approximates Sue Ellen's intent than probate of Will 2. As a result, Will 2 should not be admitted to probate.

3.   The will execution was problematic in two respects. First, Robert Jones did not sign the will by himself. If Robert had asked for help in

signing the will, the assisted signature would undoubtedly have been adequate. But because he did not, Kitty and Lisa might challenge the signature.

Second, Marilyn Smith was an interested witness. In some states, that would disqualify her as a witness; in others, it would deprive her of any benefits she received under the will, but not affect the will's eligibility for probate. Under the UPC, use of an interested witness does not disqualify the witness nor does it deprive Marilyn of her legacy, but might be relevant in evaluating any undue influence claim.

4.   The second document should not be admitted to probate because it was not witnessed in accordance with testamentary formalities, nor does it qualify as a holographic will because it was not entirely handwritten by testator. A court could invoke section 2–503 to validate the second document if the court found clear and convincing evidence that testator intended the document to have testamentary effect.

5.   Now the second document complies with testamentary formalities. Two issues remain. First, when was the instrument executed? Before admitting the document to probate, a court would have to ascertain that the second document was executed after the March 31 will. Otherwise, the March 31 will would have revoked the document by inconsistency.

Second, if the second document was executed after the March 31 will, it does not revoke that will, because it does not dispose of all of Testator's property. Instead, the document supplements the earlier will, so both documents should be admitted to probate. Laura takes the television, and Wilbur takes the remainder of the estate.

6.   The December 10th letter would be admissible only in a jurisdiction that authorizes holographic wills. The letter cannot be incorporated by reference into the July 2009 will, because it was not in existence at the time the will was executed. Nor does UPC § 2–513 validate the letter because a house is not "tangible personal property."

If the jurisdiction recognizes holographic wills, the document qualifies for probate because it was entirely in Testator's hand and Testator appears to have intended it to have testamentary effect. So long as the letter was clearly written by Testator (and not by Blanche), the letter should be admitted as a codicil to the will.

7.   Provisions (1), (2) and (4) are enforceable under the doctrine of facts of independent significance. Testator would not employ someone as a member of her household staff simply to make a bequest to that person; membership on the staff has significance

apart from its testamentary effect. Similarly, testator's choice of investments is designed to make money for testator, not simply to alter her testamentary decisions. Testator's husband's will has an effect other than altering the distribution of Testator's assets: it directs distribution of the husband's assets.

By contrast, provision (3) is not enforceable, because Testator's decisions to move statements in and out of a particular desk drawer would have no significance apart from a change in disposition of her own estate.

8.   Peter Jones would take the yacht, and the three children would take $100,000 each. Theresa would take nothing. Residuary devises abate first, followed by general devises, and then specific devises. Because there is not enough in the estate to satisfy all of Dan's devises, the residuary devise to Theresa would abate entirely. The $300,000 in cash would be divided proportionately among the general devisees (the children), while Peter would take his specific devise of the yacht.

UPC § 3–902 would reach the same result, although Theresa would have the opportunity to offer evidence that the statutory abatement scheme would frustrate Dan's intent.

9.   In many jurisdictions, the specific devise to Peter would be adeemed by extinction, and Peter would be entitled to nothing. UPC § 2–606(a)(6) allows Peter to establish that Dan did not intend ademption under these circumstances. Peter would argue that Dan intended to benefit Peter, and simply did not have time to rewrite the will after Marigold was destroyed. Peter's argument is a weak one, because (a) Peter was not a close family member and (b) a long time passed between destruction of Marigold and the time of Dan's death. If Peter could establish that ademption should apply, Peter is entitled to the entire $300,000; the other beneficiaries take nothing.

10. UPC § 2–606(a)(1) creates an explicit exception to ademption doctrine for insurance proceeds not yet paid at death, which guarantees Peter the $300,000; the other beneficiaries take nothing.

11. The gift of the china and silver has been adeemed, so the principal issue is whether Article Four, together with the memo in the drawer, is adequate to dispose of the piano. UPC § 2–513 holds enforceable a will reference to a separate writing if the writing disposes of tangible personal property and if it is signed by the testator. Here, the piano qualifies as tangible personal property, and it appears that Trina signed the writing (even though the signature is not at the end of the document). As a result, Stella would take the piano.

In the absence of a statute like § 2–513, the daughters would take the piano. The doctrine of incorporation by reference does not apply because the memo was executed after the will.

The daughters divide the remainder of the estate.

12.a.   Assuming the jurisdiction provides for apportionment of estate taxes (as most jurisdictions do), there are two paths to the same result. First, we could compute the percentage of the estate to which each beneficiary would be entitled if there were no tax liability, and then multiply that percentage by the total tax (in this case $1,000,000). Using this method, we would see that Neva's $200,000 painting represents 2.5% of the estate, so she bears liability for 2.5% of $1,000,000, or $25,000. She would have to pay that amount into the estate to take the painting (unless she authorized the executor to sell the painting and give her 97.5% of the proceeds). Bob's $1,000,000 devise represents 12.5% of the estate, so he is liable for 12.5% of $1,000,000, or $125,000. Dana's share of the estate (absent taxes) would be $6,800,000. That amounts to 85% of the estate. As a result, her tax bill would be 85% of $1,000,000, or $850,000.

Another way to reach the same result would be to recognize that estate taxes make up 1/8 (or 12.5%) of the estate. As a result, each beneficiary is required to contribute 1/8 of his or her share toward the estate tax bill. One-eighth of Neva's $200,000 share is $25,000; one-eighth of Bob's $1,000,000 share is $125,000, and one-eighth of Dana's $6,800,000 share is $850,000.

b.   The language here constitutes a direction against apportionment. If the will included this language, Dana would bear the entire tax liability. Neva would take the painting and Bob would take his $1,000,000 without worrying about estate taxation.

13.a.   James and Kimberly should take equally as Inez's intestate heirs. Harry's gift lapsed because Harry died before Inez. Typical anti-lapse statutes do not apply to bequests made to spouses. New Hampshire is an exception, and in New Hampshire, Ophelia would take the entire estate.

b.   Paula and Quentin will share equally in Inez's estate. Although the gift to Kimberly lapsed, the anti-lapse statute of every state would save a gift to siblings. Almost all anti-lapse statutes save the gift for the issue of the designated beneficiary, not for the estate. As a result, Paula and Quentin take—not Steve. Maryland is an exception, where the lapsed gift become part of the predeceased devisee's estate. In Maryland, Steve, as Kimberly's will beneficiary, would take Inez's estate.

c.(1) If Kimberly predeceased Inez, her $100,000 would be divided equally between her children, Paula and Quentin, for the reasons stated in (b). James would take the other $100,000. The UPC treats class gifts in the same way it treats gifts to individuals for anti-lapse purposes.

(2) If Ophelia predeceased Inez, her gift would lapse. Although the UPC anti-lapse statute applies to gifts to stepchildren, Ophelia was not survived by issue, so the gift to her is not saved. As a result, in most states, the entire residuary estate would pass to Aunt Fifi. (At common law, Ophelia's half would instead pass to Inez's heirs at law, James and Kimberly, but most states and the UPC have abandoned that approach).

(3) If Aunt Fifi predeceased Inez, the UPC anti-lapse statute would save her share for her issue because Aunt Fifi is a descendant of Inez's grandparents. Hence, Nora would take 1/4 of the residuary estate and Rex and Susan would each take 1/8. Ophelia would take her 1/2 of the residuary estate. In some jurisdictions (New York, for example), the anti-lapse statute applies only to issue and brothers and sisters. In that event, Aunt Fifi's gift would lapse and Ophelia would take the entire residuary estate.

d.   In most states, the survivorship requirement would be treated as evidence that Inez did not want the anti-lapse statute to apply. As a result, the estate would be distributed to Inez's heirs, James and Kimberly. UPC § 2–606, however, requires more than words of survivorship to supplant the anti-lapse statute. Hence, Nora would take 1/2 of the estate, while Rex and Susan would divide the other half.

e.   Even under the UPC, the alternative devise would be effective, and Kimberly would take.

14. Most courts would permit extrinsic evidence to resolve the "latent" ambiguity in the will: did the label "grandchild" apply to Charles. That is, the will is not ambiguous on its face, but ambiguity arises when we try to apply the language of the will to the facts in the world.

Some courts might hold, however, that there is no ambiguity: if Adam was Charles' biological father, then Charles was a grandchild.

15. The traditional answer is no. The will is clear on its face, and extrinsic evidence is not generally admissible when the will is clear. Moreover, courts will not reform wills for mistake, especially when reformation requires them to add words to the will.

The modern trend, however, is to reform wills when the scrivener admits that he made an error.

16. To prevail, Ava and Maude must first establish that John and Theresa's will contained a contract not to revoke. They must convince

a court that the words "each of us agrees to be bound by the following provisions" constitutes such a contract. Although courts are hesitant to find contractual language in joint wills, that language is sufficiently strong that many courts would find a contract.

Once Ava and Maude establish the existence of a contract, they must also establish that the contract encompassed all of John's property, including property acquired after Theresa's death. Margarite would argue—persuasively—that it makes no sense to construe the earlier will to bind John with respect to the millions of dollars John and Margarite earned after Theresa's death, especially when the result would be to deny any property to John's subsequent children and second wife.

17. Under the UPC, all of the provisions in Robin's will were revoked by operation of law. Gifts to spouses are automatically revoked, as are gifts to an ex-spouse's relatives. Jake could not serve as executor because the UPC provides that divorce revokes a designation of a spouse as a fiduciary.

Chapter Five: Contesting the Will

1.a. In most states, the jury's verdict will stand so long as there is evidence to support the jury's determination. In this case, the testimony of lay witnesses sheds doubt on Testator's capacity. The co-worker's testimony suggests that Testator was suffering from an insane delusion. This evidence would typically be sufficient to overcome any presumption of capacity created by the self-proving affidavit, and to support a jury verdict that Testator lacked capacity; medical evidence is not necessary.

b. If state law directs that the self-proving affidavit creates a presumption of capacity, a jury could reasonably find that the Testator had capacity if it rejected the testimony of the two lay witnesses as incredible. If the self-proving affidavit does not create a presumption of capacity, an appellate court might be willing to overturn the jury verdict, especially since Testator disinherited his two daughters.

c. If the trial judge permitted the lay witnesses to testify to their conclusions without testifying to the facts on which they based those conclusions, an appellate court could reverse a finding of incapacity on the ground that the trial court had improperly admitted testimony as to legal conclusions. Moreover, either an appellate court or a trial court could conclude that the jury's finding of incapacity was not supported by any evidence, because the unsupported opinion testimony of the lay witnesses did not constitute evidence.

2.a. Typically, the existence of a confidential relationship plus suspicious circumstances gives rise to a presumption of undue influence. Here, unequal treatment of the son might be treated as suspicious circumstances. But in this case, both the son and the daughter offer the same account of the will: essentially, the mother received a quid-pro-quo from the daughter. This explanation should be enough to rebut any presumption of undue influence. Some courts might conclude that it is for the jury to determine whether the influence exercised by the daughter was undue; others would conclude that the presumption of undue influence has been rebutted as a matter of law because the daughter is entitled to contract with her mother, formally or informally, to provide services in return for a bequest of assets in the mother's will.

b. In this case, there is clearly adequate evidence to support the jury's verdict that any evidence exercised by the daughter was not undue. The will was the product of a contract between mother and daughter.

3. The sons could contest the will for undue influence or for fraud. The undue influence claim would be based on the existence of a confidential relationship together with suspicious circumstances—a direct benefit to the minister. A court would be likely to conclude that the circumstances were sufficiently suspicious to justify a presumption of undue influence. In that case, the minister would be required to rebut that presumption. Testimony that the minister believed the bequest to the minister would improve Testator's chances at salvation would be unlikely to persuade a jury that the influence was not undue. The minister's efforts appeared designed to coerce Testator into making the bequests.

The sons' fraud claim depends on whether a jury would believe that the minister believed his statements to be true. If the jury finds that the minister believed his statements to be true, then it cannot find fraud. If the jury finds that the minister did not believe his statements to be true, and that he intended to deceive the testator, the sons could make out all of the elements of a fraud claim.

4. The "no-contest" provision in Testator's will would not be an effective deterrent. The sons are both Testator's residuary legatees and his intestate heirs. If the court enforces the no-contest provision, the residuary devise would fail, but Testator's sons would be entitled to the property as Testator's heirs. Traditionally, courts have not enforced "negative disinheritance" provisions unless the will provides an alternative devise, and in this case, the will provides none. As a result, even if the will contest were unsuccessful, the sons would end up with $125,000 each. The sons would have little to lose from a contest. The result would be similar under UPC § 2–101(5), discussed

in Chapter Four. If the will contest were unsuccessful and the devise to the sons were held invalid, the sons' children would take the residue. Again, the clause would create little disincentive to a will contest.

5.   The wife cannot successfully contest the will. The will itself was not the product of incapacity or undue influence. At the time the will was executed, testator's son was the natural object of his bounty, and there is no evidence that the son acted inappropriately in procuring the will.

The wife could take her elective share, but if the UPC were in force, the elective share might be small in light of the short duration of the marriage. The UPC's premarital will statute would not be helpful, because that statute gives the wife a share of assets not left to testator's descendants. Because the son is a descendant, the premarital will statute would not benefit the wife.

The wife's best claim in this situation is a tortious interference claim against the son. The son acted wrongfully in preventing execution of a new will and, as in Beckwith v. Dahl, the wife has a plausible claim that the son's instructions to the lawyer constituted tortious interference with her inheritance. (The wife might also have a claim against the lawyer for tortious interference, especially if the lawyer knew that the testator had capacity and was not acting under undue influence).

Chapter Six: Trusts

1.   Allison should not prevail. The letter is evidence that Trina intended to make a gift of the house to Blanche alone. Allison might argue that the letter to Blanche created a trust naming her as a beneficiary. After all, if Trina intended to make a simple gift to Blanche, it would not have been necessary to indicate that Blanche could live in and devise the home. Moreover, it is odd that Trina's letter doesn't appear to contemplate the Blanche might sell the house. But the words used by Trina are clearly precatory. The mere mention of a preference that Allison receive the house "if at all possible" would not be read to create an enforceable right in Allison, especially in light of the deed, which never uses language of trust.

2.   At common law, the trust would not be enforceable because the trust is not charitable, and because there are no identified human beneficiaries. The Restatement (Third) of Trusts would give Klaus a power to distribute the estate for Herbert's benefit, but not the duty. Any undistributed funds would be given to Greenblat's heirs. In most states, by statute, trusts for pets are now valid. The court or the trust document must appoint a person to enforce the provisions of the trust.

3.a. Under the law of any state, the club would not be entitled to garnish the trust proceeds. The instrument creates a support trust, and the property must be used for Adam's "health, support, and maintenance," Under no stretch of the imagination does a club tab come within the standard [unless perhaps the club had employed some unsavory enforcers who put Adam in fear for life and limb]. Similarly, Bob would not be entitled to make payments to the club because the club tab does not qualify as health, support, and maintenance.

b.   Again, because the instrument creates a support trust, Bob would not be permitted or required to give Adam the money.

c.   Here, Bob would be permitted and probably required to assist in paying the rent. Rent payments would certainly qualify as "health, support, and maintenance," and the instrument requires Bob to make payments without regard for the needs of the remainder beneficiaries. Especially if Adam had been living in a luxury apartment before the trust was created, a court is likely to hold that Bob is required to make payments to maintain Adam's standard of living. If Adam's apartment is more luxurious than his prior digs, Bob would be within his discretion to refuse payment if he determines it would hamper his ability to meet Adam's other support needs throughout his life.

In a state that has not enacted the UTC, Adam's landlord would have the same right as Bob to compel a distribution. In a state that has enacted UTC § 504(b), however, the landlord can attach Adam's interest in the trust, but has no right to compel payment if the trustee refused to pay.

4.   The answers to 3(a) and 3(b) would be the same. The spendthrift clause would reinforce the conclusion that Bob does not have to satisfy the judgment in 3(a). The spendthrift clause has no effect on Bob's obligation to limit payments to "support," thus precluding payment in 3(b).

The spendthrift clause does not affect Bob's obligation to make payments for Adam's "health, support, and maintenance" in 3(c). In a non-UTC jurisdiction, however, the spendthrift clause would have an effect: it would prevent the landlord from attaching Adam's interest in the trust, unless the jurisdiction recognizes an exception to spendthrift clauses in favor of creditors who provide necessities. Under the UTC, however, the spendthrift clause would not matter, because even without the clause, the landlord could not attach Adam's interest in the trust.

5.   The trust document gives Adam an absolute right to trust income. Moreover, with respect to principal, Bob has discretion that

is not limited by an ascertainable standard. As a result, in situation (a), Bob would be required to pay trust income to the club in order to satisfy the judgment the club has obtained. Bob would be permitted, but not required, to make payments of principal to the club if, in his judgment, such payments would be in the interest of the trust beneficiaries. But under common law, Bob would be personally liable if he paid principal to or on behalf of Adam without first satisfying the club's claim. In situation (b), Adam would be entitled to trust income, and Bob would again be permitted, but not required, to advance money to Adam from trust principal. In situation (c), Adam would be entitled to income, and Bob would have discretion to distribute principal to make Adam current in his rent payments. Adam's landlord would have the right to attach the income stream, but no right to compel a payment from principal unless Bob distributed principal to or for the benefit of Adam after being served with notice of the creditor's garnishment order.

Under the UTC, the club and the landlord have the right to attach Adam's interest in the trust, but no right to challenge Bob's exercise of discretion if he declines to distribute principal to them.

6.   A court would probably not order termination, because termination would frustrate a material purpose of the settlor. The settlor's creation of a support trust was motivated by a desire to provide for Adam for life and fear that Adam would manage an outright gift unwisely. Giving $1,000,000 outright to Adam would frustrate Settlor's material objective—to ensure that Adam has enough money for his support for the remainder of his life.

7.   In this situation, a court might order termination whether or not the remainder beneficiaries consented. If Bob was receiving fees for service as trustee, and especially if Bob was hiring investment advisors or other professionals to help him manage the trust, the cost of maintaining the trust probably exceeds the trust income, making the trust inefficient to continue. Indeed, section 414(a) of the UTC would permit Bob, as trustee, to terminate the trust without judicial approval if the trust principal diminished to less than $50,000 and Bob determined that the value of the trust was now insufficient to justify administrative costs.

8.   To the extent a court views the trust as a support trust, with an obligation on Bob's part to make payments for Adam's health, support, and maintenance, in most states the trust assets would be available to determine Adam's eligibility for Medicaid.

9.   In most states the trust income, but not the trust principal, would be available to determine Adam's eligibility. Because Bob has no obligation to pay trust principal to Adam rather than conserving it for the other trust beneficiaries, and because the trust was not self-

settled, the trust principal would not be treated as an asset of Adam's.

10. At common law, the gift to the museum would likely fail, and Alice, as the residuary beneficiary, would be entitled to the money. The issue is whether Testator had a general charitable intent, which triggers application of the *cy pres* doctrine, or whether Testator's charitable intent was specific, in which case the Museum's inability or unwillingness to use the money for the purposes specified by Testator will result in failure of the charitable trust and distribution to the residuary beneficiary. Here, where it appears from paragraph (2) of the will that Testator's charitable intent was specifically directed toward issues surrounding his native country, it would be difficult for the Museum to argue that testator had a general charitable intent.

Under Uniform Trust Code § 413, a court would be more likely to grant the museum's request because the presumption is that Testator had general charitable intent. Other charitable entities might argue that Testator's intent would be better served by another charitable use of the bequest, but the property would be unlikely to pass to Alice.

11. Here, testator's charitable intent appears to be general, and focused on the promotion of art, as evidenced by the residuary clause of his will. In this circumstance, it is more likely that even at common law, a court would apply the *cy pres* doctrine, and permit the museum to use the money for a purpose other than the one specified by testator. Alice's claim is correspondingly weaker.

Chapter Seven: Fiduciary Duties

1. The daughter would be liable for breach of the duty of loyalty if the brother does not purchase the shares and the daughter then purchases the shares herself. The sale transaction would amount to self-dealing on her part, and the no-further-inquiry rule would apply.

The daughter might contend that she breached no duty because she offered her brother precisely the same deal she ultimately took for herself. That argument ignores, however, the different position of the parties. Ownership is worth more to the daughter than it is to the son, because ownership by the daughter enables her to preserve her management position. Hence, the fact that the son turned down an option to purchase at $200,000 does not establish that the shares were only worth $200,000 to the daughter.

In this situation, the daughter should either seek express approval from her brother, or should seek judicial approval of the proposed sale.

2.   Both the husband (the income beneficiary) and the children (the remainder beneficiaries) would have claims for breach of the duty of care.

Although the trustee may have diversified the trust's stock portfolio, the trustee's decision to invest that portfolio exclusively in common stocks left the trust subject to considerable market risk, otherwise known as undiversifiable risk. The remainder beneficiaries can contend that this course of action resulted in substantial loss of principal. They should not, however, be entitled to recover 25% of the trust principal, because a reasonable trustee would have invested a significant portion of the trust principal in common stocks. Trustee liability should be limited to the amount of the loss attributable to the trustee's unreasonable decision to concentrate in common stocks. If a reasonable trustee could have invested half of the principal in common stocks, the claim would be limited to 12½% of principal. How much of the investment in common stocks was imprudent will depend on the financial condition and needs of the particular trust beneficiaries.

The trustee's decision to invest so heavily in common stocks also caused loss to the income beneficiary. A decision to invest in a portfolio that generated a return of only 2% unreasonably favors the remaindermen over the income beneficiary. Although concerns about inflation would have made it unreasonable to invest the entire portfolio in fixed-value investments like real estate mortgages, the trustee was obligated either to invest in securities that generated a higher than 2% return for the income beneficiaries, or, to the extent authorized by statute or the trust instrument, to make adjustments to assure a greater than 2% return for the income beneficiaries. The income beneficiaries would be entitled to recover from the trustee the difference between 2% and a reasonable return on a trust portfolio.

Neither the income beneficiary nor the remaindermen would be entitled to recover the value of the settlor's own business. The trustee had an obligation to sell that business in order to diversify the trust portfolio. The sale did not breach any duty to the beneficiaries.

If the value of the trust principal had increased by 25%, the remainder beneficiaries would have had no claim, because they were not harmed in any way by the trustee's action. The income beneficiary, however, would still have a claim if the trustee paid the income beneficiary only 2% of the trust portfolio each year.

3.   Under these circumstances, the modern approach, which permits the trustee to delegate investment responsibility, would not make the trustee liable for losses resulting from imprudent investment so long as the trustee acted prudently in selecting the

investment advisor and monitoring the advisor. The investment advisor, however, would be liable to the trust beneficiaries.

The trustee would probably remain liable for a decision not to make adjustments that would generate a return for the income beneficiary.

Chapter Eight: Revocable Trusts and Other Non-Probate Assets

1.   In virtually every jurisdiction, Norman's challenge will fail. The Uniform Testamentary Additions to Trusts Act permits a will to pour assets into even an unfunded revocable trust, "regardless of the existence, size or character of the corpus of the trust." Neither the absence of trust property nor the absence of duties renders invalid a provision pouring assets into a standby, or unfunded trust. Moreover, no trust ever fails for want of a trustee; a court will appoint a substitute trustee in the absence of a trustee named in the trust instrument.

The same rules that apply with respect to the pour-over provision in the will also apply with respect to the life insurance policy and the 401K plan: even if the trust was unfunded until death, the trust will become effective at Testator's death.

In some jurisdictions, execution of the trust would require formalities, but the problem asserts that Teresa "properly executed the document", so Norman cannot rely on any absence of formalities.

In the few states that have not adopted the Uniform Testamentary Additions to Trusts Act, Norman has a stronger argument. The residuary clause of the will devises her estate to a trust that was not executed with testamentary formalities. The doctrine of facts of independent significance will not validate the pour over provision, because the trust was not funded during Teresa's life, and therefore has no independent life time purpose. But does the will incorporate the trust by reference? Although the will precisely identifies the trust, was the trust "in existence" at the time the will was executed? Not really, since the trust was executed immediately *after* the will. If the trust is not validly incorporated, the residuary provision fails and will pass by intestacy. Moreover, in the absence of a statute like the Uniform Testamentary Additions to Trusts Act, his argument that the trust must fail for want of property may have legs.

Although Norman's argument is technically correct, a sympathetic court might stretch incorporation by reference doctrine to find that a trust executed immediately after the will meets the doctrine's requirements, since Teresa's intent is clear. Modern courts would probably reject Norman's argument that the trust is invalid for lack of property because the trustee is designated the beneficiary of several non-probate assets.

2. Harry should take the Microsoft stock unless the trust instrument made explicit provision limiting Sara's power to remove property from the trust. In general, if Sara has created a revocable trust, she reserves the right to revoke the trust with respect to any property in the trust simply by selling the property. Here, by selling the bearer bonds, she removed the bonds from the trust. Because she took no steps to transfer the Microsoft stock to the trust, Harry takes the stock pursuant to the terms of Sara's will.

3. Harry takes all three accounts. A will generally disposing of all of Decedent's property never revokes Decedent's account designations, whether those accounts are POD accounts, employer-sponsored retirement accounts, or IRA accounts.

4. Harry still takes the employer-sponsored retirement account, because the Supreme Court has held that the account designation controls, whatever the content of state law. With respect to the POD account and the IRA account, jurisdictions differ. The Restatement, for instance, would permit express language in Decedent's will to revoke a Totten trust designation (and presumably an IRA account), so the Red Cross would take those accounts. By contrast, California and the UPC would hold that a will cannot revoke an account designation, even if the language is express, so Harry would take those accounts. New York permits revocation by express language in the will, but that language must identify the account and the beneficiary—which this will doesn't, so the Red Cross would take the accounts.

5. Here, UPC § 2–702 would apply the 120-hour survival requirement to will substitutes as well as wills, but UPC § 2–702 is pre-empted with respect to accounts governed by ERISA.

As a result, the IRA account would pass to Ann, because Harry will be deemed to have predeceased Decedent. Bill would not share, because the UPC's pretermitted child provision (2–302) applies only to wills, not to testamentary substitutes. Harry's estate would take the employer-sponsored retirement account (unless ERISA were construed that have a 120–hour survivorship requirement like that in the UPC). Harry's estate might, or might not, be distributed to Ann and Bill, depending on Harry's will. The POD account would be distributed by intestate succession, in equal shares to Ann and Bill, because (a) the account did not designate an alternate beneficiary and Harry is deemed not to have survived Decedent; (b) as a result, the account passed through Decedent's estate; and (c) because Decedent's will named no alternative beneficiary, the account would pass by intestate succession.

6.   In this case, under UPC § 2–804, divorce would revoke the designation in the IRA and the POD account, but not in the employer-sponsored retirement account. As a result, Harry would still take the retirement account. Ann would take the IRA, and the POD account would pass to Ann and Bill in equal shares, by intestate succession (see solution to Problem 5).

Chapter Nine: Powers of Appointment

1.   The answer depends on whether S's will exercises M's power of appointment. At common law, donee's execution of a will without mentioning the power of appointment does not exercise the power. UPC § 2–608 reaches the same result with respect to special powers—and the power in this case is special, because S is restricted to appointing among his descendants.

If S's will does not exercise the power, then the powers-in-trust doctrine would be applicable, and would direct that the trust principal be distributed equally between the only two objects of the power—S's descendants, X and Y. The powers-in-trust doctrine assumes that M would rather have the property distributed to the objects of the power than to the residuary beneficiaries of M's estate, especially when M's trust names no takers-in-default and where the objects of the power form a readily identifiable class.

In some jurisdictions, particularly New York, S's execution of a will without mentioning the power of appointment is nevertheless effective to exercise the power. In states like New York, the trust principal would be distributed exclusively to X.

If the will had included a clause providing for failure to appoint, the designation of takers in default would supersede the powers-in-trust doctrine. As a result, if a court were to conclude that S's will did not exercise the power, the trust property would be distributed to Y at S's death.

2.   In common law states and under the UPC, S's will is ineffective to exercise the power and, as in Problem 1, the powers in trust doctrine would apply so that the trust principal would be divided between X and Y.

In states like New York, S's will would be effective to exercise the power, except that S has appointed to non-objects of the power. As a result the appointment to the Roman Catholic Church is ineffective. The appointment of $100,000 to X remains effective, and the remainder of the trust principal would be divided equally between X and Y (in accordance with the powers-in-trust doctrine). Hence, X would take $300,000 and Y would take $200,000.

3.   Here, S made a clear attempt to exercise the power, but part of the exercise appears to be invalid. The power is special, and the

Roman Catholic Church is not an object of the power. Nevertheless, a court would "marshal" S's own assets and the trust assets to give maximum effect to S's will: The appointive property would all be distributed to X, and the first $300,000 of S's personal assets would be distributed to the Church to equalize distributions. The remainder of S's personal assets would be divided equally between X and the Church. As a result X and the church would each take $400,000.

4.   D is entitled to H's personal $100,000 estate, but has no claim against the appointive property because contracts to exercise testamentary powers are unenforceable against the appointive property. By creating a testamentary power, W sought to assure that H could consider any changes in circumstance until H's death that might warrant a change in appointment. If H were entitled to make an enforceable contract to appoint, H could too easily relinquish the power to change his mind—a power that was significant in W's decision to make the power testamentary. As a result, D is not entitled to specific performance of H's contract to appoint. But because H did breach a contract with D, many jurisdictions would hold that D has a contract claim against H's estate. If the contract claim is measured by the value of promised performance, D's claim would be for $300,000, but because the estate's value is only $100,000, that is the maximum D could recover. In other jurisdictions, D's claim might be limited to the value of the services she provided, but that too might reach or exceed the size of H's estate.

If H had released the power, H would still have breached his contract with D. But unlike contracts to appoint, which are unenforceable, releases are enforceable. As a result, H's release of the power assures (under the powers in trust doctrine), that the appointive property will be distributed equally between D and S. H's purported exercise of the power in H's will is ineffective. D would take $150,000 of the appointive property as a result of the release, but retain a breach of contract action against H's estate. As a result, D would take a total of $250,000.

5.a. The answer depends on the approach the jurisdiction takes towards creditors' rights in appointive property. If the jurisdiction applies the equitable assets doctrine, T's appointment subjects the appointive property to creditor claims, and T's creditors would take the first $200,000 of the appointive property, while D would take the final $100,000. The same result would be reached in California, where property subject to a general testamentary power is subject to claims of the donee's creditors, whether or not the donee exercises the power.

In New York, when property is subject to a testamentary power of appointment, the property is not subject to claims of the donee's creditors. Hence, D would take all $300,000.

b.   Under the equitable assets doctrine, creditors would not be able to reach the appointive property, and the property would be equally divided, $150,000 to S and $150,000 to D. The same result would apply in New York.

In California, creditors would be entitled to $200,000, while S and D would divide the remaining $100,000, because in California, property subject to a general testamentary power is subject to creditor claims, whether or not the donee exercises the power.

c.   The property would be equally divided between S and D because the donee has given up all power of the appointive property by releasing the power. As a result, creditors cannot reach the appointive property in any jurisdiction.

6.a. When T has a general presently exercisable power, creditors have a claim against the appointive property in every jurisdiction, including New York. As a result, the creditors are entitled to the first $200,000 of appointive property. If T's will exercises in favor of his daughter, the daughter takes the other $100,000; if T's will does not exercise the power, or if T releases the power, the son and the daughter share the $100,000.

b.   When T has a special power, T's creditors cannot reach the appointive property in any jurisdiction. As a result, if T's will exercises in favor of his daughter, D takes all $300,000. If T does not exercise, or if T releases the power, S and D take $150,000 each.

Chapter Ten: Future Interests

1.   Both at common law and under most anti-lapse statutes (including UPC § 2–603), the devise of a future interest to A lapses because A did not survive T and A is not a blood relative or a spouse of T. At common law, B and C acquired vested remainders at T's death. When W died, those vested remainders became possessory. At that time, C was still alive and in a position to take her half of the trust principal. B had died, but she had devised all of her property— including her vested remainder—to the American Red Cross. As a result, C and the Red Cross would share the trust principal.

If UPC § 2–707 were in force, the remainders of B and C would not have vested at T's death. Instead, the statute implies into T's will a survivorship requirement, and then creates a substitute gift in favor of descendants of devisees who do not meet the survivorship requirement. Hence, because B died before the time for distribution of trust principal (W's death), UPC § 2–707(b)(1) creates a substitute gift in B's surviving descendants—here, in F. As a result, the trust principal would be divided between C and F.

2.   At common law, the trust principal should be distributed to B. S did not satisfy the survivorship requirement, so the principal should be distributed through the residuary clause of T's will.

Under UPC § 2–707, the trust principal should be distributed to D. UPC § 2–707(b)(1) creates a substitute gift in D, and that substitute gift takes effect even if the trust instrument includes express language of survivorship, in the absence of additional evidence. (UPC § 2–707(b)(3)).

3.   The principal should be distributed at H's death. In order to permit distribution at H's death, the class closing rule excludes J and K from sharing in the trust principal. At common law, A's share would pass to G under the terms of A's will, and G would share equally with B, C, D, and E.

Under UPC § 2–707, G would not take A's share. Instead, A's interest would be construed as contingent on survivorship, and because A did not survive, the statute creates a substitute gift in A's daughter F. As a result, F would share equally with B, C, D, and E.

4.   The principal should be distributed at D's death, in equal shares to all of D's children, including but not limited to X, Y, and Z. In this case, the class closing rule does not apply because at the time scheduled for distribution—S's death—there is no one entitled to take; T does not yet have any grandchildren. In that circumstance, the class closing rule does not apply, and distribution is postponed until the class of grandchildren closes "naturally" by the death of D. (After D's death, no more grandchildren of T can be born).

5.   The question here is whether the interest in the grandchildren is vested, subject to divestment only if a grandchild dies leaving children, or whether the interest in grandchildren is contingent.

Most courts hold, in this circumstance, that the interest in grandchildren is vested. As a result, the principal of T's trust would be divided into 6 shares, one for each grandchild. The three surviving grandchildren, D, G and H, would each take a share. The shares of E and F would pass to G by intestate succession, while the share of J would be divested in favor of her child, L. As a result, G would take one-half of the estate, while D, H, and L would each take one-sixth of the estate.

A few courts would conclude that the grandchildren held a contingent remainder, together with an alternative contingent remainder in children of deceased grandchildren. In that circumstance, the estate would be divided into 4 shares, one each for the three surviving grandchildren, D, G, and H, and one share for the child, L, of the deceased grandchild, J.

Chapter Eleven: The Rule Against Perpetuities

1.   No part of the trust violates the common law Rule Against Perpetuities. The interest in T's wife is a present possessory interest, and therefore does not violate the Rule. The contingent remainder in T's "surviving children" vests at W's death, and as a result, W can be used as a measuring life. The income interest in T's grandchildren vests at the death of T's last surviving child. Because all of T's children are alive at T's death, the children can be used as measuring lives, and the income interest is valid. The grandchildren's ultimate interest in trust principal is also valid. That interest vests indefeasibly at the death of T's last surviving child; at that point, we know precisely who will take the remainder—all of T's grandchildren. As a result, we can use T's children as measuring lives, and the interest is valid. Even if the interest might not become possessory until later, the Rule does not require that the interest become possessory within its period, but only that the interest vest within that period.

2.   The disposition of trust principal is valid. The interest in great-grandchildren vests at the death of T's last surviving child. Because the trust is testamentary, all of T's children are alive at the time the trust is created. As a result, we can use T's children as measuring lives, and the interest in great-grandchildren is valid. (Even if the interest will not become possessory until much later, the interest vests within the lifetime of T's children).

If the trust had been an irrevocable inter vivos trust, the disposition of trust principal would be invalid. T could have more children after creating the trust, so we can no longer use T's children as measuring lives; a great-grandchild could be born after the death of all children of T alive at the time the trust was executed, but before the death of an afterborn child of T.

3.   The disposition of trust principal is invalid if the trust is an irrevocable inter vivos trust. The interest in T's grandchildren does not vest until the death of T's last child. That child could have been born after T created the trust. As a result, we cannot use T's children as measuring lives, and the interest in grandchildren is invalid.

If the trust had been a testamentary trust, the interest would have been valid. All of T's children have been born by T's death, so that we can use T's children as measuring lives, and the interest in T's grandchildren will have vested by the death of T's last child.

4.a. The disposition is valid; Charlie has an indefeasibly vested remainder from the inception of the trust.

b. The disposition is valid; the interest will either vest or fail during Charlie's lifetime, so we can use Charlie as a measuring life. If Charlie survives T's last grandchild, the interest vests during Charlie's lifetime. If Charlie dies before one or more of T's grandchildren, then Charlie's interest fails. Charlie's interest cannot, however, remain contingent beyond the moment of Charlie's death. Hence, there is no violation of the Rule. The answer is the same if T's parents or siblings are alive at the time of his death.

c. The disposition is valid if both of T's parents are dead. In that case, we can use T's siblings as measuring lives (because no more siblings can be born), and the interest in T's nieces and nephews will vest indefeasibly upon the death of T's last surviving sibling (the nieces and nephews need not, by the terms of the grant, satisfy any condition precedent; the grant requires merely that they be born).

If either of T's parents are alive, the disposition is invalid because we can no longer use T's siblings as measuring lives; T could have more siblings (or half-siblings), and a niece or nephew could be born after the death of all of T's currently living siblings.

d. The disposition is valid if T's parents and all of T's siblings are dead. In that case, we can use the nieces and nephews themselves as measuring lives. Within their own lifetimes, we will know whether they have survived T's last surviving grandchild. As a result, the interest in nieces and nephews will vest indefeasibly, or fail, within the lifetime of the nieces and nephews.

If one or more of T's siblings are alive at the time of T's death, the disposition is invalid. We can no longer use the nieces and nephews as measuring lives, because T's surviving siblings could produce more nieces and nephews. We cannot use T's grandchildren as measuring lives, because T's children could produce more grandchildren after T's death.

5. The disposition is invalid. First, note what the grant means. If, at the death of T's last surviving child, no grandchildren have yet been born to the brother (a distinct possibility), distribution of the trust principal would be postponed until we know how many grandchildren will ultimately be born to the brother. As a result, the interest in the brother's grandchildren will not vest indefeasibly until the death of the brother's last surviving child. (Until that time, more grandchildren could be born to the brother). But we cannot use the brother's children as measuring lives because the brother can still have additional children. As a result, the interest in the brother's grandchildren is invalid.

If the brother has a grandchild alive at the time of T's death, the disposition is valid. The class-closing rule of convenience provides that the brother's existing grandchild will be entitled to take at the death of T's last surviving child, and any subsequently born grandchildren of the brother will be excluded. (Otherwise, there would be no way to know how much to distribute to the existing grandchild). As a result, we know that the remainder will vest indefeasibly at the death of T's last surviving child—the time of scheduled distribution. Because the trust is testamentary, T's children are all alive at the time of the grant, and we can guarantee that the interest in the brother's grandchildren will vest or fail within the lifetime of T's children.

Chapter Twelve: Administration: The Probate Process

1.　If the personal representative distributes estate assets to beneficiaries without providing notice to creditors, the PR is personally liable to the creditors for amounts wrongfully paid to the beneficiary (that is, if the creditor claims prove meritorious, the personal representative is liable).

In most jurisdictions, however, non-claim statutes extinguish creditor claims against the estate (and against the PR) if the PR provides notice to the creditor and the creditor does not act within a very short period of time.

The United States Supreme Court has held that the due process clause requires personal notice to creditors before the PR can take advantage of these non-claim statutes. Certainly with respect to decedent's suppliers, if the PR provides no personal notice, and the suppliers have valid claims, the PR will remain personally liable if the PR distributes the estate to the beneficiaries. With respect to customers, the scope of the Supreme Court's decision in the *Pope* case is less clear. The court held that notice of publication would be enough to cut off what the court called "conjectural claims"—and guaranties could well fall within that category.

2.　At common law, the injury victim would have an action against the PR (and against the employee). The PR might be able to seek indemnification from the estate to the extent that the PR's actions were taken reasonably in the interest of the estate.

Under UPC § 3–808, the injury victim would have an action against the estate, but not against the PR. The PR would be personally liable only if he is personally at fault.

If the personal representative were the only person working in the store, even under the UPC, the injury victim would have an action against the PR personally as well as against the estate.

3.　The PR's actions might subject the estate to unnecessary income tax liability. If the PR were to distribute the store and the stamp collection in kind, the recipients would enjoy a "stepped-up basis," and no income tax would ever be due on the difference between the value at decedent's death and decedent's purchase price. As a result, if the PR were to sell rather than distributing in kind, the PR might be subject to a claim for breach of fiduciary duty.

If, however, the PR offered the beneficiaries the option of distributing in kind, and the parties could not agree to a valuation or distribution of the property, then the PR would probably not be liable to the children if the PR were to sell and distribute the sale proceeds.

TABLE OF CASES

INDEX

References are to Pages